Raised from Obscurity

Raised from Obscurity

A Narratival and Theological Study of the Characterization of Women in Luke-Acts

Greg W. Forbes
and
Scott D. Harrower

Foreword by
Lynn H. Cohick

◆PICKWICK *Publications* · Eugene, Oregon

RAISED FROM OBSCURITY
A Narratival and Theological Study of the Characterization
of Women in Luke-Acts

Copyright © 2015 Greg W. Forbes and Scott D. Harrower. All rights reserved.
Except for brief quotations in critical publications or reviews, no part of this book
may be reproduced in any manner without prior written permission from the
publisher. Write: Permissions. Wipf and Stock Publishers, 199 W. 8th Ave., Suite 3,
Eugene, OR 97401.

Pickwick Publications
An Imprint of Wipf and Stock Publishers
199 W. 8th Ave., Suite 3
Eugene, OR 97401

www.wipfandstock.com

ISBN 13: 978-1-62564-119-9

Cataloguing-in-Publication Data

Forbes, Greg W.

Raised from obscurity : a narratival and theological study of the characterization of women in Luke-Acts / Greg W. Forbes and Scott D. Harrower, with a foreword by Lynn Cohick

xvi + 236 p. ; 23 cm. Includes bibliographical references.

ISBN 13: 978-1-62564-119-9

1. Bible. Luke—Criticism, interpretation, etc. 2. Bible. Acts—Criticism, interpretation, etc. 3. Women in the Bible. I. Harrower, Scott D. II. Cohick, Lynn H. III. Title.

BS2589 F66 2015

Manufactured in the U.S.A.   06/19/2015

This work is dedicated to the major
characters in both our lives:

(Greg)

Anne-Maree
Bayley
Caylen
Addy

(Scott)

Kate
Dante
Grace
Angela

Contents

Foreword by Lynn H. Cohick | xi
Acknowledgments | xv

CHAPTER 1—Introduction and Methodology | 1

    Literature Review
    The Aim of this Book
    A Methodology for Exploring a Narrative's Theological Claims about its Characters
    Structure and Content of the Book

CHAPTER 2—Women in Judaism and the Greco-Roman World | 20

    Introduction
    Preliminary Comments
    Women in Ancient Jewish Society
    Women in Second Temple Judaism
    Women in the Greco-Roman World
    Conclusion

CHAPTER 3—The Infancy Narratives (Luke 1:5—2:52) | 36

    Elizabeth
    Mary
    Anna
    Anticipating Broader Narratival and Theological Themes in Luke-Acts

CHAPTER 4—Galilean Ministry (Luke 3:1—9:50) | 64

    Jesus as the Central Narrative Character
    Calling of the Disciples (Luke 5:1–11, 27–32; 6:12–16)
    Raising of the Widow's Son (Luke 7:11–17)
    Jesus Anointed by a Sinful Woman (Luke 7:36–50)
    Women who Support Jesus (Luke 8:1–3)
    Jesus' True Family (Luke 8:19–21)
    Raising of Jairus' Daughter and the Healing of the Women with a Hemorrhage (Luke 8:40–56)
    Summary of Narratival Propositions
    Theological Propositions
    Anticipating Further Narrative and Theological Themes in Luke-Acts

CHAPTER 5—Travel Narrative (Luke 9:51—19:28) | 101

    Sophistication and Paradigms as Narratival Techniques
    The Mission of the Seventy (Luke 10:1–24)
    Mary and Martha (Luke 10:38–42)
    The Queen of the South (Luke 11:31)
    Healing of a Crippled Woman on the Sabbath (Luke 13:10–17)
    The Parable of the Lost Coin (Luke 15:7–10)
    The Parable of the Judge and the Widow (Luke 18:1–8)
    Summary of Narratival Propositions
    Theological Propositions

CHAPTER 6—Jerusalem Narrative (Luke 19:29—24:53) | 123

    The Widow's Offering (Luke 21:1–4)
    Peter's Denial and the Astute Servant Girl (Luke 22:54–62)
    On the Way to the Cross (Luke 23:26–31)
    The Death of Jesus (Luke 23:44–49)
    The Resurrection of Jesus (Luke 24:1–12)
    Summary of Narratival Propositions
    Theological Propositions

CHAPTER 7—The Purpose and Structure of Acts | 139

    Luke's Portrayal of Women in Acts
    The Purposes of Acts: Theological and Apologetic
    The Structure of Acts

CONTENTS

CHAPTER 8—The Birth of the Church (Acts 1–2) | 149

    Acts 1
    Acts 2
    Summary of Narratival Propositions
    Theological Propositions

CHAPTER 9—The Church in Jerusalem (Acts 3–12) | 157

    Ananias and Sapphira (Acts 5:1–11)
    The Seven who Serve (Acts 6:1–7)
    Tabitha—also Known as Dorcas (Acts 9:36–42)
    Mary Mother of John, and Rhoda (Acts 12:12–17)
    Summary of Narratival Propositions
    Theological Propositions

CHAPTER 10—The Church in the Greco-Roman World (Acts 13–28) | 184

    The Conversion of Lydia (Acts 16:11–40)
    Priscilla (Acts 18:1–28)
    The Daughters of Philip (Acts 21:1–16)
    Summary of Narratival Propositions
    Theological Propositions

CHAPTER 11—Summary and Conclusions | 202

    Summary of Narratival Propositions in Luke and Acts
    Summary of Theological Propositions in Luke and Acts
    A Lukan Theology of Women
    A Final Word

Bibliography | 219
Index of Names | 231

Foreword

IS THE BIBLE GOOD for women? I have been asked this question many times, and I have always been puzzled as to how to answer it. The question presumes that we both know what "good" is—it is having a choice, being independent, self sufficient, and autonomous. Of course, these "goods" are our modern Western culture's "goods," they are not necessarily the virtues of the ancient world, or of every culture around the world today. I feel that to answer such a question, one first needed to see what the ancient world thought was "good."

During the 1980s in graduate school, I began to study women in the ancient Jewish and Greco-Roman cultures of the Mediterranean world. At that time, some scholars approached texts much like miners work on a mountain, chiseling the solid rock of data, hoping to discover a gem—information about historical women's lives. There was a confidence that the reader could examine the text objectively, and that the text itself presented simple historical facts. Elisabeth Schüssler Fiorenza's *In Memory of Her: A Feminist Theological Reconstruction of Christian Origins* (Crossroad, 1983) broke new ground as she challenged the patriarchal and androcentric bias of the ancient texts. She read with a hermeneutic of suspicion, which confronted the text's portrait of women to discover a liberating note within the cacophony of patriarchal jangle. This approach continues to be influential in reconstructing women's lives from ancient sources, as seen in Robert M. Price, *The Widow Traditions in Luke-Acts: A Feminist-Critical Scrutiny* (Scholars Press, 1997).

As feminist studies proceeded, different reading strategies developed. First, minority feminist voices and postcolonial readings incorporated feminist analysis as they engaged the biblical text, as for example Musa

W. Dube's *Postcolonial Feminist Interpretation of the Bible* (Chalice Press, 2000). Second, there grew increasing skepticism about gaining access to real women's lives through the texts. Sources were seen as constructing women (and men) in gendered ways; elite male authors used women as constructed categories in their discussions about political, social, religious, and cultural life. An example of this approach can be found in Ross Shepard Kraemer's *Unreliable Witnesses: Religion, Gender, and History in the Greco-Roman Mediterranean* (Oxford, 2011). Kraemer contrasts her earlier work that was more confident in the sources' ability to present historical women with her current position, which postulates that ancient authors constructed women from their beliefs about gender and social order. These constructed women are often beyond the historian's reach.

Others, myself included, are more optimistic about the possibility of discerning historical information from texts, while recognizing the text's rhetorical power and the importance of the modern reader's perspective. In my book *Women in the World of the Earliest Christians: Illuminating Ancient Ways of Life* (Baker Academic, 2009), I examine in broad strokes the real and the ideal women of Second Temple Judaism and the emerging Roman Empire. I focus on a woman's life cycle—birth, marriage, work, family, and religion—as the ancients wrote about it. My book pays attention to ancient rhetoric, the culturally established truths about men and women, about religion and politics, to give readers today a sense of what an average woman's life might have been like. But my book was never intended as the last word; it was to be the first word, a foundation upon which careful study of specific women, especially biblical women, could be built.

Recently several works have looked with historical lens at specific women in the New Testament, and situate these women's experiences in the broader Jewish and Greco-Roman environment. Craig S. Keener's *Paul, Women and Wives: Marriage and Women's Ministry in the Letters of Paul* (Hendrickson, 1992), and Richard Bauckham's *Gospel Women: Studies of the Named Women in the Gospels* (Eerdmans, 2002) focus on particular New Testament writings as they explore women's activities and their identity as followers of Jesus. These books provide helpful snapshots of women within the Jesus movement; they invite further analysis of biblical women from *within* the narrative of the biblical text.

Raised from Obscurity takes up that invitation. Scott Harrower and Greg Forbes focus on the narrative of Luke/Acts, recognizing that texts are constructed worlds wherein the story tells the reader what is going on and what to think about those events. They argue that the narrative's characters reflect historical figures, thus linking narrative text and historical context.

Using the narratival and narratival-theological approaches, Harrower and Forbes address how the portrait of women interacts with the larger aims of Luke/Acts, and how that portrait contributes to the theological message of the biblical text. These scholars are well equipped to do this job. Harrower focused on systematic theology in his graduate work, completing his dissertation on the Trinity in Luke and Acts at Trinity Evangelical Divinity School in Deerfield, IL. Forbes has explored Luke's Gospel since his days in graduate school, and his dissertation from Deakin University, Melbourne, looks closely at Luke's parables. These two bring their complementary expertise to this project, resulting in a sophisticated, nuanced examination of women in Luke/Acts.

In the opening chapter of the book the authors lay out their methodology, discussing how they will develop narratival propositions, and from these narratival propositions, draw theological propositions. The second chapter provides a historical, social, and cultural overview of the first-century Greco-Roman world, with special attention paid to Jewish communities, especially in Roman Palestine.

Harrower and Forbes next turn to the narrative itself in Luke/Acts. Here we find detailed and extensive discussion on well-known figures such as Mary, the mother of Jesus, Elizabeth, John the Baptist's mother, and Mary Magdalene. They explore whether women are portrayed as serious disciples, for example, or as unreliable. If serious disciples, how does that emphasis play out within the wider narrative, in a woman's interaction with Jesus or with other disciples? And what does the serious female disciple reveal about God's engagement with the church, about God's character in Christ, and the church's mission to the world? A significant benefit of this approach is that it allows Luke's fundamental purpose—an account of Jesus of Nazareth, his teachings, his Passion, and his followers—to remain central as female characters are illuminated and analyzed.

Alongside insightful discussions of the main female characters, Harrower and Forbes spend time on lesser-known figures. The treatment of Rhoda is an example of the authors' careful attention to details, understanding of ancient culture, and theological prowess. Rhoda is the slave girl who greets Peter at the outer gate of the house of Mary, the mother of John, after his miraculous release from prison (Acts 12:1-17). Harrower and Forbes highlight the important role she plays in Luke's drama and bring to the fore Rhoda's low status as a slave. The household characters' skepticism and derision at her news of Peter's arrival is pointed to as typical treatment for her social class. And the chastisement of these characters is discussed as the plot reveals their blindness and Rhoda's clear sight. Luke demonstrates with her character that women might serve in ways beyond their social class or circumstances. Harrower and Forbes tie this story back to the reliable testimony given by the women at the empty tomb, who were initially ignored by the other disciples, but later vindicated as it became known that their claims of Jesus' resurrection were indeed true. This attention to detail, to the seemingly minor characters, makes the book interesting and engaging.

Harrower and Forbes discover that in Luke/Acts, women are valued as key disciples, thinkers, actors, and even mouthpieces of God. They act as important witnesses to God's commands and demonstrate faithfulness. They highlight the values of God's kingdom, which include service and humility, two typical "feminine" virtues that, then and now, are not often associated with leadership and authority.

Harrower and Forbes have synthesized decades of scholarship on Luke's portrait of women, and offer concise explanations of competing theories as they lay out their own argument based on Luke's narrative and theology. Whether readers are quite familiar with Luke/Acts, or reading it for the first time, they will find the book's format and argument straightforward and clear. And challenging, for in laying out Luke's narrative and theology as it relates to female disciples, Harrower and Forbes' allow Luke to confront, provoke, and inspire readers today to live their lives in line with the faithful pattern presented by the women in Luke/Acts. They invite the reader to be the "yes" to the question, "Is the Bible good for women?"

Lynn H. Cohick, PhD
Wheaton College, Wheaton, IL

Acknowledgments

THERE ARE MANY PEOPLE who have assisted us, both directly and indirectly, in the production of this work. First of all, we are appreciative of the helpful and obliging editorial staff at Wipf and Stock Publishers, particularly Robin Parry for his encouragement and enthusiasm for the project from the outset. We are also grateful to our friends, students, and colleagues who together provide the stimulating climate that enables theological reflection and writing.

In terms of direct input Scott would like to thank Rev. Dr. Douglas McComiskey for his formative influence with respect to methodological issues to do with Luke's Gospel. During an MA seminar class at Ridley College, Doug helpfully pointed Scott to a wide variety of literature and to the issues that attend the vexed relationship between narrative and the theology. We are both grateful to Kate Harrower and Kara Reeves who read part of the manuscript and offered helpful suggestions. Special thanks go to Gillian Asquith, who not only acted as proof-reader but was also a source of invigorating encouragement and enthusiasm. Finally, we are indebted to Lynn Cohick for agreeing to read the manuscript and write the foreword.

CHAPTER 1

Introduction and Methodology

> If one chooses to teach and preach Luke's stories uncritically, they continue to reinforce patriarchal role divisions. On the other hand, if one engages in the difficult task of reinterpreting the text from a feminist perspective, reading against Luke's intent, then the stories can be recontextualized to proclaim a message of good news for women and men called equally to share in the same discipleship and mission of Jesus.
>
> —BARBARA E. REID. *CHOOSING THE BETTER PART? WOMEN IN THE GOSPEL OF LUKE,* 205.

THE AUTHOR OF THE quote above is not alone in her negative evaluation and consequent rejection of the Lukan narrative and Luke's views of women. She is representative of several, mainly feminist, interpreters who consider that Luke's objective was to suppress the roles of women in the early church. Consequently, he portrays them as passive and silent disciples who do not enjoy equal participation with men in the mission of Jesus.

This book proposes a counter-case. It is our contention that Luke has a remarkably positive and rich view of women who are believers in the God of Israel and Jesus as Lord. We arrive at this contention by utilizing a narratival, and narratival-theological approach, the justification for which will be further explained after the literature review. This review clearly demonstrates the polarized nature of scholarship on Luke's theology of women. Our work provides a narrative-sensitive way through the impasse.

Literature Review

Works on literature, narrative, characterization, and narratival theology abound. General material in these areas include those by Robert Alter,[1] Mark Allan Powell,[2] Shimon Bar-Efrat,[3] and more specialized pieces on OT[4] and NT books[5] (particularly Mark's Gospel).[6] Specialized contributions on Luke and Luke-Acts include those by Sánchez Navarro,[7] Manuel Benéitez,[8] Étienne Mbilizi,[9] Daniel Gerber,[10] Jens Börstinghaus,[11] Willard Swartley,[12]

---

1. Alter, *The Art of Biblical Narrative*; Alter, *The World of Biblical Literature*.
2. Powell, *What is Narrative Criticism?*
3. Bar-Efrat, *Das Zweite Buch Samuel*; Bar-Efrat and Klein, *Das erste Buch Samuel*; Bar-Efrat, *Narrative Art in the Bible*.
4. Alter, *The Five Books of Moses*.
5. Poplutz, *Erzählte Welt: narratologische Studien zum Matthäusevangelium*; Frey and Poplutz, *Narrativität und Theologie im Johannesevangelium*; Dettwiler, "Studien Zu Matthäus Und Johannes"; Eisen, *Die Poetik der Apostelgeschichte: Eine narratologische Studie*; Sánchez Navarro, *Testimonios del Reino: Evangelios sinópticos y Hechos de los apóstoles*; Resseguie, *Narrative Criticism of the New Testament*; Culpepper, *Anatomy of the Fourth Gospel*; Culpepper and Segovia, *The Fourth Gospel from a Literary Perspective*.
6. This is a very fruitful field of study, but only a representative sample may be provided at this juncture. In New Testament circles, Mark's Gospel has received significant sustained attention over the past twenty years. A landmark work in this field was Rhoads and Michie, *Mark as Story*. This work (now in its third edition) and its enduring influence has now been the source of considered reflection in Iverson and Skinner, *Mark as Story: Retrospect and Prospect*. Another thorough work on narrative methodology is France, *Gospel of Mark*.
7. Sánchez Navarro, *Testimonios del Reino: Evangelios sinópticos y Hechos de los apóstoles*.
8. Benéitez, *"Esta salvación de Dios" (Hech 28,28): Análisis narrativo estructuralista de "Hechos"*.
9. Mbilizi, *D'Israël aux nations: L'horizon de la rencontre avec le Sauveur dans l'œuvre de Luc*.
10. Gerber, *"Il vous est né un sauveur," La construction du sens sotériologique de la venue de Jésus en Luc-Actes*.
11. Börstinghaus, *Sturm fahrt und Schiffbruch: Zur lukanischen Verwendung eines literarischen Topos in Apostelgeschichte 27,1—28,6*.
12. Swartley, *Israel's Scripture Traditions*.

James Dawsey,[13] Robert L. Brawley,[14] C. Kavin Rowe,[15] Charles Talbert,[16] Joel Green,[17] Karl Allen Kuhn,[18] Mikeal C. Parsons,[19] John A. Darr,[20] Robert C. Tannehill,[21] and multi authored works such as that edited by J. Frey, C. K. Rothschild, and J. Schröter.[22] Clearly there is a sustained interest in Luke's narrative, theology, and characterization. However, there has been relatively little narratological work on female characters in Luke and/or Acts.

In terms of what has been done with respect to the Lukan narrative and its theological portrayal of women believers there are three broad approaches. We have labeled these approaches the 'feminist—liberationist' perspective, the 'selective reader' approach and the 'broad positive—descriptive' stance. We will summarize each of these in turn.

First, the 'feminist-liberationist' perspective. Some of the specific work on female characters in Luke has been carried out from this perspective with the intent to provide a counter reading against the grain of Luke's Gospel. This is represented by Barbara Reid's 1997 volume *Choosing the Better Part? Women in the Gospel of Luke*.[23] In her study Reid employs a femi-

---

13. Dawsey, *The Lukan Voice*.

14. Brawley, *Centering on God*.

15. Rowe, *Early Narrative Christology*; Rowe, "History, Hermeneutics and the Unity of Luke-Acts"; Rowe, "Luke and the Trinity"; Rowe, "Biblical Pressure and Trinitarian Hermeneutics."

16. Talbert's contribution to the study of Luke's narrative and its theology revolves around the idea that Luke has a distinctive view of Jesus, and this view of Jesus has many facets. This must be borne in mind when pericopes are interpreted. Talbert notes that the Lukan use (or omission) of available materials is one of the keys to understanding the "distinctively Lukan picture of Jesus." Talbert, *Literary Patterns*, 111–12.

17. According to Green, in order to draw theology from the Gospel of Luke, the exegete needs to bear in mind two key points. First, how conclusions were drawn from narratives by readers in a Greco-Roman/Hellenistic Jewish context. Second, being attuned to the particular shape the author gives his narrative in order to achieve his larger aims. Green, *Theology of the Gospel of Luke*, 21; Green, "Learning Theological Interpretation from Luke."

18. Kuhn's particular contribution is to focus on the relationship between the narrative and the emotional elements of stories. His focus is especially on the opening chapters of Luke's Gospel. His point is that there is a "cardiography" within biblical narratives that are intended to move the reader. Kuhn, *The Heart of Biblical Narrative*.

19. Parsons locates Luke within his Greco-Roman rhetorical milieu, and explores the author's work from this standpoint. Parsons, *Luke*.

20. Darr, *Herod the Fox*. See also the more general work on characterization in Luke-Acts: Darr, *On Character Building*.

21. Tannehill, *Narrative Unity*. Tannehill, *Luke*. Tannehill, *The Shape of Luke's Story*.

22. Frey, Rothschild, and Schröter, *Die Apostelgeschichte im Kontext antiker und frühchristlicher Historiographie*.

23. Reid, *Better Part*. Examples of similar approaches were included in the 1997

nist-liberationist hermeneutic to the end that she explicitly writes *against* what she perceives to be Luke's view on women. Reid is unambiguous in clarifying her intention. She explains: "As we proceed with these stories, we will approach Luke's restrictive portrayal of women with a hermeneutic of suspicion. We will be 'choosing the better part' by looking for ways to read against Luke's intent so as to release their liberating potential."[24] Reid has also written polemically against what she believes to be Luke's portrayal of women as silent and passive contrasts to male disciples.[25] Given that Reid writes against the grain of the text, the natural result is that these leanings dampen the theological depth and integrity of her conclusions from the narrative. Reid's work was shortly followed by Jane Schaberg's provocative essay in the *Women's Bible Commentary*.[26] Schaberg writes, "The Gospel of Luke is an extremely dangerous text, perhaps the most dangerous in the Bible."[27]

The second approach to the characterization of women within Luke's narrative is the 'selective-reader' method. Loretta Dornisch may be taken as representative of this approach. Like Reid's work, Dornisch's *A Woman Reads the Gospel of Luke* was published by the Liturgical Press in the mid-1990s, and operates with a feminist reading of the text. We have categorized this approach as the 'selective reader' approach to the text because it is a fusion of historical-critical methods, a study of selected perspectives offered within the text, and the individual perspective (often based on particular experiences) of the reader. This view could also be described as a selective and biblically informed version of the reader response approach. Dornisch's description of the methodology she uses to interpret the Gospel of Luke includes comments on 'latitude' in her reading. For Dornisch this latitude allows one to move away from the majority "male or even patriarchal" reading of the text.[28] This latitude is enhanced when Dornisch brings significant personal reflection to bear upon the text. She writes:

Semeia volume which was wholly devoted to women's perspectives on the Bible. The volume was entitled "Reading the Bible as Women: Perspectives from Africa, Asia and Latin America." Essays included Rebera Ranjini, "Polarity or Parnership? Retelling the Story of Martha and Mary from Asian Women's Perspective (Luke 10:38–42); Musa W. Dube, "Toward a Postcolonial Feminist Interpretation of the Bible." Reid's more recent work includes *Taking Up the Cross: New Testament Interpretations through Latina and Feminist Eyes*.

24. Reid, *Better Part*, 95.
25. Reid, "Choosing the Better Part."
26. Schaberg, "Luke," 363–80.
27. Ibid., 363.
28. Dornisch, "A Woman Reads the Gospel of Luke," 8.

We have, then, for our reflections a first perspective of the writer or writers of Luke, a second perspective of the implied narrator or narrators of the individual story or groups of stories, and a third perspective of "certain women" who seem important in the unfolding of the text. A fourth perspective is that of women today who bring their own experience to the reading of the good news.[29]

Dornisch's work has a more positive view of the authorship of Luke's Gospel than that of Reid. Dornisch even hypothesizes that the composition of the Gospel may have included female contributors. She is thus focused on stories about, and from, women.[30] For her, such a reading provides a sound counter to pervasive views of women in the Greco-Roman world.[31] However, what her Ricoeurian approach ultimately accents is the *possibility* of a *positive reading* of women in Luke's Gospel. There is, therefore, a significant implied assumption which informs her approach to the narrative and underlies her aims. Dornish assumes that a positive view of women in Luke is not accomplished by listening to the narrative and the theology which is native to the text itself. To her mind, such a positive view must be achieved by adding to the text. Dornisch's positive view of women, therefore, is established by means of reading the text via the external lens of one's own aims, history and experience.

The third direction in studies of women in Luke may be termed the 'broad positive-descriptive' approach. These are studies which are broad in that they either include material from beyond Luke's Gospel or their survey of the material in Luke (or Luke-Acts) is from a wide-ranging perspective. These studies are positive in that they consider (1) Luke's perspective towards women to be in some sense counter-cultural and (2) Jesus' ministry meant some form of social and spiritual liberation for women.

One of the 'broad positive' approaches is represented in the seminal study by Ben Witherington III. Witherington's *Women in the Ministry of Jesus* is a survey of Jesus' view of women during his earthly ministry.

29. Ibid., 11.
30. Dornisch, *A Woman Reads the Gospel of Luke*.
31. Dornisch's position may be described as a post-modern, moderate womanist and comparative-religions position. This approach differs from Reid's. A representative passage reads as follows: "Many feminist writers see the highlighting of the role of a virgin as anti-woman, lacking appreciation of the goodness of sexuality. In the context of the culture of the time, however, the concept may have very different connotations. . . . In this story, then, Mary is a virgin, radically replacing the accepted virgin Athena. She appears in the simplicity and strength of an autonomous woman from whom the Lord requests a role radically different from the dominant roles in her society. A new concept of virgin as free person has emerged." Ibid., 16.

Witherington explores these relationships, actions, and attitudes between the birth and resurrection narratives (which he does not treat).[32] A recent work by Darrell Bock has contributed to this strand of scholarship. Bock's *A Theology of Luke and Acts* includes a section on women in Luke and Acts which concludes that women are depicted as those who model belief and testify to the grace they have received from God though Jesus.[33] These examples affirm Jesus' and Luke's positive stance towards women and their involvement in his mission. However, the theological claims about women arising from the narrative are not stated strongly. For example, although Witherington notes that the relationship that Jesus has with women is marked by positive regard, the narratival and theological claims are quite restrained given the direction and cumulative focus of the narrative. Notwithstanding this restraint, the positive regard for the narratival presentation of Jesus and his interactions with women is what sets works like these apart from the 'feminist-liberationist' and the 'selective-reader' proposals.

Richard Bauckham's *Gospel Women: Studies of the Named Women in the Gospels* seeks to provide fresh insight into particular women characters in the Gospels. Not all named women are covered (e.g., Mary and Martha), but those that do appear are treated with Bauckham's characteristic historical and exegetical rigor. While drawing on the insights of feminist biblical criticism, Bauckham is sharply critical of the feminist tendency to employ a hermeneutic of suspicion as their methodological foundation. On this approach texts are "not assumed innocent until proved guilty, but assumed guilty without a chance of a fair hearing."[34] Bauckham likens his work to a "series of deep probes,"[35] a collection of essays designed to conduct a thorough investigation into "whatever questions seemed capable of interesting answers."[36] In the main, Bauckham focuses on "the world of the text and the world to which the text makes historical reference."[37]

As expected, much of Bauckham's work is focused on the Gospel of Luke, for it is here that many of the named women in the Gospels appear. Overall, not only is his study of women 'broadly positive,' he also suggests that at times the narrative presents a gynocentric perspective in which recipients are invited to read the text from the perspective of the female

---

32. Witherington, *Women*.

33. Bock, *Theology of Luke and Acts*, 344–52. Another example of a positive view of Jesus' and Luke's perspectives on women is a very short, devotional piece by Osiek, "Accusers, Mourners, Disciples."

34. Bauckham, *Gospel Women*, xv.

35. Ibid., xvii.

36. Ibid.

37. Ibid., xviii.

character(s). He brings this to bear specifically in his study on Joanna (Luke 8:1–3) where he proposes that from this point in the narrative the text invites the reader to adopt the perspective of the women who journey with Jesus. Consequently,

> if we read on from 8:1–3 in the company of Joanna and the other women, it will not be possible to read 10:1–20, where Jesus sends out seventy-two disciples to participate actively in his own mission of preaching and healing, without assuming that the women are included among these disciples.[38]

Bauckham's text and historical-centered approach forms a contrast to that of F. Scott Spencer. Spencer's recent work is restricted to Luke's Gospel and is 'broadly positive' towards Luke's presentation of women and their relationship to Jesus.[39] The breadth that characterizes Spencer's work stems from his decades-long interaction with feminist scholarship. This means that his treatment of Luke's Gospel with respect to women is focused upon significant themes within feminist thinking. The breadth of his work is also evidenced in the scope of characters which he studies. Beyond those with whom Jesus interacts directly, he also pays significant attention to female characters including the persistent widow from one of Jesus' parables, as well as foreign women mentioned by Luke such as the widow of Zarephath, the queen of Sheba, and Lot's wife. Spencer's work is generally positive towards Luke's depiction of women, however, he argues that it is a complex and at times ambiguous depiction.[40] He states:

> I endeavor in this project to pull the pendulum back a tad from the feminist-critical pole toward the center ... still applying sharp feminist-critical analyses, but pressing through to more salutary results, to a somewhat sweeter concentration in Luke's bittersweet, 'mixed message' regarding women's agency and action.[41]

---

38. Ibid., 200.
39. Spencer, *Salty Wives*.
40. Spencer has marked similarities with an earlier work by Turid Karlsen Seim. In a statement with strong affinities to Spencer's findings Seim writes: "It is a preposterous simplification to ask whether Luke's writings are friendly or hostile to women. Luke's version of the life of Jesus and of his believers cannot be reduced either to a feminist treasure chamber or to a chamber of horrors for women's theology. It contains elements that bring joy to 'dignity studies' and other elements that give support to 'misery studies.'" Seim, *Double Message*, 249.
41. Spencer, *Salty Wives*, 4

Spencer continues with the claim that his mixed message seeks to avoid both selectivity and anachronism whilst engaging in sensitive literary and historical work:

> Short of remixing Luke's soundtrack, I see . . . no way to amplify women's virtual silence (after the birth narratives) in this Gospel. And short of anachronistic revisionism, I see no rhyme or reason to profiling Jesus or Luke as first century feminists. . . . But I do see room to expand our positive engagement with 'capable women of purpose and persistence' within their Lukan literary and social worlds.[42]

Spencer describes his methodology as one which "generally reflects an eclectic use of grammatical, historical, sociological, literary, canonical, theological, postmodern, and feminist tools."[43] However, such eclectic method arguably comes at a price. The cost is less attention on the text and its narrative and theological claims. It can also lead to quite disparate results. This problem is exacerbated by his rather wide-ranging interests (e.g., he reads Luke 1:57–58 and 15:8–9 with reference to the *gecekondu* women in Istanbul[44]).

The Aim of this Book

If these three approaches are indicative of the state of affairs, they point to a lacuna in Lukan scholarship. That is, there is a paucity of recent work which privileges the narrative and its theology of women who believe in the God of Israel and Jesus as Lord. This state of affairs is surprising given the frequent inclusion of women and the relatively prominent role (in comparison to the other Gospels) that they play throughout Luke's Gospel and Acts. In his study we intend to redress this lacuna.

So the aim of this work is to study the narrative of Luke-Acts and to clearly articulate the theology which resides within the author's characterization of women. To this end we will explore three literary and theological elements which relate to women as players in the divine drama that Luke describes. These elements are (i) the characterization of women in the narrative, (ii) narratival claims made concerning such women, and (iii) theological claims concerning women that arise directly or indirectly from the narrative. A more detailed explanation of our methodology follows.

42. Ibid.
43. Ibid., 20.
44. Ibid., 337–38.

A Methodology for Exploring a Narrative's Theological Claims about Its Characters

In the preface to Luke's Gospel (Luke 1:1–4), the author introduces his work as a narrative (διήγησις), with key concerns for order (καθεξῆς), accuracy (ἀκριβῶς) and reliability (ἀσφάλεια).[45] In so doing, Luke has carefully constructed a two-part work in which there are a number of narrative parallels both within each of the two parts and between the two parts. In terms of its balance, symmetry, and pattern, it resembles classical works such as Virgil's *Aeneid* and Near Eastern literature such as the books of Jonah and Ruth.[46] Luke informs us that his gospel is written for the purpose of strengthening the recipient's confidence in the reliability of what he has been informed or taught. In other words, Theophilus can be sure that the narrative of events surrounding the birth, ministry, death, and resurrection of Jesus is indeed trustworthy. The book of Acts will go on to provide a narrative account of those who are understood to be the legitimate followers of Jesus.[47]

It is now generally accepted that the four canonical Gospels fall within the broad genre of Greco-Roman *bioi*.[48] Luke's 'cultic biography' then follows the tradition which includes works such as Diogenes Laertius, *Lives of Eminent Philosophers*. These biographies "usually treat the career of the community's founder as the value norm for devotees and the object of their reverence and worship."[49] Talbert also notes that within this genre tradition there was a type of biography in which "(a) the life of the divine hero was followed by (b) a narrative of successors and selected other disciples. These components (a + b) were parts of a single work."[50] Such biographies with the a + b pattern were employed to legitimate particular philosophical schools of thought. This endorsement occurs via legitimating the initial witness to the founder's words and actions and also by legitimating the continuity

---

45 "[I]n describing his work as a narrative . . . , Luke identified his project as an account of many events, for which the chief prototypes are the early Greek histories of Herodotus and Thucydides." Green, *Theology of the Gospel of Luke*, 18. For the style of amateur history or biography including Callimorphus, Josephus (*Antiquities, Against Apion*) and Dionysius of Halicarnassus (*Roman Antiquities*), see Downing, "'Theophilus' First Reading of Luke-Acts," 97–100. For narrative parallels in Old Testament, Rabbinic and Hellenistic stories, see Martin, ed. *Narrative Parallels to the New Testament*.

46. On Luke's genre see Talbert, "Once Again: Gospel Genre."

47. Talbert, *Reading Luke*, 2–3.

48. Burridge, *What Are the Gospels?*; Pearson and Porter, "Genres of the New Testament," 137–42; Keener, *Historical Jesus*, 71–125.

49. Talbert, *Reading Luke*, 2–3.

50. Ibid., 3.

between the followers and the life and teachings of the hero.[51] Luke-Acts has obvious parallels with this literary form.

For the author of Luke-Acts, "narration is proclamation."[52] As highly purposeful literature, the narrator deliberately employs "history to preach, to set forth a persuasive, narrative interpretation of God's work in Jesus."[53] Therefore, not only the narrative itself and its structure, but the interpretation of the narrative is a key concern for Luke.[54] As a compiler and redactor, he has selected his material so that the narration occurs as a select sequence of events. This selection has been deliberately made so that the narrative achieves a particular theological, and thus proclamatory aim.[55] Storytelling techniques such as dialogue,[56] mode of narration,[57] repeated actions[58] including type scenes,[59] narrative specification,[60] word and phrase choice, and word or phrase repetition, alert the reader to the significant themes in the narrative.

---

51. Ibid., 2–3.

52. Green, *Theology of the Gospel of Luke*, 19.

53. Ibid.

54. Ibid.

55. Ibid.

56. Dialogue is stylized in different ways to achieve various ends. It may be long or short and include varied tones and images within. All these features contribute to dialogue being an "effective vehicle of meaning." Alter, *The Art of Biblical Narrative*, 182–83.

57. Alter (ibid., 183) states, "Perhaps the most distinctive feature of the role played by the narrator in the biblical text is the way in which omniscience and inobtrusiveness [*sic*.] are combined." The attentive reader of narrative should also pay attention to changes in narrational patterns, as this is highly significant and a means by which the narrator emphasizes a point. Alter writes: "The Bible's highly laconic mode of narration may often give the impression of presenting the events virtually without mediation: so much, after all, is conveyed through dialogue with only the minimal 'he said' to remind us of a narrator's presence; and even outside of dialogue, what is often reported is absolutely essential action, without obtrusive elaboration or any obvious intervention by the narrator. Against this norm, we should direct special attention to the moments when the illusion of unmediated action is manifestly shattered. Ibid., 184.

58. Repeated action "occurs when we are given two versions of the same event and when the same event, with minor variations, occurs at different junctures of the narrative, usually involving a different character or sets of characters. . . . The question we might ask is why he [the author] should have done this, in what ways do the two narrative perspectives complement or complicate each other." Ibid., 181.

59. "The recurrence of the same event—the sameness being defined as a fixed sequence of narrative motifs which, however, may be presented in a variety of ways and sometimes with ingenious variations—is what I have called 'type scene,' and it constitutes a central organizing convention of biblical narrative." Ibid.

60. The general lack of narrative specification in the Bible means that "when a particular descriptive detail is mentioned—Esau's ruddiness and hairiness, Rachel's beauty, King's Eglon's obesity—we should be alert for consequences, immediate or eventual, either in plot or theme." Ibid., 180.

The key concern in our study is to examine what the narrative communicates and its consequent theological message regarding women who are followers of Jesus.[61] Therefore, we hope to draw both narratival and theological proposals (see further, below) from a close following of the text itself. In this way we hope to subordinate our Australian male biases to the text. This awareness of our own situatedness means that a careful and attentive methodology is crucial to the success of our endeavor. This methodology is outlined below.

Our method will particularly draw upon the contributions of scholars who have specialized in narrative and literary critical issues. These include R. Alan Culpepper, Robert Alter, David Rhoads and Donald Michie, R. T. France, Willard Swartley, James Dawsey, Robert F. Brawley, C. Kavin Rowe, James L. Resseguie, Charles Talbert, Joel Green, John A. Darr, and Robert C. Tannehill.[62]

First, the structure of the narrative will be ascertained from the plot.[63] For example, based on the turning points in the narratival flow, we may break up the narrative of Luke-Acts into the following sections: Infancy Narratives (Luke 1:5—2:52), Galilean Ministry (3:1—9:50), Travel Narrative (9:51—19:28), Jerusalem Narrative (19:29—24:53), The Birth of the Church (Acts 1–2), The Church in Jerusalem (Acts 3–12), and The Church in the Greco-Roman World (Acts 13–28). The narrative can then be broken down into macro-sections of grouped pericopes. This macro-breakdown and pericope grouping is based upon the "prima facie coherence of subject matter and/or function in the development of the narrative."[64] That is to say, the major sections of the narrative provide their own compass for the interpretation of the passages within them.

Awareness of the larger structure of Luke-Acts and how this affects the interpretation of pericopes will aid the identification of the narratival threads (see below) which run through each section of the narrative structure. Examples of such key threads of the narrative include Christology, promise-fulfilment, and mission. Based upon these broader structures of

---

61. The exception here is, of course, the women in the Infancy Narratives who are not followers of Jesus but believers in the God of Israel.

62. Steps three through five of our methodology are a significant adaptation, drawing on the works of others cited in this paragraph, of a methodology developed by Douglas S. McComiskey in a class that he teaches for deriving theology from Luke's narrative. His methodology involves the formation of summary thematic propositions on a pericope-by-pericope basis, the translation of those narrative propositions into theological propositions, and the consideration of the cumulative body of propositions in the development of a Lukan theology.

63. This is done bearing in mind the macro-genre of the Gospels and the genre of individual pericopes.

64. France, *Gospel of Mark*, 14.

the narrative, the reader is to follow each thread (i.e., Christology, fulfilment or mission) through the narrative to see how the narrative makes certain theological propositions about these concerns.

Second, we shall note how characters are introduced into and developed within the narrative. This will take place within individual or grouped pericopes and may include several different techniques. Characterization may be developed through "indirect presentation,"[65] whereby characters are left to reveal themselves to the reader. In this case there is no comment by the narrator which may influence the reader's perception of the character. For example, Luke 7:39 records the self-talk of the Pharisee: "when the Pharisee who had invited him saw this, he said to himself, 'If this man were a prophet he would know who and what sort of a person this woman is who is touching him, and that she is a sinner.'" On the other hand, characters may be presented directly to the audience. This means that the omniscient narrator will comment on the traits of the characters or reveal their inner thoughts. For example, Cornelius is depicted as a generous and kind man: "a devout man . . . gave many alms to the people . . ." (Acts 10:2). Other narrative techniques which will be highlighted include 'explanatory discourses,'[66] scenes where the narrator uses 'sandwiching' technique and/or a 'parallel spotlight' technique,[67] and narrative 'knots.'[68]

Third, based on characterization and the broader story of Luke, we shall identify the *narratival propositions* which emerge from the text. A narratival proposition is a succinct proposal or statement that arises from the narrative, and may be either implicit or stated directly. It summarizes the main point the narrative makes about a given character or characters. The focus of the narratival proposition will vary according to the type of character presented in the story. In this way, the same story can yield different propositions with respect to different characters. For example, a narratival proposition arising from the story of Jesus calming the storm (Luke 8:22–25) is that *Jesus has power over the fierce wind and the waves of the sea*. With

---

65. Resseguie, *Narrative Criticism of the New Testament*, 126–28.

66. These are crucial for drawing out theology from the narrative. They provide "a theological framework for understanding the new thing that is happening with the coming of Jesus of Nazareth." France, *The Gospel of Mark*, 15.

67. "Not only does he enclose one story within another, but he likes to set up parallel scenes and move the spot light between them . . . so that they become mutually illuminating." Ibid., 19.

68 These are points at which multiple paradoxes come together with "special force." This allows for comparison between the beginning of the particular paradox and the unexpected final status of the elements within the paradoxes. The solution of the narrative knots is sometimes left to the reader, because the paradox may not be explicitly resolved. Ibid., 20.

reference to the disciples, the same story would lead to the proposition that *the disciples' faith in Jesus is challenged by the storm and found to be wanting.*

The examples that have been given above are narratival propositions whose contours are determined by the specific details of the text. One might say they are 'first order' narratival propositions. In addition the narrative may also yield more generalized 'second order' narratival propositions. This is so because the narrative may have inherent generalizing tendencies which cannot be ignored. These second order propositions extend beyond the particular details of the story and generalize according to major influences within the narrative. These influences may be summarized as four narratively attuned criteria:

1. Key concerns of the narrative, for example the kingdom of God, the poor and the marginalized of society.
2. The generalization will be entirely consistent with the broader ministry of Jesus in Luke-Acts.
3. The generalization will not be inconsistent with any other features of the narrative.
4. The presence of words or signs within the story which drive the proposition beyond its immediate horizons.

For example, in the story of Mary and Martha (Luke 10:38–42) Jesus explicitly rejects a socially regulated role for Mary (preparing a meal) in favor of her accepting the disposition of a rabbinic pupil. A first order narratival proposition emerging from the episode would be: *Jesus rejects socially regulated roles by allowing Mary to listen to his teachings as her first priority.* However, according to the four criteria listed above, there is evidence from the narrative that Jesus' response would not be limited purely to Mary but would be applicable to all women believers. It is clear that:

1. The kingdom of God, and the poor and the marginalized (including women) are major narratival and theological concerns in Luke-Acts.
2. Jesus consistently shows concern for the marginalized of society, and repeatedly draws attention to the necessity of listening to his words.
3. There is no evidence that Jesus either allowed a socio-religious norm to contravene, or to take precedence over, his teaching, or that he discouraged women in any way from being disciples and listening to his words.

4. The statement by Jesus that "Mary has chosen the better part," naturally points beyond the story itself to all disciples choosing the better part no matter what the circumstances.

Consequently a second order narratival proposition that emerges from this episode would be the more global: *Jesus' first priority for female disciples is that they listen to his words, even if this overturns socially regulated roles.*

At times, first order narratival propositions cannot be generalized. For example, the proposition *Elizabeth was a woman of pedigree* is specific to her character and therefore resists generalization. Due to the particular characters and events in the infancy narratives, we find numerous examples that fit this category. At other times, recognizing that the narrative has interests and goals beyond first order narratival propositions, we will endline a second order proposition after discussing the first order proposition that forms its basis.

The narratival propositions are the basis for broader *narratival threads*. A narratival thread conveys a larger picture with respect to a person or topic based upon the logic of the narratival sequence. A coherent narratival thread with reference to the proposition arising from Luke 8:22–25 would take into account previous propositions that *Jesus cured a centurion's servant* from Luke 7:1–10, and *Jesus raised a man from the dead* from Luke 7:11–17. The narratival thread from Luke 7 and 8 would be that would be that *there is no power which Jesus cannot resist and overcome: neither illness, nor death, nor creation, nor demons.*

Fourth, narratival propositions, or several narratival propositions forming a narratival thread, may lead to *theological propositions*. For example, whereas a key narratival proposition from the story of Jesus calming the storm may be that *Jesus has power over the wind and the waves of the sea*, the theological proposition may be that *Jesus is Lord over creation*. In the case of a narratival proposition not having a theological proposition emerging directly from it, it may contribute to a theological proposition in a cumulative manner in tandem with other narratival propositions, e.g., from a narratival thread. For example, the theological proposition that *Jesus is fully human* receives a strong contribution from the narratival claim "the child grew and became strong, filled with wisdom . . ." (Luke 2:40a), and a modest and indirect contribution from the passage where Jesus weeps over Jerusalem (19:41–44). In the first instance, the narrative makes a direct claim that Jesus developed as a normal yet godly person. In the second instance, we read a description of an appropriate human emotion "as he came near and saw the city, he wept over it" (19:41). The fact of Jesus crying is consistent with the first claim; however the narrative is not primarily interested in the doctrine of Jesus' humanity *per se*. The difference lies in the fact that Jesus' common humanity is a direct implication of the passage about his growth and development (2:40a), whereas the second passage (19:41) only leads to such a conclusion in tandem with other like passages. Thus, strong theological propositions emerge directly from a particular pericope and may also take into account the cumulative effect of other previous narratival propositions.

Thirty years ago R. Alan Culpepper, in his groundbreaking work on the Fourth Gospel, noted how the author can convey ideas to the reader without direct narration. This is achieved by utilizing any number of indirect signals such as misunderstanding, irony, and symbolism. In other words there is often silent communication, when the narrative generates a "surplus of meaning."[69] So, in addition to forming the basis for a narratival argument, many narratival propositions generate a corresponding theological proposition which emerges 'silently.'

It is important at this point to emphasize how narratival propositions differ from theological propositions. The crucial difference between the narratival proposition *Jesus has power over the wind and the waves of the sea*, and the theological proposition *Jesus is Lord over creation* is that the theological proposition is more broadly theological and, as it stands, is not limited to the passage at hand. Moreover, a theological proposition is stated atemporally, whilst many narratival propositions have temporal referents. To cite the next story in Luke as an example, the story about Jesus and the Gerasene demoniac (Luke 8:26–39) gives rise to the first order narratival proposition that *Jesus has power over the Legion*. A second order proposition flows naturally from it: *Jesus has authority over the demonic realm*. A theological proposal from the story would have no temporal or story reference point. It may be *Jesus is Lord over the demonic realm*. Consequently, a theology of female disciples in Luke-Acts will necessarily be derived from both narrative and theological propositions.

On occasions our work will endline second order narratival propositions which closely approximate theological propositions. One such example is *God reverses the fortunes of the lowly who are open to him, including women*. This close approximation between narratival and theological propositions exist because what sometimes distinguishes a second order narratival proposition from a first order narratival proposition is that its generalizing force is grounded in a theological theme (e.g., the kingdom of God). Such second order narratival propositions are often inherently theological and thus require no deeper theological interpretation (although it may require rewording), in order to produce an a-temporal theological

---

69. Culpepper, *Anatomy*, 199.

proposition. Consequently, when such narratival propositions are endlined it is not the case that the theological interpretation of Scripture has been privileged over and above the narrative. Rather, we are recognizing the fact that second order narratival propositions are often inherently theological.

Fifth, in addition to theological propositions, theological progression can be determined as theology emerges from the narratival argument and the accumulation of theological propositions. That is, our theology of female disciples in Luke-Acts will be an evolutionary one that will build on what has previously been stated. This will include elements of continuity and discontinuity, thus giving rise to a rich and multi-layered theology.

In sum, our methodology can be diagrammed as follows:

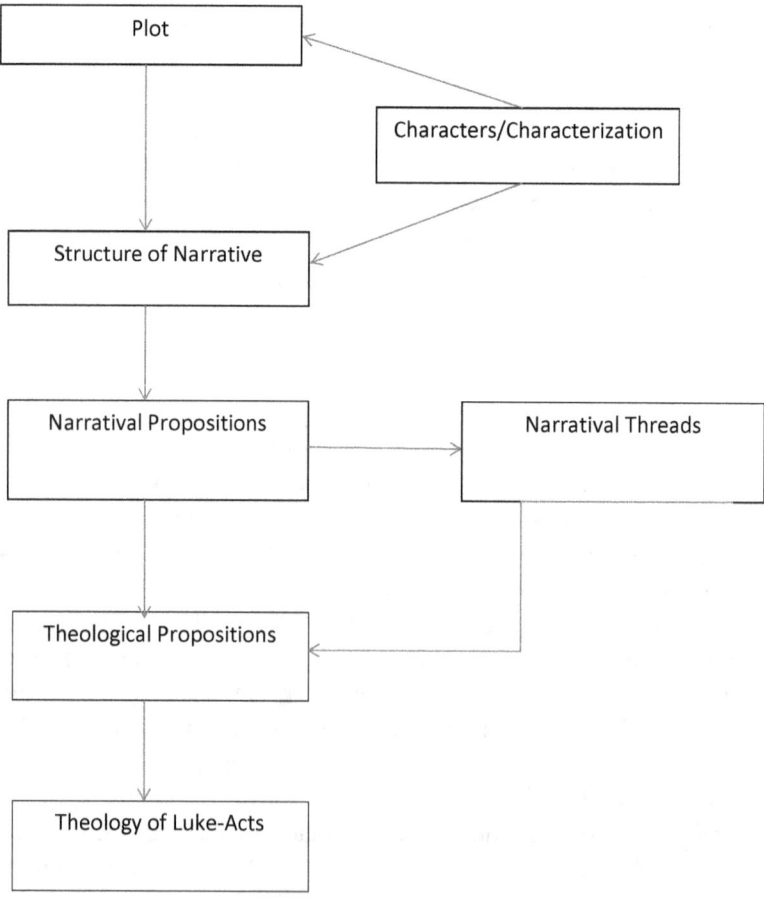

A consistency criterion

In this connection, our methodology works with a strong consistency criterion. This criterion rests on the assumption that Luke has an overall narratival and theological framework that governs Luke-Acts. This assumption is formed on the basis of Luke's stated concern for accuracy, order, and reliability in the opening preface (see above). Theophilus can hardly have assurance of the reliability of what he has been informed[70] if the narrative and its characterization lacks coherence.

The consistency criterion is a negative criterion in that it does not guarantee that a proposal is true. That is, such a proposal will need to be substantiated by reference to the work as a whole. However, if a proposal is found to be discordant with any narratival and theological thread, and/or the overall narratival and theological framework, then it must be regarded as questionable.

Characters are deployed throughout Luke-Acts in order to express the author's theological ideas within his narrative framework. This does not mean, however, that characters will be presented in a monochrome mode. Characters may be presented in a dynamic manner because they are caught up in the storied interaction between the narratival-theological threads. A character may be initially portrayed in one instance in a manner which serves one narratival-theological thread but in another situation a similar character may be employed to communicate a message concerning another thread.

The way that Luke portrays Roman soldiers illustrates this point. Roman soldiers are not 'flat' characters, i.e., they are not monochrome in their characterization and can undergo development. At times soldiers form part of the narrative thread of Gentiles demonstrating faith (to varying degrees) in Jesus (see Luke 7:1-10; 23:47; Acts 10:1-49). Other Roman soldiers beat and mock Jesus (Luke 23:22, 36-37)[71]. In the latter situation, the soldiers are serving the narrative thread of human sinfulness against God. This complex portrayal of the Roman soldiers is not due to inconsistency on the author's behalf. Their characterization varies according to their role in particular narrative threads within Luke's overall framework. Hence, the Roman soldier characters may be represented in various ways for different purposes without contradiction.

It is important to note that these character descriptions (and accompanying theologies) are always in conversation with the major narratival

---

70. Or, *taught,* depending on the force of κατηχήθης. See the discussion in Nolland, *Luke,* 1:10-11.

71. Admittedly, this brutality is downplayed significantly in Luke's account (cf. Mark 15:16-20; Matt 27:28-31; John 19:1-3).

and theological threads which run through the established framework of Luke-Acts. As stated above, this framework is a function of Luke's concern for order and reliability as he reflects on various accounts of events available to him. Given this intent stated in the preface, the reader is encouraged to assume that the author has a consistent theology throughout his work and consistently portrays his characters in the service of his theology. Thus it is reasonable to assume that the narrative and its proposals will not contain internal contradiction. So, the proposition that *Roman soldiers are models of faith* is not contradicted by another narratival proposition that *Roman soldiers brutalized and crucified Jesus*. Both these propositions serve different narratival and theological threads.

If, however, a narratival proposition is being considered which is not consonant with any other narratival proposition or thread, doubts about its viability would naturally arise. For example, the proposition *Roman soldiers are ideal apostles* appears to be in conflict with key aspects of the narrative such as Jesus' selection of the twelve disciples for the sake of mission to the world (and the criteria established for Judas' replacement in Acts 1:12–26), together with the silence with regard to Roman soldiers taking on this role in Acts. So, by adhering to Luke's overall narratival-theological framework and the narratival threads that serve it, we hope to work in a manner which may be resisted and falsified if it falls outside of these bounds. The strength of this point is that this criterion not only functions as a negative criterion, it also avoids monochrome characterization by being attuned to character complexity.

Structure and Content of the Book

As stated above, our aim in this volume is to explore the Lukan narrative and theological characterization of women who are followers of Jesus. Our approach is narrative-critical with theological aims. The book is structured according to the major structural outline of Luke-Acts (as discussed above under our methodological approach). Chapters 3–6 deal with women in Luke's Gospel. Chapter 7 looks at some introductory matters concerning Luke's portrayal of women in Acts, including the purpose of Acts and its narrative and literary progression. Chapters 8–10 study the narrative of Acts as it pertains to women. Chapter 11 draws the study together by way of conclusion, and offers suggestions regarding the potential contribution of our work to both a canonical 'theology of women,' and the discussion of women in Christian ministry today.

Each of the chapters that deal with the Luke-Acts narrative is structured similarly. In general, only pericopes that deal with women are investigated, although there are exceptions. For example, in chapter 4, at the beginning of Jesus' Galilean ministry, several narratival propositions regarding Jesus and his ministry are examined. This is so because although women as disciples are the focus of our study, women as characters serve Luke's central narratival focus on the identity and work of Jesus and how people respond to him. This christological section provides the broader context with which the narratival material on women interacts.

Within each chapter material is normally treated sequentially following the order of Luke's narrative. Introductory issues that pertain to each pericope are discussed before the narratival propositions are presented. The narratival propositions appear in italics and are followed by a discussion of that proposition. At the end of each chapter there is a summary of the narratival propositions, followed by a list of theological propositions that arise from them. At times, we depart from the above structure in an attempt to be sensitive to the narrative and particular characterization. For example, in the Infancy Narratives each of the female characters is treated separately. The narratival propositions are summarized, and the theological propositions presented for each in turn. In Luke 8:1–3 each of the three women mentioned is discussed in turn by way of introduction, but the narratival propositions are presented with respect to the women as a group.

Before we commence our narratival analysis, we first of all turn to the Jewish and Greco-Roman historical-cultural context of the recipients of Luke's work. Our purpose here is to assess how women were viewed in the ancient world, and the extent of their participation and leadership in religious and community activities. In this way we can better appreciate how the original recipients of Luke's work would have been impacted by his characterization of women.

CHAPTER 2

Women in Judaism and the Greco-Roman World

Introduction

THE PURPOSE OF THIS chapter is to examine attitudes to, and the role of, women in the religious and cultural life of the ancient Jewish and Greco-Roman world. This is undertaken in order to anticipate possible initial audience expectations regarding the role and characterization of women in Luke-Acts. It is important to emphasize 'possible,' because it is impossible to say with any certainty what any particular reader may anticipate and expect regarding women's roles. This is so because the literary evidence itself, particularly in the Greco-Roman period, evidences many differing attitudes to women, and it is reasonable to expect that this diversity of views would be represented in Luke's readership as well. Nevertheless, to the extent that it is possible to map a cultural norm, it should be possible to speak in broad terms regarding audience expectations.

Our task will be to describe and assess the role of women in both Judaism and the wider Greco-Roman world. The former is necessary because Luke-Acts itself is an intensely Jewish document. That is, it presents Jesus and the early church as a continuation of the story of Israel, and indeed the fulfilment of the Jewish hope of salvation.[1] Women characters in Luke's nar-

---

1. Bock, *Theology of Luke and Acts*, 121–48, 279–89; Moessner, *Jesus and the Heritage of Israel*; Tyson (ed.), *Luke-Acts and the Jewish People*; Brawley, *Luke-Acts and the Jews*.

rative are therefore participants in this wider story and their role and status must first of all be assessed against the canvas of Judaism.

But if we take the intended recipient 'Theophilus' seriously, and there is good reason to think that we should,[2] then we are dealing with a person of relatively high standing in the Greco-Roman world, and it is this milieu which provides his foremost frame of reference. Nevertheless, if Theophilus is a 'God-fearer,' as many would argue, then the OT and Second Temple Judaism provides another significant contribution to his set of values and ideals.

Preliminary Comments

Until recently, assessments of the role of women in both religious and cultural life in the ancient world have suffered not so much from the paucity of source material—although there have been significant advances in this area in more recent times—but have been hampered by two main factors. First, the bias and/or lack of interest of contemporary male scholars has skewed both the evidence and the direction of such studies. Second, there is the issue of bias within the sources themselves. These sources were written, translated, and transmitted predominately by men, and aristocratic men at that, who were largely ignorant of the lives that women led.[3] For these authors, women were considered important only to the extent that they impacted the lives of men.[4]

We must also avoid any simplistic assessment of the role of women, and particularly exercise caution against unwarranted generalizations. Class, ethnicity, and the location of women geographically and temporally clearly affected the extent of their involvement in religion and society. There is also the problem as to whether documents depicting women's roles are descriptive or prescriptive. Do they reflect the author's perception of things, or the desire for the way things should be?[5] Not only does the evidence present a complex picture, as we shall see similar evidence can also produce varying conclusions.

---

2. See Forbes, *God of Old*, 307–27; Bock, *Luke* 1:14–15; Nolland, *Luke* 1:xxxii–xxxiii; Garland, *Luke*, 34–35. This is not to say that Theophilus was the only intended recipient, but that he was the primary recipient and possibly Luke's patron. See Alexander, *Preface to Luke's Gospel*, 52–57, 190–97.

3. Kraemer, "Women in the Religions of the Greco-Roman World," 127–33. Levine (ed.), "Women like This," xii; Percy, *Christian Women Writers*.

4. Percy, *Christian Women Writers*, 33.

5. Levine, "Women like This," xii–xiii.

We will begin with women in Jewish thought and literature, first briefly examining the OT data before moving on to Second Temple Judaism. The data from the wider Greco-Roman world will then be investigated.

Women in Ancient Jewish Society

With respect to outlining the role of women in ancient Jewish society there are a number of inherent difficulties, for not only does the OT span a millennium, it contains numerous forms of literature each with its own subtleties of interpretation.[6] Furthermore, the OT was authored by males offering a male perspective.[7] Consequently women predominately appear as subordinate characters in the OT drama. Of course there are exceptions. Apart from the Jewish matriarchs, there are a number of significant women that we encounter. Rahab gave refuge to the spies in Jericho, and was extolled as a hero in later Jewish thought.[8] According to rabbinic tradition she married Joshua and was the ancestor of Jeremiah and other prophets.[9] Several women were said to be prophets (or prophetesses) including Miriam (Exod 15:20)[10] and Huldah, the latter who was also "keeper of the wardrobe" (2 Kgs 22:14). Other OT heroines include Deborah, Jael, Ruth, and Esther. Among these only Deborah stepped outside clearly defined cultural roles in assuming a position of judge during the era of the tribal confederacy (Judg 4–5).

In one sense one could argue that the above accounts are possibly indicative and representative of wider participation by women in key roles in the life of the nation, as the literature is hardly exhaustive and is unable to document every particular instance of the key involvement of women.[11] However, this is not the view of the majority. The above instances are normally viewed as atypical and their atypical nature may in fact be the rationale for their inclusion in the literature.

It is beyond doubt that in ancient Jewish life women's labor contribution was centered in the domestic sphere, where to produce and nurture children was the major avenue to security and prestige. Conversely,

---

6. For example, narrative explains what did happen rather than convey normative behavior. Law, on the other hand, is prescriptive but not always obeyed. See Emmerson, "Women in Ancient Israel," 371–72.

7. Bird, "Women (OT)," 951–52.

8. Jos. *Ant.* 5.2.

9. *b. Meg.* 14b, 15a. In the Christian tradition Rahab is regarded as an example of faith (Heb 11:31; 1 Clem 12:18) and good deeds (Jas 2:25).

10. See Burns, *Has the Lord Indeed Spoken*.

11. Emmerson, "Women in Ancient Israel," 371, raises the question.

infertility was a mark of public disgrace and viewed as a sign of divine disfavor. Women's roles in work and leadership outside the home were dependent upon several factors, including geographic location, seasonal factors, and other exceptional circumstances (war, famine, etc.).[12] Greater religious and social freedom was available to older women who were no longer tied to familial duties.[13]

Whereas women were regarded as members of the covenant people, this participation was dependent to some extent upon the males that surrounded them in family relationships.[14] Nevertheless, this did not absolve a woman from the necessity of obedience to the Law.[15] The view that women were regarded as the mere property of their father or husband[16] has been called into question. It is probably more correct that a woman, though not having independent legal status, was "part of her husband's person, so that the husband and wife constituted a single legal unit."[17]

Ancient Jewish androcentrism is further evident in the use of masculine grammatical forms for generic speech, and male dominated cultic life. Notwithstanding the enigmatic reference to women who served at the entrance to the tent of meeting (Exod 38:8; 1 Sam 2:22), who are unnamed and whose precise task remains elusive,[18] women were generally excluded from the centers of holiness and cultic activity. The reasons for this may have been complex, but can be attributed largely to purity concerns.[19]

So, while all women were regarded as part of the covenant community, and some women are presented as having key roles in the OT narrative, most would agree with Emmerson that, despite this, the OT supplies "unequivocal evidence of inequality between the sexes."[20] Although there are limited examples of women's independence and power (see above), these

---

12. See Meyers, *Discovering Eve.*.

13. Bird, "Women," 954.

14. Wiley, *Paul and the Gentile Women*, 81. This patrilineal nature of Jewish society is evident in the male dominance in genealogies and genealogical narrative. See Bird, "Women," 953, who indicates a ratio of approximately 12:1 male to female in the OT genealogies.

15. Emmerson, "Women in Ancient Israel," 378–79.

16. For example, Wiley, *Paul and the Gentile Women*, 82.

17. Wright, *God's People in Gods Land*, 221.

18. For a discussion, see Durham, *Exodus*, 486–88.

19. Emmerson, "Women in Ancient Israel," 379. See also Wiley, *Paul and the Gentile Women*, 83. Cohen, "Menstruants and the Sacred," analyzes the purity texts with respect to women in Leviticus and their application in later Judaism and Early Christianity.

20. Emmerson, "Women in Ancient Israel," 372.

do appear to be the exceptions. This inequality finds expression within the religious community and especially in its leadership.

Women in Second Temple Judaism

As we move closer to NT times (second century BC onwards) a similarly complex picture emerges. On the one hand, there is some evidence of the prominence of women in Jewish apocryphal texts, particularly the revelatory status accorded to them in such works as *Jubilees, Joseph and Asenath*, and the later portions of the *Testament of Job*. To some extent this phenomenon is also mirrored in the targums and rabbinic midrashim. However, it is difficult to extrapolate the roles and status of women in contemporary Jewish society from such literature. Clearly for these writings to have their intended effect they must not be culturally subversive regarding their portrayal of women. On the other hand, neither should we make too much of the evidence and find clear and defined leadership roles for women in religion and society. We are dealing here with a genre of literary fiction, not historiography. So the evidence is at best indirect. What the literature does show is, at the very least, that portrayals of women in Second Temple Judaism as oppressed and excluded may be simplistic and caricatured.[21]

The Jewish treatment *par excellence* of the female hero is undoubtedly the book of Judith, the righteous widow who by her wisdom, wealth, and resourcefulness traps and defeats the enemy leader Holofernes.[22] By contrast, in the book of Tobit males dominate in religious matters and women are assigned to the domestic arena. The exception is the character Anna, who is given a little more autonomy and gains employment in "women's work" (2:11).[23]

Women characters in the Jewish apocryphal/deuterocanonical works such as Deborah, Edna, Judith, Susanna, and the mother who circumcised her sons (2 Macc 6) not only embody Torah, but in their wisdom, courage, and piety teach Torah to following generations, and thus help construct Jewish religious identity.[24] This is especially so for the mother-martyr character in 2 Maccabees 7, who encourages her sons to suffer martyrdom rather than

---

21. Chestnut, "Revelatory Experiences," 107–25.

22. See Pervo, "Aseneth and Her Sisters," 145–60. As to whether women were possibly responsible for the writing of such novels, see Lefkowitz, "Did Ancient Women Write Novels?" 199–219; Kraemer, "Women's Authorship," 221–42. Lefkowitz deems it unlikely, whereas Kraemer is more open to the possibility.

23. See Bow and Nickelsburg, "Patriarchy with a Twist," 127–43.

24. Craven, "Women As Teachers of Torah," 275–89.

transgress Torah. She appears as the instructor of Torah, the hero of the people, and is ultimately "portrayed as a woman who possesses masculine virtues."[25]

On the other hand, in Ben Sira we see not just an affirmation of traditional women's roles, but also a rather negative depiction of women as someone that the man must control. Loss of control of women, whether one's own wife or in improper relations with other women, means a corresponding loss of honor, and Ben-Sira does his utmost to avoid the presence of shame.[26]

Although Philo (c. 20BC–AD50) treats the issue of women incidentally it is clear that he views the female as mentally inferior,[27] selfish, audacious, and given to seduction.[28] Given that he is decidedly more negative than the biblical (OT) material on women, Wegner contends that his views stem more from Hellenistic than Hebraic influence.[29] He is more positive regarding the Therapeutrides (female Therapeutics), a group of well educated, ascetic women who engaged in the allegorization of Scripture. But this is likely the result of them sharing a common exegetical technique.[30]

Amy-Jill Levine rejects the neat dichotomy of women suppressed in Judaism and liberated in Christianity, and is especially critical of earlier studies of Swidler and Witherington.[31] With respect to Second Temple Judaism, she argues that the restriction of women based on purity issues is exaggerated, and the evidence that women were restricted from leadership roles and forbidden to be disciples of a great teacher are entirely lacking.[32] Furthermore, the appearance of women at various points in the Gospel narratives is not remarkable but reflective of the norm of Jewish life and society.[33]

In supporting Levine's proposals, there is both literary and inscriptional evidence indicating that some women held the position of *archisynagōgissa* (fem. form of *archisynagōgos*). Although some have indicated that this may be an honorific description, or possibly indicating the wife of a synagogue

---

25. Habner, "Living and Dying for the Law," 75–92.
26. Camp, "Understanding a Patriarchy," 1–39.
27. *On the Embassy to Gaius* 319.
28. *Hypothetica* 11.14–17.
29. See Wegner, "Philo's Portrayal of Women." Wegner's proposal in this respect is questionable, given that our analysis indicates that attitudes to women in the Greco-Roman world were arguably more positive than those in Second Temple Judaism.
30. Cohick, *Women in the World of the Earliest Christians*, 198–99, 249–54.
31. Levine, "Second Temple Judaism."
32. At this point Levine's argument is one from silence and she produces little supportive evidence of her own.
33. Levine, "Second Temple Judaism," 20–21.

ruler, it is unlikely that the feminine form of a masculine noun would indicate a different function. More likely it does indicate some form of leadership and organizational role in the synagogue.[34]

Like Witherington, others are not as optimistic as Levine regarding the role of women in Second Temple Judaism. Emmerson, for example, concludes that there was a definite deterioration in the view of women in the Second Temple period.[35] Terrien contends that women lived a socially reclusive life, with a status slightly above that of a Greco-Roman slave,[36] whereas Tribble concludes that in the post-exilic period, women were "impure, subordinate and inferior human creature(s)."[37]

In assessing the role of women in first-century Palestinian society we have four main sources: the Gospels (which we will not discuss here because Luke's Gospel is the focus of this study), Josephus (who says very little about women, but what he does say is largely negative),[38] the Dead Sea Scrolls, and the early rabbinic material.

The previous consensus that the Scrolls envision a community consisting entirely of male celibates, has recently been called into question by some female scholars.[39] Lynn Cohick, for example, contends that the Qumran literature portrays a mixed gendered community, citing women's involvement in taking oaths, giving testimony, and receiving education in the law.[40] However, it remains to be seen if her proposals will convince the wider group of Scrolls scholars. The consensus to date is there is very little material on women and their religious-cultural involvement in the Qumran community.

With respect to the rabbinic material, here we encounter a problem with dating. However, as Witherington contends, the material that was codified in the Mishnah (c. A.D. 200) certainly dates from an earlier period,

---

34. Cohick, *Women in the World of the Earliest Christians*, 210–14. See also Levine, "Synagogue Leadership."; Brooten, *Women Leaders in the Ancient Synagogue;* Keener, *Acts*, 1:628–29.

35. Emmerson, "Women in Ancient Israel," 391.

36. Terrien, *Till the Heart Sings*, 85–86, 121–22. Terrien maintains that temple segregation, the mere presence of the Court of Women, was a tangible manifestation of their inferior religious status.

37. Tribble, "Women in the OT," 963–66.

38. E.g., Jos. *Ag. Ap.* 2:200–201.

39. See Cohick, *Women in the World of the Earliest Christians*, 199–209; Wassen, *Women in the Damascus Document;* Schuller, "Women in the Dead Sea Scrolls," Grossman, *Reading for History in the Damascus Document.*

40. Cohick, *Women in the World of the Earliest Christians*, 199–209.

and it is reasonable to suggest that it provides a helpful window into the role and status of women at the beginning of the Christian era.[41]

According to the rabbinic literature, in general the Palestinian woman's sphere of influence was confined to the family. She was allowed to hold and inherit property, but a male heir had priority. It was disputed among the rabbis whether a woman should be able to teach or be taught the law,[42] although there is evidence that some did become skilled in both the written and oral Torah. Having said this, it was considered inappropriate for a woman to become a rabbinic pupil. A woman could not hold office in the temple because of purity issues, could not recite the daily *Shema*, nor could make pilgrimage to Jerusalem for the annual feasts.[43] Also disputed among the sages was the validity of women's legal testimony. So, while there is not uniformity of opinion in the rabbinic material on all issues regarding women, a negative assessment of women is probably the dominant picture.[44] Palestinian Jewish society was certainly one of the more patriarchal in the Mediterranean basin at the time.

Women in the Greco-Roman World

In ancient Greek literature women characters were featured merely to highlight the heroic values of the men. Furthermore they were the object of men's desires and heroic actions.[45] There is some evidence from classical Greek art works of aristocratic women having various roles in religion, funeral rites, and wedding ceremonies. However the evidence indicates that the women of ancient Greece had civil rights roughly comparable to a slave, excluded from life in the *polis*, and largely confined to the domestic realm.[46] Although the Greek romantic novels do portray the power of women, this

---

41. Witherington, *Women*, 1–2.

42. Not all endorsed the view of R. Eliezer (late first century A.D.) in *m. Sotah* 3.4—"R. Eliezer says: If any man gives his daughter a knowledge of the Law it is as though he taught her obscenity." For various views, see Keener, *Acts*, 1:632–34.

43. Although, as Emmerson, "Women in Ancient Israel," 378, contends, the original obligation on male pilgrimage only (Exod 23:17; Deut 16:16) was probably more for practical reasons (i.e., women's roles in the domestic sphere) rather than denoting any inequality as such.

44. Witherington, *Women*, 10.

45. Percy, *Christian Women Writers*, 12,18. See also Cantarella, *Pandora's Daughters*, 63–76.

46. Percy, *Christian Women Writers*, 20, 30–32.

power is evident in terms of their sexual appeal. This gives them an apparent power, but the women rarely rise above this stereotypical quality.[47]

Greek philosophers held divergent, and at times contradictory, views regarding women. On the whole, though, they held to a range of gender inequality views in which males were superior to women. Plato indicated that women were inferior to men, advocated their subordination, and believed that evil men could be reincarnated as women.[48] Xenaphon was a little more charitable to females, whereas Socrates insisted that the female was not inferior to the male, apart from lacking wisdom.[49] Aristotle believed that women are mis-born males who lack the authority which is innate to men. Furthermore, for him, default female psychology and virtues fall short of their ideal instantiation as found in men.[50]

Moving into the Greco-Roman period we are immediately confronted with complexity.[51] This complexity is in part a product of changing times, in part ambiguous evidence, in part differences in attitudes between the literary and epigraphic evidence,[52] and in part a reflection of geographical differences.

With respect to the last mentioned it is apparent that the rights and status of women differed not only according to social status (see below) but also to geographical location. In Rome, Egypt, and Asia Minor, for instance, the education of women was more highly regarded than in Greece or Judea. With respect to political influence, women in Egypt were more prominent, while in religious affairs women in Egypt, Asia Minor, and Macedonia had more prominence than their counterparts in Greece or Rome, although this did change somewhat with the increase in prominence of the Oriental cults in Rome and its colonies.[53]

---

47. Pervo, "Aseneth and Her Sisters," 145–46.

48. Plato, *Laws*, 10.904b.

49. Plato, *Rep.* V.449a–472a. Xenaphon, *Sym.*2.9. See also Cantarella, *Pandora's Daughters*, 52–62.

50. For example, see Aristotle, *Politics*, book 1, chapters 12 and 13. For trends in the recent discussion on this, see Schollmeier, "Aristotle and Women: Household and Political Roles." Nielsen, "The Private Parts of Animals: Aristotle on the Teleology of Sexual Difference."

51. For a balanced and careful study of women in the Greco-Roman period, see Arlandson, *Women*, 14–119.

52. Cohick, *Women in the World of the Earliest Christians*, 28–32.

53. Witherington, "Women," 957–61. This area of research has recently been explored in a number of works including Rüpke, *A Companion to Roman Religion*; Thompson, *The Role of Vestal Virgins in Roman Civic Religion*; Takács, *Vestal Virgins, Sibyls, and Matrons*; Green, *Roman Religion and the Cult of Diana at Aricia*; Warrior, *Roman Religion*.

With respect to the overall role and value of women in the Greco-Roman world there is clarity on some points. First, daughters were less desired than sons and consequently were more likely to be exposed. Having said this, daughters were considered an integral part of the family and did have some rights of inheritance. They sometimes received education, albeit a lesser standard than male children.[54]

Second, a virtuous wife was considered a great asset to the family and to the *polis*, yet her role was to remain in the shadow of her husband, to be obedient to him, and to preserve family honor.[55]

Third, there is widespread agreement that we should avoid making unwarranted assumptions about women's roles based on the presence and worship of female deities.[56] Although female deities were prominent in Greco-Roman religion this does not, in itself, argue for prominence of women in society. Percy, in fact, proposes that "such women could only exist as human impossibilities[;] . . . [they existed] in Greek mythology because their existence in real life was an impossibility."[57] This needs to be held in tension with the sentiment reflected in a prayer to Isis "you have made the power of women equal to that of men."[58]

Fourth, there is clear evidence of the involvement of women in religious cultic activity.[59] The example *par excellence* of this is undoubtedly the Vestal Virgin. Young girls between six and ten years of age, perfect in pedigree and physical form, underwent a rigorous selection process. If successful she was committed to serve a minimum thirty year term of chastity. Her role was to attend the sacred hearth fire of Rome and to ensure that it burnt continually. In this way a Vestal Virgin embodied the virtuous and chaste ideals of Roman society. She "was repressing or controlling her reproductive potential, redirecting that power for good and stability of Rome."[60] In terms of legal status, a Vestal Virgin was free from legal male control and had the power to act independently in forming a will.[61]

54. Cohick, *Women in the World of the Earliest Christians*, 33–64.
55. Ibid., 65–97.
56. Kraemer, "Women," 131.
57. Percy, *Christian Women Writers*, 29.
58. *Poxy* 1380, lines 214–16, cited by Meeks, *First Urban Christians*, 25, who adds that even so, male priests still outranked and outnumbered priestesses in religious cults.
59. See Kraemer (ed.), *Maenads, Martyrs, Matrons, Monastics*; Kraemer, *Her Share of the Blessings*; Schultz, *Women's Religious Activity*.
60. Cohick, *Women in the World of the Earliest Christians*, 166.
61. For a discussion of the role of a Vestal Virgin, including the penalty for unchastity, see Sawyer, *Women and Religion*, 68–70; Cohick, *Women in the World of the Earliest Christians*, 162–66.

The participation of women in religious pursuits is also evident in the Bona Dea cult festival, held twice annually. This festival was open to women only, irrespective of age and status. Anything male, including statues and animals, was not permitted in the vicinity. This is not to say that this significant Roman deity, who was regarded as the protector of the Roman state, was only worshiped by women,[62] for both the epigraphic and literary evidence indicates otherwise. Nevertheless women held the positions of *magistrae*, who oversaw cultic sacrifices and offerings, and *sacerdotes*, the function of priestess.[63]

In fact, the sources indicate that women regularly served as *magistrae*, *sacerdotes* and *ministrae* of many religious cults. Not only did they engage in such ritual duties, many also donated large sums of money to the cult, thereby increasing their honor and esteem. It also appears that while religious cults were open to both male and female worshipers, certain cultic rights were limited to one particular gender.[64] Women as well as men were involved in rituals designed to consolidate the military and political power and stability of Rome, and in one instance the prayers of Roman matrons were sought to influence the campaign against the Carthaginian general Hannibal.[65]

Although the various religious cults clearly offered cultic roles for women from all levels of the social strata, this was not necessarily an accurate portrayal of women's roles in wider Greco-Roman society. Some consider that they were exceptional and certainly not reflective of social roles. As Alicia Batten states:

> the Greeks and Romans lived in a gendered universe, with a clear hierarchy of male over female, and in which the male social identity was generally associated with public activities while that of the female was aligned with the domestic . . . .[66]

With respect to education, the intentional schooling of Roman women began around 200 BC, and by 100 BC it was not uncommon for aristocratic women to be educated in literacy, numeracy, language, history, and the classics.[67] One of the most legendary women in this respect was Cornelia, mother of Gracchi (second century BC) who was fluent in the Greek language

---

62. As indicated by Sawyer, *Women and Religion in the First Christian Centuries*, 70–71.

63. Cohick, *Women in the World of the Earliest Christians*, 166–73.

64. Ibid., 178–79.

65. Ibid., 183.

66. Batten, "Neither Gold nor Braided Hair," 491.

67. Percy, *Christian Women Writers*, 46, who concedes that this education was probably at a lower academic level from that given to men.

and demonstrated rhetorical competence and eloquence.[68] A statue was even erected in her honor, a rare tribute for someone of her time. It is also of note that much of her acclaim revolved around her standing as a mother,[69] which indicates that as a heroic figure she had not been androgenized.

Some well educated women of elite social rank were also schooled in philosophy. The attitudes of male philosophers to this phenomenon were varied. Some believed that women involved in such pursuits actually became an honorary male, others felt that it contributed to society in a positive manner by assisting the woman to further their role as mother and wife and uphold family honor. Some looked upon them with disdain, linking such pursuits with sexual promiscuity,[70] others saw their philosophical activity as an unacceptable invasion of male space.[71]

Many of the legal restrictions placed upon women were considered to be for their protection. Nevertheless, discerning the difference between altruism and male self interest in this respect is not easy.[72] With regard to restrictions on work, only two occupations were forbidden to women: Senate politicians and provincial governors, and soldier.[73] However, when the Romans encountered the occasional woman warrior, one of the most famous being Boudicca (mid first century AD) who engaged the Roman army in Britain, they tended to regard such women as aberrations and violations of the natural order.[74]

The particular work that Greco-Roman women undertook was dependent to a large degree upon their social status. The rural poor undertook manual labor whereas the urban poor may have been shopkeepers or artisans. Those of higher status could be involved in merchant trade. We find an example of the latter in the book of Acts, where Paul and Silas encounter Lydia, a worshiper of God (σεβομένη τὸν θεόν). She is a commercial trader dealing in purple cloth, a luxury item for the wealthy and the royal. She is obviously a woman of considerable means, who runs her own household (thus likely to be a widow) and leads in their baptism. The text also presents her as a benefactor to the apostles, providing accommodation for

---

68. D'Ambra, *Roman Women*, 143–46. A bronze statue was erected in her honor in Rome c. 100 B.C. It was exceptional for a woman to receive this public acclaim.

69. Cohick, *Women in the World of the Earliest Christians*, 156.

70. This was likely due to the woman being involved with males outside of those in her own family. See Cohick, *Women in the World of the Earliest Christians*, 248–49.

71. Ibid., 242–48.

72. Arjava, *Women and Law in Late Antiquity*, 254–56.

73. Cohick, *Women in the World of the Earliest Christians*, 225–49.

74. D'Ambra, *Roman Women*, 161–62.

them and utilizing her home (obviously quite large) as the base for church gatherings (Acts 16:11–15).[75]

Indeed, it was benefaction and the patronage system that provided significant opportunities for elite women to make an impact in religion and society. Because patronage was "in many respects gender-blind,"[76] women could deliberately, or as a by-product of their benefaction, increase their honor and presence in the public arena. The result was often inscriptions in praise of their worthy deeds, public acclaim by clients, and sometimes the right to hold the office of city magistrate. Women patrons thus won for themselves liberty to speak and act in political and religious affairs.[77]

So, it is quite apparent that greater freedom was available for women who were affluent and well situated, although to some extent this freedom was dictated by the influence of their husbands or fathers. In addition, most of their activity and influence was likely to be indirect.[78] Nevertheless, there is evidence that women could function as magistrates, exert political influence and serve as benefactors or patrons. Epigraphic evidence near Pompeii indicates commercial activity of women to be similar to that of men.[79] There is also first-century epigraphic evidence that women did hold positions of influence. Iunia Theodora was commended not only for her hospitality and care of Lycians who came to Corinth, she also worked tirelessly for their cause in provincial government circles. Her work thus went beyond that of public benefaction, and saw her active in the traditional male circles of commerce and government.[80] Another prominent woman was Claudia Metrodora, who held magistracies on the island of Chios and was well-known for her benefactions including the donation of public baths. She directed the imperial games, held the office of *gymnasiarch*[81] four times, and appears to have twice held the highest office of the city *stephanophoros*.[82] Both these

---

75. Ibid., 188–91; Peterson, *Acts of the Apostles*, 458–62; Bock, *Acts*, 530–35.

76. Cohick, *Women in the World of the Earliest Christians*, 320.

77. One of the most famous female benefactors was Plancia Magna of Perge. See Boatwright, "Plancia Magna of Perge," 249–72. See also Cohick, *Women in the World of the Earliest Christians*, 285–320. Cohick argues that it is under the banner of patronage that we should understand Paul's relationship to Phobe (Rom 16:1) and Lydia (Acts 16:12–14), and the women (Mary Magdalene, Joanna, Susanna and others) who supported Jesus and the twelve (Luke 8:1–3).

78. Ibid., 142–43. We see such indirect influence in the Gospels' portrayal of Pilate's wife (Matt 27:19) and the role of Herodias and her daughter in the execution of John (Mark 6:14–29).

79. Wiley, *Paul and the Gentile Women*, 86.

80. Kearsley, "Women in Public Life," 191–98.

81. A leader in education including literacy and gymnastic activity.

82. The local lead magistrate. Ibid., 198–201.

cases are evidence that upper-class, wealthy Roman women could move with some freedom in a traditionally male domain.

Conclusion

So, what are we to make of such conflicting attitudes, and also the data at our disposal? The varying analyses of the religious and cultural roles of women in both Judaism and the wider Greco-Roman world is, to some extent, mirrored by the attitudes of ancient writers themselves. On the negative side women were the target of the satirical wit of Juvenal. In his eyes, women were quarrelsome, unfaithful, gullible, and conniving.[83] This is a stark contrast to the view of the Roman philosopher Musonius Rufus, who considered the sexes as basically equal and argued for the value of teaching daughters as well as sons.[84]

In contemporary scholarship it appears that one's assessment of the role of women in the Greco-Roman world is dependent to a large degree on how one views the exceptions to the patriarchal norm. Some, most often female scholars, make much of the exceptions and present a view of gender roles that are fluid to a point and, at the very least, resist neat categorization. Others, on the other hand, mention the exceptions as exceptions and do not regard them as sufficient evidence to deconstruct existing paradigms of a world that was overwhelmingly patriarchal and androcentric. Here again we encounter the problem of the source material, for the sources do not always depict the female norm, but give space to the exceptional, the hero, and the wealthy elite.[85]

What then may we conclude with any degree of confidence? First, in terms of the source material: inscriptions, everyday business documents, and private correspondence do present a more variegated picture of women's roles than the literary evidence. This is not surprising given that literary texts were written from an androcentric perspective and were often designed to inculcate the patriarchal norm. Second, the domestic sphere belonged to the woman, whereas the public domain belonged to the man. This curtailed the opportunities for women to speak in public, and

---

83. See Percy, *Christian Women Writers*, 49–54, for a selection of quotes. Of course, as Cohick, *Women in the World of the Earliest Christians*, 124, remarks, we must be careful of equating satire with historical accuracy. Nevertheless, for the satire to be rhetorically effective, it must have some credence in reality.

84. Wiley, *Paul and the Gentile Women*, 87–88.

85. Cohick, *Women in the World of the Earliest Christians*, 26.

although there were exceptions they were generally viewed as irregular.[86] Third, social location was a key factor. Where the patriarchal boundary was 'transgressed' it was normally the wealthy elite women who transgressed it. Finally, the prevalence of patronage and benefaction goes a long way to explaining the disparity between societal norms and daily practice. In the end, the ambiguities present in the source data may well reflect the ambiguities and tensions regarding women's roles in Greco-Roman society itself.[87]

There was certainly a softening of attitudes to women in the Hellenistic period as opposed to the classical era in Greece.[88] Yet even a sympathetic author such as Cohick admits that by the Greco-Roman period "[there was not] an egalitarian paradise[;] . . . . at the highest levels men made the decisions, women as a group had fewer opportunities for self-expression than did men."[89]

So, in terms of the focus of our study and the goal of this chapter with respect to that, can we determine what the expectations of the initial readers of Luke-Acts would have been regarding women's roles in religion and society? As mentioned at the outset, any conclusions in this respect must be provisional. First of all, a Palestinian reader is likely to be less attuned to an elevated role of women. Although the data is evaluated differently by modern scholars, it does appear as though first century Palestine was more strongly patriarchal than other societies in the Mediterranean basin.[90] This is particularly the case with respect to women's involvement in cultic activity.

On the other hand a Hellenistic Jew, with more direct Greco-Roman influence, would probably have a greater awareness of prominent women, and have some acquaintance with women's involvement in cultic affairs. The same would apply, possibly to a greater degree, to those from wider Greco-Roman society who were attracted to Jewish monotheism (God-fearers). So Theophilus, as a likely member of the wealthy elite himself, would have been aware of women who played key and important roles in religion and society.

Given the public performance of the Gospels—that is, a public reading in the home of a more well-to-do sympathizer or patron such as Theophilus[91]—the original recipients of the Gospel of Luke are likely to be a diverse group of people, both male and female, from a variety of social stations. Insofar as it is possible to speak of common expectations regarding

---

86. See Keener, *Acts*, 1:634–37.
87. Hylen, "Women's Roles," 3–12.
88. Keener, *Acts*, 182.
89. Ibid., 324–25.
90. Arlandson, *Women*, 117–18.
91. See Alexander, *Preface to Luke's Gospel*, 187–212.

women's roles in this regard, and here we reiterate previous cautions in this respect, the expectation of most would likely have been: (i) the political and social sphere outside of life in the home was a realm in which only men and wealthy elite women moved; (ii) women's involvement in religious cultic activity was not so narrowly limited.

Bearing in mind these findings, we are now in a position to examine Luke's characterization of women. We begin with the Infancy Narratives.

CHAPTER 3

The Infancy Narratives (Luke 1:5—2:52)

LUKE'S NARRATIVE OPENS WITH an 'infancy gospel.' This subsection of the author's greater story recounts the origins of John and Jesus. Luke presents several Jewish exemplars, including their attendant emotions, to provide the context within which Jewish piety will find its culmination in God's new work though Jesus and the Holy Spirit.[1] We shall now explore the infancy narratives and their narratival claims with regards to the women characters of Elizabeth, Mary, and Anna. Following this, the theological concepts which arise from the narratival propositions will be outlined. The narratival propositions appear in italics as paragraph headings.

Elizabeth

The priest Zechariah and his wife Elizabeth are the first characters introduced into the Lukan narrative (Luke 1:5). They are presented against the backdrop of Palestinian history ("in the days of King Herod of Judea"), thereby initiating Luke's concern to portray the events surrounding the birth and ministry of Jesus Christ as the drama of God acting on the world stage (cf. 2:1–2; 3:1–2).

---

1. Nolland, *Luke*, 1:13.

The Infancy Narratives (Luke 1:5—2:52)

Elizabeth is a woman of pedigree

Zechariah was of the priestly order of Abijah, and reflecting common practice for the Jewish priesthood, he had married a woman of priestly descent (Luke 1:5-6).[2] This itself was not a restriction placed upon priests, with the only Levitical command insisting on marriage to a virgin, that the woman be undefiled in any manner, and not a widow (Lev 21:7-15). Consequently, Elizabeth is introduced from the outset as someone who has the highest pedigree, possibly reinforced by her sharing the name of Aaron's wife (Exod 6:23).

Elizabeth is an exemplar of Jewish piety

Together with Zechariah, Elizabeth is presented as an exemplar of Jewish piety (Luke 1:6). This is stressed by a rather overloaded Greek sentence in which it is said that "they were both righteous in the sight of God" (ἦσαν δὲ δίκαιοι ἀμφότεροι ἐναντίον τοῦ θεοῦ), "living according to all the commandments and regulations of the Lord" (πορευόμενοι ἐν πάσαις ταῖς ἐντολαῖς καὶ δικαιώμασιν τοῦ κυρίου), and doing so "blamelessly" (ἄμεμπτοι). This characterization is important as far as the ensuing narrative is concerned, for throughout his account Luke portrays Jesus and his faithful followers as law-observant Jews (2:23-24, 27, 39, 46; 16:17; 17:14; 19:45, 47; 20:1; 21:37-38; 23:56; 24:53). Such law observance should not be construed as a legalistic emphasis on the minutiae of the Torah devoid of compassion and grace—as per the religious authorities who encounter scathing criticism as a result (15:1-3; 7:36-50; 18:9-14)—but a heartfelt response to the God of Israel who had revealed himself in the life of the nation. This portrayal even goes beyond the Gospel narrative and continues in Acts, where the early disciples are engaged in temple worship and practice (2:46; 3:1, 11; 21:17-26). Consequently, Elizabeth and her husband Zechariah are not presented in terms of an outmoded form of piety that will be replaced by a new spirituality of those who follow the Messiah Jesus, but as living examples of what it means to be a faithful follower of God, and thus paradigmatic for the ensuing narrative.

This is quite different from Mark's narrative, where the reader's first encounter with the law as such is decidedly negative due to the legalistic and unsympathetic reactions of the scribes and Pharisees to Jesus (Mark 2:6-12, 16-17). There is also a contrast to the Johannine prologue's stark juxtaposition of the law which came through Moses, and grace and truth through Jesus Christ (John 1:17). The reader of Luke is thereby required to avoid

---

2. Bock, *Luke*, 1:76.

categorizing piety without reference to Jewish structures and institutions, and is consequently prepared in a particular way to grapple with Luke's major theme of promise-fulfilment. For Luke, the Old Testament and Jewish hope of salvation is not discontinued by the life and ministry of Jesus, but rather it finds its concrete fulfilment in Jesus and (in Acts) the church. Thus, having the opening characters of the infancy narratives scrupulous with respect to the law not only serves narrative purposes, it also plays an important role in Luke's theological program. In fact, as we have already indicated, narrative should not be divorced from theology, for unlike Matthew who proof-texts much of his theology, Luke's theology is more subtly expressed via narrative.³

Elizabeth is infertile, but experiences God's reversal

The reader is also informed that Zechariah and Elizabeth are childless, and this is due to Elizabeth being infertile (στεῖρα). Such unfortunate couples, particularly the woman, were viewed with disdain in Jewish society. The pious couple, or woman, without child immediately evokes memories of Sarah (Gen 15:1–6; 16:1–6; 18:1–15), Manoah's wife (Judg 13:1–24), and Hannah (1 Sam 1), the parallels with Sarah stressed by Luke's description of Zechariah and Elizabeth being advanced in years. Given this 'type scene' and the favor shown to these women of old, the reader is expectant regarding a positive outcome for Elizabeth.⁴ Not only so, there is expectation of something significant with respect to God's salvation plan resulting from this. The offspring from the other previously infertile women, Isaac, Samson, and Samuel, each played key roles in God's dealings with Israel.

Readers well-versed in their OT scriptures may also recognize an incongruence here. The covenant explicitly promised that sterility and infertility would not befall those who were obedient to God's ordinances (Deut 7:12–14).⁵ Yet at the outset of Luke's narrative we are confronted with a couple blameless before the Lord, yet without child. If God is to be faithful to his covenant, then we would expect that the situation be reversed.⁶

---

3. See Bock, *Proclamation from Prophecy and Pattern*; Coleridge, *Birth of the Lukan Narrative*; Rowe, *Early Narrative Christology*.

4. Tannehill, *Narrative Unity*, 1:18

5. Garland, *Luke*, 65. Garland further claims that it is as if the curse against Babylon (Isa 47) regarding widowhood and loss of children, has fallen upon Israel. However, rather than referring to infertility, loss of children may equally relate to devastation in war.

6. Especially so given the reversal theme in Luke. See Brawley, *Centering on God*, 182–211; York, *Last Shall be First*.

Elizabeth is unlike her husband who doubted

The narrative takes the expected positive turn when Gabriel, the angel of the Lord, appears to Zechariah during his priestly ministrations and announces that God has responded to their prayers. "Your wife Elizabeth will bear you a son and you are to name him John" (Luke 1:13). Moreover he is to play a significant part in God's redemptive purposes; his prophetic vocation is to be carried out in the spirit and power of Elijah (1:8–20).

Zechariah's first response is that of fear and terror (1:11). Although this is a typical response of those who are confronted with the divine (cf. 2:11), given the way the narrative later progresses, Zechariah also features as a type of those who are confronted with Jesus' mighty works and are amazed and perplexed (5:26; 7:16; 8:37). His second response of disbelief is perhaps understandable from a human point of view. Zechariah has questions regarding the likelihood of all this given both his and Elizabeth's age (1:18–20). His request for a sign ("How will I know that this is so?") has biblical precedent (Gen 15:3–8; 18:11–12; Judg 6:37; 2 Kgs 20:8; Isa 7:11), but ironically the sign he receives is a form of judgment. Zechariah should have realized that he was not challenging a mere human representative, but a divine messenger, and so his questioning expresses his underlying disbelief. Consequently, he is struck mute until the time of the fulfilment of the angelic oracle. So, notwithstanding Luke's previous depiction of him as a righteous and blameless man, Zechariah is ever so slightly diminished in the eyes of the reader. The reader is also challenged not to emulate the unbelief of Zechariah but to trust the divine word.

Zechariah acts as a foil for the response of his wife Elizabeth. No reason is provided for her self-seclusion (περιέκρυβεν ἑαυτήν), but the lack of clarity in the narrative tends to evoke a sense of mystery. This sense of mystery undergirds the significance of what is taking place.[7] In contrast to her husband there is no narratival indication of unbelief or surprise on her behalf, only a response of praise for her having conceived (Luke 1:24–25). Again, not only does her infertility and subsequent pregnancy mirror an OT model, so does the praise and thanks that she offers to God for dealing with her disgrace (Sarah in Gen 21:6; Rachel in Gen 30:23). In this way, we see that recurring pattern (e.g., birth of children to infertile women) across the Testaments is a key component of the Lukan proclamation. Fulfilment is thereby not limited to explicit narratival discussion, but is conveyed by subtext to the extent that the reader is able to identify the intertextual echoes.

---

7. Bock, *Luke*, 1:97–98, has a summary of the various proposals regarding her motive for seclusion.

Elizabeth shows gratitude to God

Elizabeth construes her pregnancy as God's personal favor upon her in taking away her public disgrace. To this extent her response is limited and indicates that she has not perceived her place in terms of God's wider dealings with his people.[8] Nevertheless, her brief statement of gratitude performs an important narratival function in anticipating the Magnificat where Mary's more detailed praises find expression (Luke 1:46–55).[9]

Elizabeth is filled with the Holy Spirit and prophesies as a reliable spokesperson for God

After the corresponding announcement to Mary regarding the birth of her child, where Elizabeth's conception in her old age is a sign to Mary that all things are possible with God (Luke 1:36–37), Elizabeth herself again features in the narrative when visited by Mary. This draws the two narrative strands together and arguably serves to subordinate John to Jesus.[10] Upon Mary's greeting, "the child leaped in Elizabeth's womb" (1:41), thus conveying not only a sense of the divine orchestration of events, but also the key relationship that the two children will have.[11] It also confirms the previous announcement that Elizabeth's baby would be filled with the Holy Spirit "even before his birth" (1:15).[12]

At this point Elizabeth is said to be "filled with the Holy Spirit" (1:41), a description that is highly significant for Luke's narrative and theology. For Luke, the Spirit is inseparably linked with the prophetic word (1:67—Zechariah; 2:25–27—Simeon), characterizes the baptism performed by the Messiah (3:16), descends on Jesus and guides his public ministry (3:22; 4:1, 14, 18; 10:21), is the gracious gift of the Father (11:13), and empowers those called to testify to their faith (12:12). The Holy Spirit also characterizes the life of the early church in Acts: he is responsible for its birth and growth (2:1–38; 9:31), he emboldens and empowers believers (4:8, 31; 6:10), is the mark of maturity (6:3, 5), gives revelation (7:55; 10:19), directs mission (10:44–48;

---

8. Coleridge, *Birth of the Lukan Narrative*, 48.

9. Tannehill, *Narrative Unity*, 1:17. Tannehill notes that the imbalance between Elizabeth's brief statement of thanks and Mary's lengthy canticle that follows has narratival significance. It not only highlights Mary's faith in contrast to Zechariah's doubt, but further underscores the greater significance of Mary's child.

10. Nolland, *Luke*, 1:62; Bock, *Luke*, 1:138.

11. Also possibly confirming that Elizabeth's child John will be filled with the Holy Spirit from conception (1:15).

12. Tannehill, *Narrative Unity*, 1:23.

13:2; 16:7), informs key decisions (15:28), and instigates the prophetic word (20:22; 21:11).

Prophecy is a key theme for Luke and is the mark of the hand of God orchestrating events according to his divine plan. God does not work "in a corner" (Acts 26:26), but with the aid of human instruments. Such human instruments not only prophetically proclaim and witness to the plan and its fulfilment at its various stages, but are themselves participants in the unfolding drama. It is noteworthy, therefore, that not only is Elizabeth the first person in the narrative to be filled with the Spirit, she is also the first to prophesy. In fact, like others in the infancy narratives, and in the wider narrative of Luke-Acts, it is the filling of the Spirit that results in a prophetic utterance. Further, as one who prophesies, Elizabeth is to be regarded as a reliable spokesperson for God.[13] The contrast between the silence of distrustful Zechariah and the prophetic work of Elizabeth highlights this facet of her relationship with God and others. The depiction of Elizabeth under the Spirit's power not only confirms the divine instigation and control of the events surrounding the birth of the two children, she also anticipates the later faithful disciples of Jesus who will be likewise empowered.

The importance of prophecy is further demonstrated in that for Luke, Jesus is the prophetic Messiah who is not only the ultimate successor to Moses (Deut 18:15 and Luke 9:35), but also carries out his ministry in the mould of Elijah and Elisha (4:24-30; 9:28-33). It is significant, therefore, that Elizabeth's prophetic action sets the tone, not only for the songs that follow (Magnificat [1:46-55], Benedictus [1:67-79], Nunc Dimittis [2:28-32]), but also for the ministries of John and Jesus. In using the language of fulfilment, she not only picks up one of the key terms from the preface (1:1) and thus aligns herself with Luke's stated purpose, but helps contribute to the certainty that the reader feels regarding the positive outcome of other narratival predictions.

The reader should by now be alert to the significance of this woman in the working out of the divine plan. Further, given the contemporary cultural and religious restrictions faced by women,[14] somewhat of a reversal is evident that will find increasing expression as the narrative progresses.

---

13. Ibid., 1:22.
14. See chapter 2.

Elizabeth rightly identifies Jesus as Lord

Also significant is the Christological statement in identifying Mary as "the mother of my Lord." While it is ultimately the resurrection that will vindicate Jesus as Lord (Acts 2:36), Luke is not averse to inserting the resurrection title back into his Gospel narrative (Luke 7:13, 19; 10:1; 11:39, etc.). In using this title of the as yet unborn Jesus, Elizabeth becomes a proto-disciple and anticipates the response of those who will later recognize and respond to the divine identity of God's Messiah.[15] Furthermore, the joy that characterizes both Mary and Elizabeth is not only typical of the joyful strain that runs through the infancy narratives, it is programmatic for those who are the recipients of the blessings that will issue from the messianic ministry of Jesus.[16]

Elizabeth is faithful and obedient to God

Following the Magnificat, the birth of John the Baptist is narrated (Luke 1:57–66). Elizabeth's joy is now supplemented by that of her neighbors and relatives (1:58), thereby fulfilling the statement of the angel in 1:14. Significant for our purposes here is that Elizabeth responds in obedience to the angel's initial directive in naming the child John, opposing the others who wish[17] to name him Zechariah after his father. Thus she continues in the vein of the obedient servant of God who responds positively to his initiative and instructions. In the abandoning of naming conventions, the narrative also hints that traditional values and concepts are no longer a given in this new work of God.[18]

---

15. Garland, *Luke*, 93. Not all agree. Bock, *Luke*, 1:137, for example, contends that although κύριος later takes on significant connotations, here it is nothing more than a title of respect. It appears that Bock has muted the claims of the narrative at this point. If Luke retrojects the title into his narrative and editorial comments, then it raises the question of why have a less developed nuance here, especially given the "supernatural" flavor of the infancy narratives.

16. Bock, *Luke*, 1:140.

17. The imperfect ἐκάλουν is here taken as conative ("trying/going to call"), but it may also reflect the name they were actually using (so Garland, *Luke*, 104). It is unclear who is intended to be the subject of the third person verbs here. Given the way the narrative develops, it is obviously not Zechariah or Elizabeth, so presumably the other relatives are in mind. On the naming of a child at circumcision, see Brown, *Birth*, 369.

18. Ibid.,105.

THE INFANCY NARRATIVES (LUKE 1:5—2:52)

Summary of Narratival Propositions regarding Elizabeth

The characterization of Elizabeth plays an important narratival and theological function. In terms of narratival propositions, she is a woman of exceptional pedigree, an exemplary Jew, and one who, although infertile, plays a key role in God's salvific purposes. Elizabeth responds in obedience, is joyful and thankful. She is filled with the Holy Spirit and makes prophetic statements that are Christological and reinforce other narratival threads. In many ways Elizabeth anticipates the faithful disciple of Jesus: obedient, filled with the Holy Spirit, and a conveyor of the prophetic word. In this way she embodies the narrator's concerns, and so forms an important link between the stated purpose in the preface and the unfolding of later events.

Theological Propositions arising from the Characterization of Elizabeth

Given Luke's portrayal of the character and role of Elizabeth against the backdrop of cultural expectations regarding the role of women in religion and society, the reader is left wondering whether God is going to involve women in his plan in new and significant ways. Indeed, as the narrative unfolds, the following theological propositions emerge:

1. God's is able to reverse the infertility of some couples.
2. God fulfils his promise to bestow the Holy Spirit in the end times.
3. The Spirit enables believers to speak prophetically on God's behalf with respect to salvation history and the identity of Jesus.
4. Being a mouthpiece for God is neither determined nor inhibited by gender or age.

Mary

Immediately after the angel Gabriel's reintroduction into the plot, Mary is introduced as a protagonist (Luke 1:27–28). As Mary plays a role in Jesus' origins and in the fulfilment of God's plans for the world, her character serves two purposes in the infancy narratives. Obviously Mary is essential to the story of God's work in the birth of his Son. However, she is also employed by the narrator to communicate many other important theological points to the readers/hearers. In terms of her character role, her appearance is not limited to participation in select 'type-scenes' in the narrative.[19] Rather, the way in which Mary plays her part is theologically apposite. That is, Mary is in many ways a model of a desired response to the unexpected ways in which God may work in and through the lives of the faithful. The responses which are modelled by Mary suggest ongoing theological truths for Luke's audience. These realities about God and his desires for the world are communicated through the interactions between Mary and God, Mary and Jesus, and Mary and other characters. These theological truths are communicated by narratival propositions, which in turn form the basis for theological propositions.

Mary is a woman of lowly social status

Gabriel appears to Mary, thus creating tension in the account. Will his announcement be similar to that received by Zechariah? What will the response be, both by angel and recipient? Gabriel is commissioned by God and sent to Nazareth, an insignificant place in Palestine let alone the Roman Empire. Hence the focus of Luke's account moves away from the temple in Jerusalem to Nazareth in Galilee. By means of this geographical shift, the power of God is surprisingly focused on a remote place, and upon a person of very low status—a woman. She is a virgin whose sole reference point is her engagement to a man. Her name is Mary. No genealogy of her own is given— unlike both Elizabeth (a descendent of Aaron) and her betrothed (from the line of David)—she has no pedigree or clan which would recommend her as a key character in the story. Mary's description is at first quite minimal. Though the focus of the narrative is on her, in fact more description is given regarding Joseph. Nevertheless her story does not stand alone. The account of Mary is tied to the previous one by the words "in the sixth month." This reference to Elizabeth's conceiving serves not only to connect the two narratives but also the women themselves as part of God's larger story.

---

19. 'Type scenes' are "certain fixed situations which the author is expected to include in his narrative and which he must perform according to a set order of motifs -situations like the arrival, the message, the voyage, the assembly, the oracle, the arming of the hero, and some half dozen others. The type-scene of the visit, for example, should unfold according to the following fixed pattern: a guest approaches; someone greets him, gets up, hurries to meet him; the guest is taken by the hand, led into the room, invited to take the seat of honour; the guest is enjoined to feast; the ensuing meal is described." Alter, *The Art of Biblical Narrative*, 50–51.

THE INFANCY NARRATIVES (LUKE 1:5—2:52)

Mary experiences an unexpected religio-cultural reversal which is sanctioned by God's presence and activity

Mary's initial characterization is broadened dramatically via the angelic greeting, where her description and status are taken in unexpected directions. She receives acclaim from the angel: "Greetings, favored one!" (Χαῖρε, κεχαριτωμένη—Luke 1:28). In the eyes of both the angel and God, she is not merely a young virgin pledged to a man. She is those things, yet she is also marked out as a unique character in that she is the recipient of divine favor, and also the recipient of those actions which will express that favor.[20] Κεχαριτωμένη may be translated as "favored one" or "you who have received grace." Either translation captures the fact that the term totally redescribes her as a character, for her status has been radically altered by God's disposition towards her. In fact, κεχαριτωμένη "functions as a name for Mary."[21] The angelic greeting therefore serves as a narratival marker that Mary as a character has transitioned from obscurity to particular divine focus. The narrative of course raises the question: what is the nature of this favor?

The favor of the Lord is expanded upon by the words that immediately follow: ὁ κύριος μετὰ σοῦ—"The Lord is with you!" Few individuals have had their relationship with God described in these terms. The preceding Zechariah story highlights the fact that he was one amongst the very few Israelites who ever had the opportunity of entering the innermost parts of the temple. These few men from a single tribe were the favored ones under the Mosaic and Levitical system to operate the temple cult. And only a few from amongst these men could enter the sanctuary where God's presence was to be found. But Mary is described as the one with whom the Lord is pleased and therefore present with her. The narrative proposes a surprising religio-cultural reversal: God is pleased with, and present with Mary in contrast to his response to the unbelief he found in the person of Zechariah. Though Luke is on a whole positive towards the temple in much of his account, in this instance the faith of the priesthood associated with the temple is not shown in a positive light.

Mary, who was one amongst the excluded, is now included in the most intimate of relationships. She is accorded the Edenic blessing of God's presence. Furthermore, Mary has God's presence without the privilege of Levitical pedigree nor male gender. Whereas a complex set of procedures is part of the description of Zechariah's entry into the temple, Mary has God's presence without fuss. Most significantly, God is at the center of this

---

20. Green, *Luke*, 86–87.
21. Ibid., 87.

reversal. He brings it to be, commands its announcement, and thereby sanctions it. The angelic words that Mary is "blessed among women" compounds Mary's change in the eyes of the narrator. This is confirmed by her response.

Mary responds in a manner not unlike that of Zechariah: "How can these things be, since I am a virgin?" (1:34). The angel explains the miraculous conception as the work of the Holy Spirit and the power of the Most High. The repetition of favor (1:28) is significant in providing the rationale for the different response to her questioning. Mary is favored and not rebuked.

God reverses the fortunes of the lowly who
are open to him, including women

A theme which is accented in Mary's song is that of God the deliverer who reverses the fortunes of the weak, the oppressed and the excluded. This reversal motif is communicated via Mary who serves as an example *par excellence* of what he will do with others. She is a character in the divine drama illustrative of the change of status of those who formerly have been excluded. The days of exclusion have ended given God's new work. The proud, rich, and powerful will oppose God, Jesus and the humble throughout the narrative. They will not succeed. People like Mary will be the recipients of God's gracious action whereby they are set in a new relation to him, to each other and the socio-religious order of the day. The divine reversal of the mighty and the lowly is "not to obliterate the powerful so that the lowly can achieve the positions of honor and privilege to which they previously had no access. Rather, God is at work in individual lives (like Mary) and in the social order as a whole in order to subvert the very structure of society that supports and perpetuates such distinctions."[22]

By this point in the narrative, the narrator has mounted an impressive scriptural and historical argument that God's new divine action will have far-reaching consequences. These consequences will be socio-religious in nature and their sole justification lies in their theological grounding. In Mary's case (as with Hannah), God reframes those characters in the narrative who may have once been considered lowly. This means that the reader will have to cope with reading characters such as Mary in a new way, for the narrator expects the reader/hearer to change their view of the lowly and excluded characters whom Mary represents. In particular, a first century Jewish and Greco-Roman view of the status of women is being challenged by the reframing of the theological position and value of these characters.

---

22. Green, *Luke*, 105.

THE INFANCY NARRATIVES (LUKE 1:5—2:52)

The reader is expected to appropriate this change of perspective as an aspect of their participation in this new initiative of God.

The scene ends in a matter of fact manner, which roots the events described in the plane of ordinary history: "Mary stayed with Elizabeth for three months, then went home" (Luke 1:56). This section thus concludes with the narratival proposal that Mary's character stands out as a model of a person of faith in the practicalities of the everyday. This extends the range of her character into ordinary family activities. Mary is thus involved in common domestic life as well as being a model believer, the mother of God's Son, and an authoritative interpreter of Scripture and salvation history.

Mary is unexpectedly drawn into God's plan to reverse the fortunes of Israel and the whole world

The angel continues to speak, announcing that not only is the Lord with Mary, he has included her at the epicenter of his new work in the world. This is a unique moment in salvation history. The author has framed the whole story within the context of the brutal subjugation of Israel and the entire world under a foreign power. The story occurs "in the days of Herod, king of Judea" (Luke 1:5), and the birth of Mary's son is introduced by the reference to the power of Rome to rule and to decree: "Now in those days a decree went out from Caesar Augustus, that a census be taken of all the inhabited earth" (2:1).

In this context of oppression, the angelic discourse explains the magnitude of the ensuing events. Mary is told that she will conceive in her womb, and bear a son. Ironically, where Elizabeth had a need for a son, Mary had no such need.[23] This announcement does not resolve any predicament on Mary's behalf, and it will not remove any shame from her as it will from Elizabeth (1:25). In fact, the events which the angel announces to Mary place her in a difficult predicament that was not of her own choosing.

She is commanded to call her son "Jesus." This new character, "Jesus," will "be great and will be called Son of the Most High, and the Lord will give him the throne of his father David" (1:32). The assumption the narrator wants the hearer/reader to make at this point in the discourse is that Mary will be the mother of the child that belongs to Joseph, who is of David's household. Human lineage is assumed. Presumably their son will rise up as warrior-king and reclaim the Davidic kingdom and rule in the fulfilment of the Davidic covenant (2 Sam 7). However, the promise and its narratival expectations are enlarged by the description of her son as the one who

---

23. Ibid., 84.

would rule "over the house of Jacob forever, and of his kingdom there will be no end." The announcement of this son, the greater-than-David son, places Mary in a surprising salvation-historical relationship to Elizabeth and her son. This relationship will be played out later in the account. The implied narratival proposition is that Mary's son is greater than Elizabeth's son. The larger significance of this episode is that the period of God's silence with respect to Israel and her salvation is now broken. The angelic visitation to Zechariah is not an isolated incident. In fact, it functions as a prelude to the angel's greater announcement to Mary.

Mary is a righteous Jewish woman (who necessarily has no child)

In what appears to be a stark piece of dialogue, the narrator presents an immediate and humanly insurmountable narrative impediment to Gabriel's announcement. She says she is "a virgin" (Luke 1:34). In Mary's mind her virginal purity is a clear obstacle to what Gabriel is saying.

Nevertheless, her virginal purity is likely meant to convey a wider sense of righteousness, and in this sense she parallels the description of Zechariah and Elizabeth. The elderly pair were "righteous in the sight of God, living blamelessly according to all the commandments and regulations of the Lord" (1:6). The implicit narratival proposition is that Mary is also an upright Jew in her devotion to God and his ways.

However, the two women do not have every feature in common. Whereas Elizabeth is infertile, Mary is a virgin. This leads to Mary's question, which seemingly parallels Zechariah's protest. The angel, however, answers without rebuke despite the similarity between Mary's answer to that which previously incurred the angel's wrath. Gabriel's answer here is descriptive rather than reproachful, and the lack of indictment in his answer is another surprising turn in the narrative. The implicit reason for his lack of rebuke appears to be that there is something about Mary which differentiates her as a character and the nature of her response from that of Zechariah. In one sense it can be explained by the previous statement "you have found favor in the eyes of the Lord." Although we are not told much of Mary's life nor piety previous to this episode, the implication is that Mary does not doubt God. Her belief withstands the unnatural promise given to her. In truth, the announcement to Mary is far more unusual than a woman bearing a child in old age, for there is ample OT precedent for the latter.

Mary's child will be conceived in a unique and unprecedented manner. Two points are made in order to assure her of the truth of the fact that the Holy Spirit will conceive a special child of God within her. She is given both the story of Elizabeth, as well as assurance of the unlimited nature of God's power (1:36–37). What Mary has to do is to trust God amidst what will be an unusual, and therefore surely difficult, journey towards the fulfilment of God's plan. Mary is thus presented as a faithful woman who will need to remain faithful to God in trying social and religious circumstances.

Mary is the mother of the divine-human Son of God

The annunciation to Mary is that "the child to be born . . . will be called the Son of God" (Luke 1:35). The identification of the child as the "Son of God" draws upon the theme of his kingship as per Luke 1:32. This includes the facts that "He will be great, and will be called the Son of the Most High, and the Lord will give him the throne of his ancestor David." However, the child's greatness is not limited to earthly power alone. In Luke 1:35, "we have a different understanding of what it means to be the Son of God, tracing it to divine intervention at conception and a resulting special nature."[24] The sentence structure of 1:35 suggests the veracity of the claim regarding Jesus' nature. The "therefore" (διό) which links "The Holy Spirit will come upon you, and the power of the Most High will overshadow you" and "he will be called the Son of God," indicates that Jesus' sonship cannot be understood aside from the claim to his divine origins.[25] Thus this "Son of God" is not merely a functional term, rather it is anchored in the co-claim that Jesus is the "Son of the Most High" (1:32). The infancy narratives thus present Mary as the mother of a unique child who is divine. Bearing God within oneself is perhaps the highest calling a human being could receive. The manner in which Mary carries (!) out this calling is another key aspect of her characterization.

Mary's service follows an exemplary Davidic pattern

The narrator gives the reader some measure of confidence in Mary by means of allusions to the faith of another unlikely servant of God, namely David. Given the focus on David (Luke 1:27, 32) in this short pericope, the narrator may be drawing from the pinnacle of Israel's history to make a point about the kind of people the Lord seeks as servants. The author may be suggesting that the inclination of Mary's heart parallels David's heart (1 Sam 13:14). Two lines of thought suggest this parallel. First, Luke has followed the sequence of thought in 1 Sam 13:14. This OT verse reads: "The

---

24. Tannehill, *Luke*, 50.
25. Kremer, "Sohn Gottes," 144, see also 43.

Lord has sought for Himself a man after his own heart, and the Lord has appointed him as ruler over his people . . . ." Luke parallels this verse by making much of Mary's disposition. She clearly is a person after God's own heart. This is made explicit by Mary's posture of self-abandoning availability to God (Luke 1:38) and is employed to confirm her characterization as the exemplar servant of the Lord. Mary says: "Here I am, the bond servant of the Lord; may it be done to me according to your word." Second, Luke presents Mary as the one whose son will take up the mantle of the rule "of his father David." Just as David was the exemplary person through whom God achieved his purposes, Mary is presented as the exemplar of trust and piety through whom the David story is advanced. The placement of the Mary story after Zechariah's story strengthens this narrative conclusion. The Zechariah story serves to highlight the fact that in both David's own day and Mary's own day the cult and leadership of Israel had failed God. Therefore, in Mary, as with David, God has again chosen an unlikely character through whom he will rescue his people from internal and external oppression.

The exemplary nature of Mary's character is further broadened and confirmed via the story of her visit with Elizabeth. The contrast of her departure scene (to Elizabeth) with Gabriel's departure scene (from Mary) affords the opportunity to fill out her character a little. Whereas Gabriel leaves her peacefully, Mary leaves the scene with haste—she is not merely a passive character. She is also capable of deliberate and intentional action. Mary "arose and went in a hurry" to the hill country where her relative Elizabeth lived (1:39).

In the next scene the focus of the narrative remains upon the interactions of the women, whose exchanges are described without reference to men. The significant details of the story pertain to Elizabeth's recognition and acknowledgement of Mary's privileged status as "the mother of my Lord."[26] This recognition is driven by God as the divine Spirit fills Elizabeth who for this reason "cried out with a loud voice" exclaiming "Blessed are you among women and blessed is the fruit of your womb!" (1:42). Elizabeth also confirms that Mary, in contrast to Zechariah, is blessed because of her belief: "And blessed is she who believed that there would be a fulfilment of what had been spoken to her by the Lord" (1:45). At the outset of Luke's narrative this bracketing technique drives the second order narrative proposal that *Mary is the model believer*.

---

26. See above under Elizabeth.

Mary is the first person to link Israel's salvation history with God's actions in her own time

Mary's role is not limited to being a model of piety, nor is her character merely expanded to being the unique person within whom the Son of the Most High will be conceived. Mary also plays the role of the first authoritative interpreter of Scripture in the light of God's new work. That is, Mary is the first one to interpret the words of God in Scripture as they relate to her situation and Israel's predicament. Her interpretation is authoritative and goes unchallenged in the rest of Luke's narrative. Indeed, it sets the theological frame of reference for the entire plot.

By way of a strong contrast, prior to Mary's speech Zechariah the priest does not interpret his experience with reference to salvation history. He only does so after Mary, and his interpretation is subservient to the narratival and theological framework she has provided. Where he is mute and must communicate with only signs, Mary (who has no official training nor priestly position) is the first person to reflect theologically on Scripture and on Jesus. Mary's interpretation of Scripture is "a virtual collage of biblical texts."[27] Mary comments upon God's covenantal defence of his people by the employment of a wide range of texts. The narrator presents Mary as a character who handles Scripture capably. She evidences a high degree of intent and nuance by which she relates the texts to each other and to her theology of God and his actions. The texts she uses include portions and themes from of the Torah (Gen 17:19; Deut 10:17–18), the Psalms (Pss 24:7; 34:2ff; 35:9; 107:9; 138:6); and the Prophets (Hab 3:18; Zeph 3:17).

Mary is also a witness to God's work in history. Significantly, this witness now necessarily includes her own story. Though initially she was minimally described, by this point she is vitally and maximally incorporated into the larger story of what God has done and has promised to do. Her trust in the Lord is again presented without equivocation. This leads to a response of utmost joy in the opening stanza: "My soul magnifies the Lord, and my spirit rejoices in God my savior . . . ." (Luke 1:46).

Mary is a valid communicator of Scripture and interpreter of salvation history

Mary's song (Luke 1:46–56) is suggestive for the reader/hearer because in it she provides the lens through which to interpret God and his actions. She comments on the actions of God in and through her with respect to key

---

27. Green, *Luke*, 100.

theological themes in the OT. Mary rightly describes God as Lord (1:46), the Savior (1:47), who powerfully lifts up the humble and brings down the proud (1:48, 51–53), who is mighty and holy (1:49), merciful (1:50, 54), and faithful (1:54–55). This is theological reflection of the highest order. Her hymn is a profound "declaration of faith."[28]

Mary's song follows a pattern of female leadership through song in the Israelite tradition. These include Miriam (Exod. 15:19–21), Deborah (Judg 5:1–31), Hannah (1 Sam 2:1–10), and Judith (Jdt 16:1–17). In particular, Mary echoes Miriam's Song after the Israelites were saved from Egyptian bondage and pursuit, for both songs heavily accent the salvation of the Lord. However, there is a stark contrast between them. In Miriam's case her song was short and overshadowed by that of Moses. In Luke's birth narrative there is no male authoritative figure whose song overshadows Mary's. Indeed, the praise of another woman provides its backdrop. The role of women in the opening scenes of Luke's Gospel is thus quite remarkable. The narrative clearly proposes that the theological reflection of these women is authoritative and a model of scriptural interpretation.

Mary's fate initially appears to be determined by the decrees and ancestries of men

The first five verses of chapter 2 provide a discrete account of the historical process by which Mary found herself in Bethlehem. In this narratival unit she is the last to be mentioned in a scale of characters. The most powerful are mentioned first. Caesar Augustus, who decrees that "the entire world be registered" (Luke 2:1) is followed by Quirinius who was the "governor of Syria" (2:2). These two powerful men are followed by a man of theologically significant pedigree. The text describes his links to David in an emphatic manner: "Joseph . . . he was of the house and lineage of David" (2:4). Mary's link with David is not intrinsic, but rather by association with Joseph.

Joseph travels "to the city of David, which is called Bethlehem, because he was of the house and lineage of David," and Mary accompanies him because they are betrothed. In fact Mary is described as "his betrothed, who was with child." Ironically, only the first of these two clauses ("his betrothed") applies to Joseph: Mary is betrothed to him, but does not owe her pregnancy to him. An imperial census and other characters in the narrative will assume that the child whom Mary carries is Joseph's child. However, this is not the case, and the reader is aware of this irony. This creates narratival tension for the omniscient reader. This tension is reinforced by the

---

28. Bock, *Luke*, 1:160.

way in which Mary is described as a passive "nobody" which would be appropriate for her socio-religious context.

Mary is active and caring despite adversity

Here the character of Mary transitions from passive to active. By means of repetition she is characterized as a birth-giver. The following unbroken line reads: "the days were completed for her to give birth, and she gave birth to a son, her firstborn" (Luke 2:6b–7a).

Luke records Mary's actions, the actions of a young mother. She wraps Jesus in "swaddling cloths" and places him in a manger (2:7). Despite the surprising nature of her conceiving she has thoughtfully prepared for the birth and is giving the child all the care a normal child would receive. Mary acts in these ways despite the adverse circumstances she experiences. By contrast to Elizabeth, when the time came for the child to be born Mary was in a foreign location, without relatives to comfort her and did not even have appropriate lodgings. Mary was a young virgin in a difficult situation. Yet this did not prevent her from acting with care and love. This is an intimate scene in which a young woman stands out in difficult times. Unbeknownst to her, she was playing her part in a divine plan as she prepared and settled the baby in such a way which would be a sign to the shepherds (2:12). What is particularly noteworthy is that even in the scene when the child is born, Mary is the primary character in the story. This is of enormous significance given how the remainder of the narrative presents the person of Jesus. It is also striking that this story was not redacted in order to give Jesus prominence over Mary. For the narrator, the focus on Mary and her actions is deliberate. On the one hand, her actions may appear unremarkable, as she does what any caring mother would do. But the narrator has chosen to include her actions because they highlight the kind of virtues which God seeks in his people. He has resisted other pressures which may have come to bear on the narrative in order to focus on Mary, who is clearly portrayed as a model of the ideal response to God.

Luke's presentation of Mary parallels the efforts of authors in the Greco-Roman world who provided their audiences with positive ethical models to imitate. Lucian wrote *Demonax* as a record of Demonax's life so that "young men of good instincts who aspire to philosophy . . . may be able to set themselves a pattern from our modern world and to copy that man, the best of all the philosophers whom I know about."[29] The ethical significance is intended to make a profound impression on the reader who is expected to take this ethical teaching on board and apply it to their own context. The narratival rhetoric is thus fashioned with the intention of influencing the reader in a particular manner.[30] In this sense Mary is clearly presented as a positive ethical witness to God's work.[31]

Mary engages in on-going theological reflection despite personal dislocation

Following Jesus' birth and swaddling, there is a stark shift from the manger to "the fields . . . at night" (Luke 2:8). Another group of lowly people has received divine revelation. Their response is a contrast to Mary's; they "were deeply frightened." The angel tells them that "a savior who is Christ the Lord" has been born (2:11). The shepherds are given a very precise sign in order to find the child. Mary's post-labor work—her ordinary work of swaddling and settling—will be the sign. No more is required for the sign, only the fruits of Mary's work. The shepherds' hasty travel leads them to "Mary and Joseph" (2:16). Mary is mentioned first as she has consistently been the primary interest of the narrative to this point. The newborn child is merely mentioned in passing and receives no further attention in this section of

---

29. Lucian, *Demonax* 2, in *Lucian 1* (trans. A. M. Harmon), cited in Tannehill, "Acts of the Apostles and Ethics," 271. In the same manner, Acts employs Peter, Stephen and Paul as positive role models. Tannehill observes that they are presented as "faithful witnesses of the Lord Jesus . . . though their roles in history may in some ways be unique, the qualities they exhibit may be exemplary, giving their stories continuing ethical significance." Ibid.

30. The force of the literary technique whereby a positive ethical model is presented with the clear expectation of imitation is called the narrative's "rhetoric." The author's use of this technique is an example which illustrates the way in which the theology embedded in a given piece of literature is communicated via these techniques. For this reason, a study of Luke's narratives will necessarily include a study of his theological themes. Ibid.

31. Importantly, her characterization includes key exemplary virtues which are hallmarks of a Spirit-led ministry. This anticipates the role which Peter plays via his speeches around the Pentecost event in the book of Acts. Tannehill writes that Peter's ability to contextualize God's work is one of his Spirit-led "outstanding qualities." These "outstanding qualities" make him exemplary. Peter was empowered in such a way that he "demonstrated the ability to interpret both the Jesus events [his resurrection and installation as Messianic King] and the immediate circumstances in which he speaks as the work of God illuminated by the prophesies and precedents of Scripture." Tannehill, "Acts of the Apostles and Ethics," 272.

the narrative.³² The same scant attention apples to Joseph. The attention falls upon the angelic message and Mary's response to it (2:17-19). These two threads, message and response, are drawn together by Mary's continuing engagement with the message. "Mary stored up all these things, trying in her heart to penetrate their significance" (2:19) Mary's response to the revelation is singled out as unique.³³ She anticipates the good soil spoken of in Luke 8:15, epitomizing the best response to the words of God, as she is one of those who "when they hear the word, hold it fast in a good and honest heart and bear fruit with endurance." In this way she is a contrast to those who are amazed at the revelation but are not recorded as continually ruminating upon it.³⁴

Mary is a key figure who ensures the pious context of Jesus' infancy

Mary is a pious Jew and she ensures the development of Jesus accordingly. Luke 2:21 reads: "when eight days were fulfilled and the time came to circumcise him, he was called Jesus, which the angel called him before he was conceived in the womb." This verse highlights Mary's obedience to God in ensuring that Jesus was given the name which had been revealed to her alone. The circumcision further serves to highlight that "in the infancy narrative . . . the Christian movement was cradled in pietistic Judaism."³⁵ Mary's role in ensuring this pious context is re-affirmed by the plural verbs used in 2:22 ("they brought him to Jerusalem to present him to the Lord . . .") and 2:27 ("when the parents brought in the child Jesus to perform for him what was customary by the law . . ."). Jesus' Jewish purity and righteousness was not the work of Joseph alone. Mary was an instrumental player in Jesus' dedication, thereby contributing to Jesus being ritually holy and set aside for the Lord. Jesus' messianic vocation has been given its fitting beginnings.

A fascinating insight into Luke's view of Mary is revealed in the story of the presentation of the baby in the temple. This episode begins with an enigmatic under-statement with respect to Mary. The verse opens with "when the days of their purification according to the law of Moses were fulfilled,

---

32. Nolland, *Luke*, 1:109.

33. ". . . while Mary is part of the 'they' who were amazed, her further response is separated out for special attention. The shepherds' words are added to her other experiences of the revelation of God and safely stored up in Mary's mind (cf. Gen 37:11; Dan. 7:28) as she seeks to understand fully what was being made known in these acts of revelation." Ibid., 1:112.

34. Garland, *Luke*, 124-25.

35. Ibid., 125.

they brought him to Jerusalem to present him to the Lord . . ." (Luke 2:22). Levitical law required only that females be purified, so why does Luke write about "their" purification? David E. Garland contends that "Luke presents it as a 'family matter' probably because he does not want the spotlight to fall solely on Mary."[36] The significance of this is quite striking. Mary's presence and influence upon the narrative has been such that at this point the narrator may have had to artificially dampen down the focus upon her so that the character of Jesus not be overshadowed.

Mary is continually receptive to the Spirit's teaching about her son

Mary and Joseph are met at the temple by a man named Simeon (Luke 2:25). Luke emphasizes the piety of Simeon and makes repeated reference to the Holy Spirit in this short pericope. Simeon was "righteous" as well as being "devout" and was also "waiting for the consolation of Israel." The agency of the Holy Spirit is paramount in this story. In sequential verses, the Spirit is explicitly referred to as the one who stands behind Simeon's piety (2:25), the unusual revelation that "he would not see death before he had seen the Lord's Christ" (2:26), and Simeon's entrance in to the temple "in the Spirit" (2:27). Simeon's prayer is astounding and has high praise and expectations for the child (2:30–32). The response by the baby's parents is depicted minimally (2:33), but there is no sense of resistance to the oracle concerning their son. Their silence is equivalent to the earlier statement concerning Mary "treasuring these things in her heart" (2:19). The author wants to emphasize the virtue of hearing God's words, taking them to heart, and continuing to walk before him faithfully even in uncertain circumstances. Further, the reticence to speak more about the parents also serves a literary purpose to shift the focus from the immediate circumstances to the persona of Jesus and his future role in God's expanding salvation to the nations.

Mary is a tragic figure

At this point in the narrative Luke chooses to include a scene which will thicken his description of Mary. It provides further content to her initial characterization as a consistently pious Jewish woman. This particular fleshing out of Mary's characterization is initiated by the fact that Simeon has challenging words for her. He does not only bear good tidings. Following a blessing, Simeon says to Jesus' mother: "'This child is destined for the fall and rise of many in Israel and as a sign to be opposed so that the thoughts

---

36. Ibid., 135.

of many hearts might be revealed. And a sword will pierce your own soul too.'" (Luke 2:34-35). The narrator has employed a striking 'word-motif' by means of the reference to the sword "piercing" Mary's soul. This piercing-motif plays two roles. First, it draws together Jesus' infancy narrative and his death scenes. Second, the concrete image of a sword draws together Jesus' piercing on the cross and his mother.[37] Therefore, the suffering of Christ on the cross must be understood as it relates to Jesus and to his mother. This demonstrates how deeply Mary is woven into the narrative about Jesus. Mary is not a peripheral protagonist, she is a central character. This centrality means that Luke will make strong use of her characterization to communicate his message to the audience. Mary's relationship with Jesus means that she will suffer a death of sorts of her own as she loses him to God's purposes; her suffering will parallel Jesus' own travails for the sake of God's mission. Thus Mary is a consistent reference point throughout the narrative.

Mary's piety does not exempt her from conflict and misunderstanding with Jesus

The story of Jesus remaining behind at the temple in Jerusalem is the final episode of the infancy narratives. This story is a bitter-sweet ending to this section as it anticipates the conflict which will characterize much of the Jesus' story hereafter. In this paradoxical conflict story Mary's character begins to develop a greater complexity. The reader is taken to Jerusalem and back to a setting in which religious life is the central concern. The story begins with a focus on Jesus' parents but by the end of the story the focus is upon Jesus and Mary.

The episode notes the piety of Jesus' family as they dutifully "went year by year to Jerusalem for the feast of Passover" (Luke 2:41). This positive portrayal opens with a picture of routine and faithfulness. This is a striking contrast to the disorder and family conflict which follows. The tension in the narrative builds as "the child Jesus stayed behind in Jerusalem, and his parents did not know" (2:43). The tension builds further by noting the parents' assumption that Jesus was with the travelling party, then after a day passed initiating a search for Jesus amidst his "relatives and acquaintances" (2:44). The futility of their search leads to the disquieting line "they did not find him" (2:45).[38]

---

37. Alter, *Art of Biblical Narrative*, 94-95.

38. From a literary point of view, this may anticipate the inability of the women to find Jesus in the resurrection scenes.

Jesus is an active character in the narrative for the first time in verse 46. He is found "in the temple seated in the midst of the teachers listening to them and asking them questions" (2:46). The scenes which Luke has created do not include any visual indicators which may detract from the focus on Jesus. Jesus has transitioned from a baby to a maturing boy. This boy is the center of attention.

The author describes the Jewish teachers in terms of their reaction to Jesus' actions and words: "All who heard him were astonished at his understanding and his observations" (2:47). By means of this astonishment Jesus joins the narrative's procession of unexpected characters. Zechariah, Elizabeth, Mary, Simeon and Anna were all ordinary people whom God involved in his plans in an extra-ordinary manner. In one sense Jesus stands in continuity with these characters, yet atypical features are evident as well. For example, at one level Jesus is a twelve-year-old boy who is chastised by his parents and ultimately obeys them, yet he is a boy of strange origins who acts most strangely in a public setting. The reader/hearer is left wondering.

However, parental amazement quickly turns to chastisement. Mary transitions out of participation in the peoples' amazement about Jesus' authority and knowledge, and moves into the role of a challenger. As a challenger she is depicted as an antagonist who directly confronts her son. Her challenge undermines his stature from authoritative teacher to that of unruly child. "Child," she begins, "why have you done this to us?" (2:48). She apportions blame and wrongdoing to Jesus, as his actions have caused great distress to both her and Joseph. The depth of her pain is emphatically underscored when she says to him "Look, your father and I have been in great distress looking for you." He is the reason for their pain and angst.

Mary chastises Jesus, only to be rebuked by him. This dialogue heightens the tension in the narrative. First, there is tension between the pious picture of Mary in the birth narrative and the presentation of her rebuking the adolescent Jesus in the temple scene. Second, Mary in turn is rebuked by her twelve-year-old son. Not only is Mary rebuked by Jesus, but she is rebuked with reference to a key point on which she is an expert witness: the issue of Jesus' origins. The true nature of Jesus' origins entails a life which leads to the clash between Jesus and his mother. Mary has to adjust to the reality in which she has been an important participant. This story illustrates on a small scale what Simeon had prophesied regarding the piercing of Mary's soul. The reader does not know all that it will involve. However, here we have a taste of Mary losing Jesus to God's own purposes, higher purposes that Mary cannot as yet perceive.

The narrative indicates that God has acted in a way that entails a great reversal of relational patterns within his people. The story of the adolescent

Jesus illustrates its consequences for his familial patterns, just as Mary's interpretation of salvation history and of the Scriptures has consequences for societal and gender roles.

Summary of Narratival Propositions regarding Mary

Mary is a major character in Luke's Gospel, with the narrative providing a robust presentation of her person. Mary is a righteous Jewish woman whose religio-cultural status is low, with her fate, at least initially, appearing to be determined by the decrees and ancestries of men. However, Mary's status and prospects are unexpectedly reversed by God's presence and activity. The reversal is sanctioned by God himself and is consistent with his historic practice whereby he reverses the fortunes of the lowly who are open to him, including women.

Mary's reversal of fortunes draws her into God's larger plan to reverse the fortunes of Israel and the whole world. She is chosen by God to be the mother of the divine-human Son of God. Her response to God's new work includes faith and astute scriptural interpretation. Indeed, Mary is the first person to link Israel's salvation history with God's actions in her own time. By means of making the connections between God's past work and his present work through her, Mary is also valid interpreter of salvation history and is furthermore able to communicate this to others.

Despite the dramatic and unusual circumstances which surround and change her, Mary is the model believer, who is active and caring despite adversity. This is expressed in her ongoing theological reflection despite personal dislocation, her participation in ensuring the pious context of Jesus' infancy, and a continual receptivity to the Spirit's teaching about her son. Mary's piety does not exempt her from conflict and misunderstanding with Jesus. Indeed, she is a character whose life is tinged with tragedy.

Theological Propositions arising from the Characterization of Mary

The characterization of Mary communicates theological propositions about God, those whom God includes in his saving work, and the interpretation of Scripture. These theological propositions are:

1. God may choose unexpected people to achieve his purposes. His sovereign choice may generate a reversal of socio-religious status and expectations.

2. God's Spirit is the source of the divine-human person who was conceived within Mary.

3. God approves of those who respond to him with purpose and care despite loss, suffering and a limited understanding of his plan.

4. A woman may be a sound interpreter of Scripture. A woman may be the primary theological interpreter of Scripture and salvation history in her context.

Anna

The celebration of the birth and circumcision of John is balanced in the narrative by the presentation of the baby Jesus in the temple and the encounters with Simeon and Anna.[39] These encounters form a "complementary pair of witnesses."[40]

Anna is a woman of exemplary piety

For such a minor character in Luke's Gospel, Anna receives significant "biographical attention."[41] Like Elizabeth, Anna is presented as a woman of exemplary piety,[42] although forming a parallel with Zechariah rather than Elizabeth since her piety is explicitly linked with temple worship and practice (Luke 2:36–38). In this sense she anticipates the devotional life of the early Christian community in Jerusalem, who continually met in the temple and were committed to fasting and prayer (Acts 2:42).[43]

Is also apparent that the infancy narratives are flavored abundantly by the OT, and the early narrative is distinctly positive in its presentation of Jewish customs and institutions. As Tannehill states, "The story is shaped to attract our sympathy to devoted men and women who have waited long for the fulfilment of Israel's hopes and who are now told that the time of fulfilment has come."[44] Anna is a character type who, along with Zechariah

---

39. Tannehill, *Narrative Unity*, 1:16. Serrano, "Anna's Characterization," 480, shows how both Simeon and Anna, as those close to death, function as symbols of fulfilment when they prophesy about Jesus. The old era is passing away, yet there is continuity between the old and the new activity of God.

40. Garland, *Luke*, 137.

41. Serrano, "Anna's Characterization," 464.

42. Anna is the embodiment of the piety of the *'anāwîm*. Ibid., 469.

43. Ibid., 472.

44. Tannehill, *Narrative Unity*, 1:19.

and Elizabeth, represents the hopes and aspirations of a people expectant that God would intervene to fulfil his ancient promises to his people.[45] In this connection, the mention of her practice of fasting and prayer is meant to evoke the sense that, at present, all is not as it should be.[46]

Anna is a prophetess

In contrast to Elizabeth who is not explicitly termed a prophet, Anna is given the prophetic label and her prophetic voice is summarized by the narrator as "she came and began to praise God and to speak about the child to all who were looking for the redemption of Jerusalem" (Luke 2:38).[47] It may be of note that the redemption of Jerusalem is mentioned rather than the people of Israel as a whole (cf. 1:68; 2:25). This could be a poetic substitute along the lines of Isaiah 40–55,[48] or it may have narrative significance in that it prepares for the city's tragic rejection of Jesus and its subsequent destruction.[49]

Anna as a "prophetess," echoes the OT heroines Miriam (Exod 15:20) and Deborah (Judg 4:4), together with Huldah (2 Kgs 22:14) and Isaiah's wife (Isa 8:3). This designation, along with her exceptional piety, prepares for her "inspired identification of the child,"[50] and in terms of the larger narrative of Luke-Acts she anticipates the daughters of Philip in Acts 21:9. Being a prophetess indicates that Anna, like Zechariah, Elizabeth, Mary and Simeon, speaks under the inspiration of the Holy Spirit and therefore is a reliable spokesperson for God.[51]

The description of Anna as a prophetess, given the OT background and the cumulative force of the portrayal of the female characters in the

---

45. Ibid., 1:39.

46. Green, *Luke*, 151, states, "Fasting constitutes a form of protest, an assertion that all is not well."

47. Tannehill, *Narrative Unity*, 1:39, notes that the description of Anna in terms of her tribal lineage, as well as her piety and expectant hope, mirrors quite closely the statement by Paul in Acts 26:6–7 regarding the hope of the twelve tribes. In this way the "author is still wrestling with the hopes and fate of such devoted and expectant worshipers of God."

48. Serrano, "Anna's Characterization," argues that in her characterization, Anna embodies the nation of Israel as represented in Isaiah 40–55. She was a young virgin, then married, and now widowed. From this place in exile she looks forward to the redemption of Jerusalem, a redemption God is about to achieve through the birth of the child Jesus.

49. Tannehill, *Narrative Unity*, 1:35.

50. Nolland, *Luke*, 1:122.

51. Tannehill, *Narrative Unity*, 1:22.

infancy narratives, yields a second order narratival proposition: *Women may engage in prophetic utterances and be reliable spokespeople for God under the inspiration of the Holy Spirit.*

Summary of Narratival Propositions regarding Anna

Anna is a woman of exemplary piety who forms part of a group eagerly anticipating the redemption of the nation. She is a prophetess, committed to prayer and fasting in the temple. Her status as a prophet, together with her exemplary piety, confirms the reliability of her statements about the child Jesus. Anna's prophetic activity indicates that women may engage in prophetic utterances and be reliable spokespeople for God under the inspiration of the Holy Spirit.

Theological Propositions arising from the Characterization of Anna

1. God employs pious women as his prophetesses.
2. Godly women are able to make correct theological claims.
3. Age and gender are not impediments to a person being the means through which God speaks into a specific situation.

Anticipating Broader Narratival and Theological Themes in Luke-Acts

The cumulative effect of the narratival proposals with reference to Mary, Elizabeth, and Anna in the infancy narratives, and the theological propositions that arise from these first three female characters, set the theological framework and tone for what follows in Luke-Acts. A particular narrative space has been opened by means of these foundational stories of women believers in God. In this space Luke will tell unexpected and new stories about God's relationship with women in salvation history. By the end of Luke 2 it appears that God is relating to women in a new way. In a like manner, women relate to God, God's people, God's word, and God's mission in a new way.

Some examples of the way that Luke utilizes the narrative space he has constructed in the infancy narratives with respect to the Third Gospel include: participation of women as the disciples of Jesus (8:1–3), women as the recipients of Jesus' ministry of compassion (8:40–56), several male-female story pairings (13:10–17 and 14:1–6; 7:11–17 and 8:49–56), and women as heralds of the resurrection (24:1–12).

We also see this narrative space filled out in various ways in Acts. In his Pentecost sermon Peter appropriates Joel's promise of the outpouring of the Spirit as foundational for the new people of God (Acts 2:16–21). Both sons and daughters, and God's male and female servants will be God's prophetic mouthpieces (Acts 2:17–18). This new work of the Spirit finds expression through key women such as Lydia, Priscilla, and Phillip's daughters.

The women characters in the infancy narratives also serve as a bridge between the ministry of women in the OT and the developing roles of women in the early church. In the former time female involvement was occasional and proportionately small. In the infancy narratives women are front and center in the events of God's saving purpose.

The density of Luke's description of Mary and the height of her standing in the infancy narratives indicates that Luke intends her to be understood as a paradigmatic character beyond this introductory section. In a given narrative, a paradigm is a concrete example which represents a constellation of beliefs, values and works. A paradigm serves as model which approximates the role that rules play in a given community.[52] There are different kinds of paradigms and various uses to which they are put. For Luke, Mary is an *anterior paradigm* for a positive response to God's new work, serving as a guide for the responses of those who will follow her in the narrative. Thus, as a paradigm of an appropriate response to God, she sheds light on the attributes of other disciples (both positively and negatively). This means that the theme of discipleship is partly explored in the light of Mary's belief, the high value she gives to the will and words of God, and finally by her obedient responses to God.

In addition to Mary being an anterior paradigm, she is also an *explanatory paradigm*. As an explanatory paradigm, Mary epitomizes a body of beliefs in that she gives them concrete expression. For example, in the character of Mary Luke also provides a paradigm for those who will suffer personal loss because of a close relationship with Jesus. Though the specific nature of this loss will vary, the new community that is devoted to Jesus will bear the marks of suffering as did its founder and his mother.

---

52. Bearsley, "Mary the Perfect Disciple," 464–68.

CHAPTER 4

Galilean Ministry (Luke 3:1—9:50)

Jesus as the Central Narrative Character

ALTHOUGH WOMEN ARE THE focus of our narratival study, the author's main interest as far as women go is how they relate to Jesus, to the kingdom of God, and to the new people of God. That is, women as characters serve Luke's central narratival concern which is to advance a particular view of the identity and work of Jesus and how people respond to him. In this context, women are presented in a variety of circumstances and relationships.

Luke has arranged his biography of Jesus in such a way that chapters 3–9, which follow his infancy narratives (Luke 1–2), focus on Jesus taking up his vocation as the Spirit-led Messiah. By means of these chapters Luke set Jesus up as the central character of the narrative. All the other aspects of the narrative, including those that pertain to characters and characterization, serve its christocentric purpose. Hence, a Lukan view of women can only be understood in relationship to who Jesus is. In the interest of being attentive to Luke's narrative, and to understand what Luke has to say about women in the context of his story, our study will continue by following the overall flow and interest of the narrative at this point—which is to highlight the life and person of Jesus as the Spirit-anointed Messiah. In this way we hope to be sensitive to Luke's authorial concerns. As women appear in the narrative their characterization and narratival roles will be discussed in their storied context.

The ministry of Jesus is the ministry of the God of Israel

From a narratival perspective, Luke 1:16–17 and 1:76 pave the way for the opening of chapter 3. The angel of the Lord has characterized the ministry of John as that of a forerunner: "He will turn many of the people of Israel to the Lord their God. And he will go before him in the spirit and power of Elijah, to turn the hearts of fathers to their children and the disobedient to the wisdom of the righteous -to make ready a people prepared for the Lord" (1:16–17). Later in that same chapter, Zechariah confirms this vocation for his son. Zechariah speaks directly to John and says, "And you, child, will be called a prophet of the Most High, for you will go before the Lord to prepare his ways" (1:76). The anticipation which fills Zechariah's words to John is expressed in the prophet's ministry.

Luke chapter 3 opens with a description of the historical time, location and those authorities which provide the backdrop for John's mission. In this context, "the word of God came to John the son of Zechariah in the desert" (3:2). This word from God sparks John's proclamation and ministry of baptism "around the Jordan." The citation from Isaiah echoes the previous remarks in the infancy narratives and signifies their fulfilment: "Prepare the way of the Lord, make his paths straight. Every valley shall be filled, and every mountain and hill shall be made low. . . . . And all flesh shall see the salvation of God" (3:4–6). The identity of the Lord for whom John prepares the way may be one of two. The Lord the God of Israel is referred to clearly fourteen times in the infancy narratives up to 1:76. However, in 1:43 another "Lord" has been introduced.[1] This other κύριος is introduced as a character through Elizabeth's exclamation: "but why am I so favored that the mother of my Lord should come to me?" The identity of this Lord is revealed as the narrative unfolds. Even as an unborn babe he is referred to in exalted tones: Gabriel speaks of him as "the Son of the Most High," (1:32) and "the Son of God" (1:35). Jesus' introduction as "Messiah, the Lord" (2:11) is confirmed by his status as a faithful Israelite full of "amazing understanding" of the Law and intimacy with God as Father (2:41–52). This presentation in chapter 2 provides the bridge whereby the eschatological coming of the Lord God of Israel is embodied in the ministry of Jesus as Lord. C. Kavin Rowe rightly identifies the significance of the use of κύριος for Jesus in the Lukan narrative for how Jesus' relationship to God is understood and for how his ministry relates to the promises of YHWH.

---

1. "Luke 1:43 thus creates the presence of another κύριος who actually now exists in the narrative. With this new presence and repetition it is becoming ever more difficult to determine exegetically whether the κύριος for whom John is preparing is the God of Abraham or the babe yet to be born." Rowe, *Early Narrative Christology*, 70.

> The doubleness and ambiguity of the κύριος at the beginning of the narrative creates a shared identity and the structure and movement of the story prepares us to follow the way of the Lord of Israel as his coming is embodied in the life and person of the Lord Jesus. Thus as the narrative advances and the focus shifts formally from promise to active fulfilment, we know that in the life of Jesus we can also see the God of Israel's presence and visitation of his people.[2]

Hence the narrative clearly portrays Jesus as Lord. His relationship to the Lord God of Israel has not been precisely articulated to this point. On one level, there is an identification between the two Lords, however it is not such a strict identification whereby the Lords substitute for one another. Nor are they rival Lords. In chapters 3 and 4, the author handles the relationship between the two Lords and their identification via "Son of God" language. Though ambiguity remains, their relationship contains notions of source, intimacy and likeness.

The arrival of the Lord will have a determinative impact on all people

One of the consequences of the fact that Jesus is Lord is that people must prepare for his arrival. John facilitated this arrival by calling people to participate in "a baptism of repentance for the forgiveness of sins" (Luke 3:3). The call for repentance suggests that the arrival of the Lord will be significant and have detrimental consequences for those who do not repent. For those that do repent the day of "salvation" will have dawned. The narrative also introduces a variety of characters who will be impacted by the arrival of the Lord. These are background characters which are typical of ancient narrative, including Jewish crowd members, tax collectors and Roman soldiers.

The narrative then gives shape to the form the visitation of the Lord will take, and in so doing indicates that the identity of the Messiah continued to be a burning question in people's minds. For example, on hearing John's message "the people were filled with expectation, and all were questioning in their hearts concerning John, whether he might be the Messiah" (3:15). John refuses this mantle by means of contrasting his ministry with the ministry of the "more powerful" one. "I will baptize you with water; but one who is more powerful than I is coming; I am not worthy to untie his sandals. He will baptize you with the Holy Spirit and with fire. His winnowing fork

---

2. Ibid., 77.

is in his hand, to clear his threshing floor and to gather the wheat into his storehouse; but the chaff he will burn with unquenchable fire" (3:16–17). This contrast serves the narrative by clarifying that a person other than John will be the Messiah and that this Messiah is greater than John. Further, the Messiah will have unique power for salvation and condemnation. His power will be such that he will affect the salvation of some which at the same time will be a powerful judgment and condemnation of others. Thus the narrative more concretely aligns the visitation and work of God with the work of the coming Lord, the Messiah. The present narrative thus further promotes the idea from the infancy narratives that the Messiah is the one through whom God will visit the world for the sake of the salvation of his people and the condemnation of his enemies. Hence, the presentation of Jesus' Lordship takes on a strongly functional aspect, whereby the reader equates the actions of the Lord Jesus with the actions of the Lord God. For this reason Dunn states that Luke's primary purpose is to "present the events he narrates as the completion of God's saving purpose for Israel."[3]

Jesus is set apart from other people because God delights in him as his Son and will empower him through his Spirit

In Luke 3:21–23 Jesus is introduced as an adult character in the narrative, being "about thirty years old" when he began his ministry (Luke 3:23). Jesus is dramatically set apart from the other recipients of John's baptism by three supernatural occurrences that uniquely attend his baptism and anointing.[4] These are: "the heaven was opened" (3:21); "the Holy Spirit descended upon him in bodily form like a dove" (3:22); "and a voice came from heaven, 'You are my Son, the Beloved, with you I am well pleased'" (3:22). The opening of the heavens indicates that divine revelation is going to occur.[5] The Spirit's descent upon Jesus recalls the Isaianic Servant's endowment of the Spirit in Isaiah 42:1 and 63:14. The descent of the Spirit upon Jesus is a decisive narrative moment because it stresses that Jesus' ministry is to be carried out in the power and authority of the Spirit.[6] The voice from above also

---

3. Dunn, "book of Acts," 389.
4. Marshall, *Luke*, 152.
5 Ibid.
6. "Jesus was baptized with the Spirit and lived under his lordship." Ferguson, *Holy Spirit*, 46. Commenting on 3:23, which reads: *Jesus was about thirty years old when he began his work*, Calvin states that with reference to his human nature, "When Christ was preparing to preach the Gospel, he was introduced by Baptism into his office; and at the same time he was endued with the Holy Spirit . . . that he comes as a godlike man . . . in whom the power of the Holy Spirit reigns." Calvin, *Harmony*, 1:204.

recalls Isaiah 42:1 and links this story to the transfiguration voice via the use of Psalm 2 and the LXX semantics underlying "chosen" and "delight."[7] The cumulative effect is to set Jesus apart from all the other characters in the story. Not only is Jesus set apart by actions of God and the Holy Spirit, but he also receives a series of designations, notably "my Son, the beloved," which determine him as unique by virtue of who and what he is.

Jesus is the story's standout character in part because he is the second Adamic Son of God

The genealogy which follows the annunciation and anointing of Jesus also serves to cement Jesus' status and role as the premier character in the narrative. This alerts the reader to pay special attention to this character in the stories that follow. By means of Luke 1:35, this genealogy and the temptation narrative which follows shortly in 4:3, 9 ("Son of God . . . Son of God"), Jesus' identity as the Son of God is emphasized. He is the Son of God in the sense that, like Adam, he is "a direct creation of God."[8] Like Adam, Jesus' identity is not reliant on a human father. Thus, it is hard to avoid the conclusion that Luke's christology has Adamic overtones. This focuses the scope of the reader's interests and expectations for how Luke's story will unfold. At the outset of his Gospel, Luke explains that the "orderly account" which he writes to Theophilus is about "the events that have been fulfilled among us" (1:1). Given the events and genealogy of chapter 3, the reader now knows that Jesus is key to the circumstances of fulfilment amongst the earliest "eye-witnesses and servants of the word" (1:3).

Jesus is the faithful Israelite, a true and righteous son of Israel who is also the Son of God

That Jesus is the premier character and interest of the story is again reinforced by the opening of chapter 4. "Jesus, full of the Holy Spirit, returned from the Jordan and was led by the Spirit in the wilderness, where for forty days he was tempted by the Devil" (Luke 4:1–2). The same Spirit which descended upon Jesus at his anointing leads Jesus into the wilderness (4:1), strongly echoing the Exodus narrative where God's theophanic presence led his people in the desert. In the story that follows, Jesus will not fail as Israel did. He will act as both the main protagonist as well as acting in a heroic manner. Jesus will be God's empowered and faithful follower because he

---

7. Nolland, *Luke*, 1:161–63.
8. Talbert, *Reading Acts*, 49.

is "full of the Holy Spirit" which is proper to him as the Messiah.[9] As such, Jesus will be the one who resists the Devil and his temptation to receive glory without having to carry out God's mission via the cross. This dramatic story ranges across human needs and desires, kingdoms of the whole earth, and trust in God. Jesus recognized that during these tests the Devil was attempting to

> deflect him from his single-minded commitment to loyalty and obedience in God's service, and interprets the devil's invitation as an encouragement to question God's faithfulness. Israel had manifested its doubts by testing God, but Jesus refuses to do so (cf. Deut. 6:16).... By facing these tests and proving his fidelity, Jesus has demonstrated unequivocally his faithful obedience to God and thus to engage in ministry publicly as God's Son.[10]

Ultimately Jesus stands upon the words of God, and eventually his trust in God exhausts the Devil's schemes: "the Devil finished every test" (4:13). Jesus emerges famished yet faithful to God. Thus, by means of a story about the struggle for faithfulness in the wilderness, Luke presents Jesus as the one who succeeds where Israel had failed. Given the way the earlier chapters of Luke accent the promises of God to his people, the reader cannot miss the fact that Jesus responds faithfully to God and is thus the heir to these covenant promises. As the Son of God he reflects God's faithful character. By recording that Jesus passed the tests at hand, the narrative proposes that Jesus is the faithful Israelite, the true and righteous son of Israel who is also the Son of God.

God's Spirit is the source of authority and power behind Jesus' vocation as Messiah

The faithfulness of God and the empowerment by the Spirit confirm Jesus as Messiah in the Nazareth announcement (Luke 4:14–30). The faithfulness of God has been declared at the outset of the story by Mary (1:46–55), who announced that God's new era had dawned and that Jesus was the extraordinary character through whom God would faithfully fulfil his promises. The Nazareth Manifesto now makes God's faithfulness known to other characters in the narrative.[11] In this episode, Jesus' ministry is once again aligned

---

9. Johnson, *Luke*, 81.
10. Green, *Luke*, 196.
11. "Thus the eschatological significance of Jesus' appearance is already known to Mary and Elizabeth within the narrative and to Luke's readers outside the narrative. Now Jesus makes this known more broadly, to the people of his own hometown. At the

with the power of God's Spirit. The story unit begins: "Jesus returned to Galilee in the power of the Spirit . . ." (4:14). This alignment between Jesus and the Spirit reminds the reader that Jesus' ministry is the outworking of the Holy Spirit's empowerment at his anointing and temptation (3:21—4:13).[12] Thus, the significance of the words "The Spirit of the Lord is upon me" in the Nazareth Manifesto (4:16-30) is to reveal the extent of Jesus the Messiah's dependence upon the Holy Spirit.[13] The Spirit's guidance of Jesus' ministry and person is later reinforced at the critical juncture where Jesus is beginning his final journey to Jerusalem towards the cross (10:20-21). At this juncture, Jesus is "rejoiced in the Holy Spirit" and praises God for his work. This event reinforces the fact that Jesus' ministry and journey towards the cross are carried out as the Spirit-anointed Messiah.[14]

Jesus is the promised Spirit-led Messiah who will exercise a liberating teaching ministry

The Nazarethan Manifesto also contributes to another narratival thread that particularizes the nature of Jesus' Spirit-led ministry: Jesus' teaching and preaching. This particularization is achieved in two ways. First, Luke 4:15 and 4:44 bracket the Manifesto by recording Jesus teaching in synagogues. Second, the reading of Isaiah beginning in 4:18 is alluded to at the end of this narrative block in 4:43 with Jesus' words that "I must proclaim the good news of the kingdom of God to the other cities also; for I was sent for this purpose."[15] In his Nazareth announcement, Jesus declared to the others in the synagogue that the Scripture he read aloud had been fulfilled "in your hearing" (4:21). The fulfilment relates to the arrival of the Spirit-anointed

---

same time, he embraces his divine mission for himself." Ibid., 214.

12. Evans and Gasque, *Luke*, 70. Green, *Luke*, 230.

13. "Luke 4:18 being of programmatic significance: Jesus quotes Isa. 61:1 to show that the Spirit of God rests upon Him as anointing his work. This verse to some extent counterbalances Matt. 12:28 which attributes Jesus' exorcisms to the Spirit of God; the parallel in Luke 11:20 has instead 'the finger of God.'" Marshall, *Luke*, 177-80. Significantly, the "finger of God" in Luke's Gospel has a different divine referent. Woods attributes this, and the work of the "finger of God," to God the Father rather than God the Holy Spirit. See Woods, *Finger of God*, 223-25. Woods writes: "With the 'finger of God' expression, God the Father is acting with power and mercy through Jesus his spirit-anointed Son (Acts 2:22; cf. Lk. 8:39)[;] . . . the phrase 'finger of God' at Luke 11:20 refer[s] to God the Father himself in a non-instrumental sense, because the Holy Spirit is already involved in miracles through the authoritative word of command and release."

14. Green, *Luke*, 422.

15. Tannehill, *Narrative Unity*, 1:60-61.

One who will "proclaim release to the captives and recovery of sight to the blind, to let the oppressed go free, to proclaim the year of the Lord's favor" (4:18). By means of this declaration, the narrative proposes that Jesus designated himself as the promised Spirit-led Messiah who will exercise a liberating teaching ministry.

The stress on the identity of the one born to Mary is continued throughout this entire section. The people respond to Jesus' declaration with amazement and a significant question regarding Jesus' identity. "Is this not Joseph's son?" (4:22).[16] The answer is, of course, that he is more than Joseph's son. He is the Spirit-anointed Messiah. The people of his hometown had to reconcile his identity as the carpenter's son with his apparent messianic claims. The reader has to do the same. A multi-faceted messianic understanding of Jesus is central to Luke-Acts. Michael Bird observes that

> Unique to Luke-Acts is that Jesus is "Messiah the Lord" (Luke 2:11, 26; cf. Acts 2:36) and Messiah of God (Luke 9:20; 23:35 cf. Acts 4:26). Luke also wishes to show the continuity of the church with the promises of Israel and to demonstrate how the work of Jesus and his followers represents the fulfillment of these promises. The Lucan Jesus, then, is simultaneously the "leader and savior" of Israel, the Jewish "Messiah" (Acts 5:31, 42) and the "Lord" of all who believe in him including the gentiles (Acts 10:36, 19:10, 17; 20:21).[17]

Jesus' proclamation of the kingdom of God and bringing it to bear in people's lives has wide-ranging effects. These include healing, reconciling, rescuing, and teaching. That this is an Isaianic ministry of liberation is expanded by what follows in the narrative. The phrase *despite resistance from his own people* could now be added to the previous narratival proposition. As well as embarking on a mission of liberation, Jesus also reveals those secret desires and inclinations which people harbour in their hearts, particularly those which are not aligned with God. The first of many attempts at assassination follows. This dramatic end to the Nazareth Manifesto demonstrates that Jesus is faithful to God even under the threat of death. Tannehill summarizes the episode as follows: "in the first scene in the narrative of Jesus' mission, Jesus announces 'words of grace' but encounters the violent rejection which prophets can expect in their homeland. The good news which Jesus preaches is already shadowed by a conflict that will persist to the end of Acts."[18]

---

16. Contra Green, *Luke*, 215, who reads their question in positive light.
17. Bird, "Messiah of God," 69.
18. Tannehill, *Narrative Unity*, 1:73.

> *Jesus understood his purpose as "proclaiming the good news of the kingdom of God"*

Jesus' ministry is given further shape and material content by means of three episodes which round out chapter 4. These episodes introduce the concept of the kingdom of God, which has only been implicit in the narrative to this point. These three episodes are Jesus' confrontation with an evil spirit in a synagogue (Luke 4:31–37), the healing and deliverance of many at Simon's home (4:38–41), and preaching about the kingdom of God in synagogues (4:42–44). The direction of the narrative brings these episodes together by means of recording Jesus' own purpose statement as a summary of his activity. This is achieved in 4:43, where Jesus resists the pressure to continue ministering in one locale. He broadens the geographic scope of his ministry by means of sharpening its focus: "I must proclaim the good news of the kingdom of God to the other cities also; for I was sent for this purpose." The thrust of the narrative is clear: Jesus understood his purpose as "proclaiming the good news of the kingdom of God." This proposition has a programmatic effect on the remainder of Luke's two-part narrative.[19]

The proclamation of the kingdom is accompanied by setting people free from affliction, whether it be physical or demonic in nature. In the service of this mission Jesus encounters a variety of people, and these encounters are opportunities for a deeper revelation of Jesus' identity. For example, when Jesus confronts the evil spirit in Capernaum (4:34), the demons ask Jesus: "What do you have to do with us, Jesus of Nazareth? Have you come to destroy us? I know who you are: the holy one of God." The demonic voice suggests to the reader that Jesus is a divine being, far superior to all the other characters in the narrative.[20] Thus the narrative makes the point that announcing the kingdom of God is fitting for Jesus because he is clearly more than a mere man.

---

19. Schnabel, *Early Christian Mission*, 1269, notes: "the phrase 'the kingdom of God' is, in Luke's account in the book of Acts, a summary of the Christian message. Paul sought to convince his visitors that the crucified and risen Jesus is the Messiah and fulfills the meaning and the promises of the law and the prophets[:] . . . some Jews 'were convinced'[;] . . . they converted to faith in Jesus as the Messiah."

20. For Gathercole, *Preexistent Son*, 152, this suggests that Jesus is "a pre-existent 'holy one.'"

GALILEAN MINISTRY (LUKE 3:1—9:50)

Jesus can and does bring full release from demonic and physical affliction through bringing the kingdom of God to bear on a person's life

The story of deliverance is a story is told with little detail; we are simply introduced to a man possessed by a demon. It takes place in the synagogue, a public setting (Luke 4:31–37). The next story occurs in the private setting of Peter's house. The transition from one location to another is matter of fact: "after leaving the synagogue, he entered Simon's house" (4:38). Immediately after identifying the location of the story, Luke introduces Peter's mother-in-law. She is the first woman to be mentioned as benefitting from Jesus' saving actions. The home was the primary realm of activity and influence for a woman in first century Palestine. Thus, this woman—like the man in the preceding story—is introduced in an arena that was appropriate to her social role. Therefore, it is fitting that her restoration to health involves restoration to her usual social roles. The woman was "suffering from a high fever" (4:38). Jesus "stood over her and rebuked the fever, and it left her." The consequence was full health: Luke relates that "immediately she got up and began to serve them" (4:39).

The story is written to impress upon the reader the proposition that Jesus can and does bring the saving action of God, God's kingdom, to bear on a person's life. The stories about the deliverance of the man in the synagogue and the woman in the home are therefore not stories about gender roles. Luke's concern is to highlight the impressive nature of the kingdom which Jesus announced via demonstrations of its saving power in the lives of many. As we suggested in our earlier chapter on women in Roman Palestine, there were clearly delineated realms of activity and influence for men and women. Therefore, we would expect that a public itinerant such as Jesus would tend to encounter women in homes. This is not indicative of Jesus' or Luke's stance on the roles of women or how women may serve within the kingdom of God. It merely reflects the realities within which the story of Jesus is told. This explains the relative paucity of stories about women immediately following the infancy narratives. Luke's narrative is driven by a concern to highlight Jesus and also the various realms in which Jesus is active. That Jesus interacts with people in rough proportion to their participation in first century Palestinian culture gives credence to Lukan characterization, because it would appear that history is not overridden by theology. The narrative is not driven by anything close to twenty-first-century gender theology, but rather by a historically attuned theology of Jesus' anointed ministry and status.

Calling of the Disciples
(Luke 5:1–11, 27–32; 6:12–16)

Chapter 4 ends with Jesus who resolutely "kept on preaching in the synagogues of Judea" (Luke 4:44). Chapter 5 is directly linked to Jesus' preaching in that it depicts various responses to his ministry. The response of characters such as the disciples and some sinners is positive towards Jesus. Their positive response is matched by the negative response of the Pharisees, who react against him. The entire literary unit of 5:1—6:49 is best described as "Calling and Controversy."[21]

> *Jesus' call receives an obedient and proper*
> *response from Simon Peter*

Luke 5:1–11 is a commission story.[22] In this passage Jesus avails himself of a fishing boat in order to continue preaching to large crowds. This boat belonged to Simon. The encounter between Jesus and Simon is presented as a result of Jesus' need rather than a preference for, or prior relationship with Simon. After finishing his teaching Jesus enabled a miraculous catch which elicited fearful reaction from Simon Peter: "Depart from me, Lord, for I am a sinful man!" (Luke 5:8). Jesus responded by calming the fisherman's fear and giving his life a new direction: "Do not be afraid: from now on you will be catching people" (5:10). Jesus' words are decisive and so is Simon's response: Simon and those with him "left everything and followed him" (5:11). The main idea of 5:1–11 is that the disciples are confronted with Jesus' power and glory via the miraculous catch of fish. Moreover, although Simon Peter's deep sense of unworthiness in the presence of Jesus compels him to desire separation from the divine, Jesus has both words of reassurance and a call to mission.[23]

Several features of this story are significant for a study on discipleship and female disciples. First, Simon Peter's response to Jesus echoes Mary's obedience to God's word. At the suggestion that he "put the nets into deep water" (5:4), Simon says "Master, after laboring through the whole night, we did not catch a thing, but at your word I will let down the nets." The phrase "At your word" is important; obeying Jesus' words is a key marker of ideal discipleship. This has already been established through the character of Mary. Mary's response to the angelic announcement was centered around

---

21. Garland, *Luke*, 223.
22. Talbert, *Reading Luke*, 63–64.
23. Garland, *Luke*, 223.

the phrase κατὰ τὸ ῥῆμά σου ("according to your word"—1:38). Peter's response echoes this closely, with ἐπὶ δὲ τῷ ῥήματί σου (5:5). In this way, "Peter's obedience recalls Mary's submission to the divine word (1:34–38)."[24] Thus Mary's character provides the reader with a model response of obedience which is the prototype for ideal responses to come.

Second, Mary's pattern of response to God earlier in the narrative means that her character, her character traits (her portrayal) and her words (her function in the narrative) continue to have a background impact on the narrative. When the story of the calling of the first disciples is narrated (6:12–16), one notes its brevity and lack of detail. One would expect that as future leaders of the Christian movement they would be introduced with at least as much detail as Mary. So, at this point in the narrative, given this minimal description of the disciples, Mary is maintained as one of the dominant characters. It also means that Mary's model of hearing and responding to God continues to function as the paradigm of the ideal response to God. Mary's role is that of a particular kind of *type*. A type is a model used in literature in which a character is

> demarcated by either or a combination of traits (which may be physical, psychological, or moral) which are stable traits. These traits are known to the reader and are particular to the role the character will play. A type can also be representative of a social group which can be described according to a limited set of traits, a particular kind of activity, a personal condition, and/or a social standing. Types may refer back to models or exemplars in the past.[25]

The archetype of a trait is the one who is the source of that trait; so God, for example, is the archetype of goodness. The prototype is the person who perfectly instantiates the traits in question. In Luke's Gospel, for example, Jesus is the prototype of faithfulness and righteousness. There may be negative prototypes such as "the disciples who do not believe."[26] In the narrative so far, Mary has prominently played the role of the prototype of faithful response to God.

Narrative critics have taken a number of positions on the function of the disciples as characters. Howell, for example, states that the implied reader is "called to stand with the implied author and Jesus and evaluate all characters, even the disciples, according to the ideological criterion of

---

24. Ibid., 227.
25. This is our translation of Sarasa, "Una indicación," 263.
26. Ibid., 263–66.

whether they accept Jesus and his teaching."[27] At the other end of the spectrum, authors such as Verseput, claim that the reader is taught to be faithful to Jesus by means of the disciples who are not role models but are presented "as a foil to educate the reader in the mighty power of Jesus."[28] Our position is that the disciples function in such a way that allows the implied reader to observe this character group and to judge whether or not they have responded positively to Jesus and his message.

As a character Mary is not presented a foil for Jesus and his teaching, although this does not mean an absence of conflict with him (e.g., see Luke 2:41–52). Rather, her function in the narrative is to be a prototype of discipleship. In this way she parallels the role of the beloved disciple in the Fourth Gospel.[29] Therefore, the selection of Simon as the first disciple does not mean that exemplary discipleship includes the characteristic of being male. Rather, Simon and the male disciples fit into Mary's model of ideal discipleship. Drawing on the narratival presentation of Mary, the central criterion for discipleship at this stage of the narrative is hearing God's word, trusting him and obediently participating in his mission. For this reason the disciple's positive response to Jesus is highlighted: "they left everything and followed him" (5:11).

Jesus selects twelve apostles from a larger group of disciples

By leaving everything,[30] Peter would "share in the total insecurity, exposure to danger, and slander which were the fate of his master."[31] But Peter is one of a number who are called. Others were astonished by the miraculous catch which Jesus' effected, including "James and John, the sons of Zebedee, Simon's partners" (Luke 5:10a). The three men "left everything and followed him" (5:11).

The story of Levi's calling is recorded a little further on in Luke 5:27–29, which in turn is closely followed by the selection of the twelve (6:12–16).

---

27. Howell, *Matthew's Inclusive Story*, 234.

28. Verseput, "Faith of the Reader," 21.

29. Sarasa, "Una indicación."

30. Peter did not leave his own family destitute: "The meaning of 'everything' is clear from the account of Levi leaving everything (5:28). He leaves his custom booth, but he still has a home and has the means to throw a banquet (5:29). Leaving their occupations is required because the disciples are to share Jesus' mission and fate and cannot be encumbered by business interests." Garland, *Luke*, 230. The phrase "they left everything and followed him" (5:11) contributes to understanding the role and authority of the women who supported Jesus financially (see on 8:1–3).

31. Hengel, *The Charismatic Leader*, 78.

The choosing of the twelve follows a series of accounts which confirm Jesus' vocation, the power of the kingdom of God, and his relationship to the law (5:12—6:11). The twelve are those "whom he also designated apostles" (6:13). This story chronicles a series of actions by Jesus. He "went out to the mountain to pray, and spent the night praying to God. When morning came, he summoned his disciples and chose twelve of them . . ." (6:12-13a). Jesus selected a smaller group of twelve out of a larger band of disciples. The fact that there are twelve disciples, (not to mention the larger group), means that there has been a growing band of disciples who are unnamed up to and including the account of 6:12-16. This raises a number of questions. Whom did this larger group of disciples include? Where did they come from? Are women included in his first group of disciples? Did Jesus choose them all, or did they follow of their own volition? Are there two types of disciples—those who understand and those who do not understand?[32]

Luke does not directly answer these questions at this stage of the story.[33] His depiction of the disciples is very slim up to this point, and both the portrayal and the function of the disciples in the narrative await further development.

> Although Jesus has called a few persons to be his disciples, these new followers have had almost no role thus far in the narrative. The focus has been instead on Jesus, the shape of his ministry, and the division he is causing in Israel as he attracts diverse responses. . . . Thus far, those whom Jesus has called have left all

---

32. Studies in Matthew's Gospel have pointed out that disciples are variously portrayed in the First Gospel. "[N]arrative critics who have done substantial work on the portrayal of the disciples affirm what redaction critics have already noted, namely, that the disciples are characterized by 'little faith.' In addition (and counter to redaction criticism in general), narrative critics have seen a tendency to *misunderstand* as characteristic of the Matthean disciples." (Brown, *Disciples,* 18). Kingsbury, *Matthew as Story,* 136, states that throughout the narrative the disciples display weak faith—"little faith." Kingsbury highlights the narrative thrust that though the disciples receive particular insight into the kingdom of heaven and Jesus' identity, they "on other occasions . . . show that they can falter in their understanding and this engenders conflict between Jesus and them." (Ibid., 138). Kingsbury particularly points to disciples' conflict with Jesus in Matthew 16:21—28:20 where the disciples misunderstand Jesus' suffering and sonship. Their struggle with Jesus "has to do with the disciple's imperceptiveness, and at times resistance, to the notion that servanthood is the essence of discipleship." (Ibid., 129). This is a very significant point because it suggests that Matthew employed those characters who are designated as "disciples" to be the ones who would exemplify failure to understand what being a disciple is all about.

33. For a narrative approach to the depiction of the disciples with reference to God and Jesus as the archetypes and prototypes for such a life in John's Gospel, see Ramirez, "Los primeros."

to follow him (5:1–11, 27–28), but their identity and purpose as disciples has remained underdeveloped.[34]

The pattern of minimal description of the disciples continues even once the "apostles" are set apart. Again Green notes: "This pattern is repeated again: Jesus names apostles, but gives no explicit assignment; instead he launched immediately into his ministry of gracious word and deed, speaking especially to his disciples in the hearing of 'the people.'"[35] He continues:

> The segregation of twelves as apostles from the larger gathering of disciples serves little immediate, qualitative function. Jesus' teaching in 6:17–49, for example, is not restricted to this (or any other) group (cf. 7:1). Even the later sending of the twelve apostles as missionaries (9:1–10) does not mark their particular role in God's purpose, for that is paralleled in the subsequent sending of the seventy-two.[36]

At this point the reader is waiting for the sketch of the ideal disciple or apostle to be filled out.[37] This begins to occur immediately after the selection of the twelve, with the teaching contained in the so-called Sermon on the Plain (6:17–49). However, it is important to note that this teaching is directed to the wider group of the disciples (6:20), and not merely to the twelve. With respect to women in particular, their discipleship is featured at different points in the following three chapters, and will come to fuller expression with the story of Mary and Martha in chapter 10.

Jesus reconstitutes Israel and thus claims all of Israel as his own

The point the narrative makes via Jesus' selection of the twelve relates to the sphere and breadth of Jesus' work. Jesus' formation of a new leadership for Israel occurs in a context of conflict. The anger of the scribes and Pharisees throughout Luke 5:1—6:11 means that the older leadership of Israel has not understood the time of God's visitation and the offer of forgiveness. Thus, the selection of twelve apostles is highly suggestive and is clearly meant to indicate a restorative function with respect to the twelve tribes of Israel.[38] By means of electing twelve, Jesus "made visible to everyone His claim upon

34. Green, *Luke*, 257.
35. Ibid.
36. Ibid., 258–59.
37. Matthew's Gospel also creates this tension for the reader/hearer. See Paschke, "Matthäus 5,13–16." In the Gospels, this tension is heightened by the misapprehension of the disciples. See Fischer, *Les disciples*.
38. Garland, *Luke*, 273.

Israel, and He did so in such a way that it was evident that He did not merely claim a select group but the whole people in all its divisions."[39] The whole people necessarily includes men and women, and so the selection of the twelve men does not reflect an androcentric concern.

The character of Judas does not reflect the characteristics that Jesus expects in his disciples

The inclusion of Judas in the list of the twelve apostles is the first hint of Jesus' suffering and death. The passion is thus introduced via the one who would betray Jesus. Interestingly, this occurs in the context of Jesus establishing a new leadership for Israel, for Judas is one of the twelve men who are typologically connected with the twelve patriarchs. By means of highlighting the inclusion of Judas, and the descriptor "who became a traitor" (Luke 6:16) in this list, the narrative implicitly points out that categories such as "apostle" are not idealized cartoons or titles which guarantee those key markers which Jesus seeks in his people, namely faith, obedience, and faithful service. The inclusion of people in these categories will necessarily include the realities and the vicissitudes of the human self. This suggests that Luke's characters and his characterization have a correspondence to reality.[40] Thus when a character (e.g., Mary) instantiates a characteristic such as obedience in a manner which is not at all faulty, it cannot be rejected by the reader as a fantasy. Furthermore, as the portrayal is realistic and not folkloric, the reader is encouraged to identify with the character(istic) and not ignore it as beyond their reach.

Raising of the Widow's Son (Luke 7:11–17)

Jesus shows concern for a marginalized woman's plight

The next time a woman features in the narrative is in Luke 7:11–17, a uniquely Lukan story. It matches the preceding episode (Luke 7:1–10) in which Jesus acts to help someone in a relationship with a person who has dire needs. In this story Jesus helps a Jewish woman, whereas in the preceding story the main character is a Gentile man. Thus the author has

39. Karl Regensdorf, cited in ibid.

40. "Reality, even reality as relatively simplified and as interpreted in the form of Luke's narrative, is not so rudimentary; . . . not all Pharisees can be characterized negatively and . . . even a disciple, even one named an apostle in obedience to God's design, can oppose God's purpose." Green, *Luke*, 260.

constructed a Gentile-Jew as well as a male-female pairing. The pairing accentuates the wide embrace of God's care: "The effect of the former is to affirm God's saving work for Gentiles (particularly soldiers); the effect of the latter is to affirm Gods saving work for Jews and women (particularly widows). In both cases the rest of the community is encouraged to recognize this affirmation."[41] The particular focus here on the raising of the dead and near dead anticipates the response to be given to the enquirers sent by John the Baptist in the following pericope (7:22).[42]

Jesus encounters a funeral procession at the gate of a town called Nain. "As he approached the town gate, a dead person was being carried out—the only son of his mother . . ." (7:12). The tone of the narrative becomes graver with ". . . and she was a widow." The way in which this story is told places the woman rather than the son at the center of concern.

> Surprisingly in a social context in which females are typically identified in relation to males, this dead man is presented as "his mother's only son." Following this, the focus of attention is on her: *she* was a widow, the crowd was with *her*; Jesus saw *her*; had compassion on *her*, spoke to her, and, finally, gave the dead man brought back to life to *her*.[43]

The other surprising aspect of this scene is that Jesus takes the initiative to help her without being asked to do so. The text is explicit in attributing compassion to Jesus. Such was the strength of his compassion for the woman (rather than the son) that he is moved to unrequested action.[44] In fact, Jesus' action to help the woman is one of the few stories in Luke which attributes emotions to Jesus. When these occur, they are especially significant. In this instance the story highlights Jesus' concern for the widow.

The story of the widow and her son is significant to Luke's Gospel because at this point in the narrative this particular episode is chosen to be the event and evidence that God is visiting his people. God's eschatological visitation in Jesus is confirmed and described by the authorial choice to

---

41. Tannehill, *Luke*, 127.

42. Green, *Luke*, 289.

43. Ibid. Green describes the significance of the woman as a character in order to epitomize the kind of person who is the recipient of Jesus' message: "She who was husbandless and sonless and in mourning, she who epitomizes the 'poor' to whom Jesus has come to bring good news is the real recipient of Jesus' compassionate ministry. In fact, it is not too much to say that 'healing' in this instance, although it entails the miraculous raising of this young man from the dead, should be interpreted as the restoration of this woman within her community."

44. "In contrast to many healing stories, no one requests Jesus' help. He takes the initiative out of compassion for the widow." Tannehill, *Luke*, 128.

include the crowd's exclamation "God has visited his people" as a response to Jesus' ministry (7:16). The theme of the visitation of God was inserted at the very beginning of the narrative in Zechariah's song (1:68). The use of ἐπεσκέψατο ("visited") here in 7:16, together with the theme of God's powerful work and presence, have therefore been used by the author to signal the connection between the opening of Luke's Gospel and a key moment within it. The fact that the moment which pinpoints God's visitation to his people involves a story focused on a woman suggests not only that the author himself has special concern for women, but by means of this narratival alignment he wants to communicate that this is also a divine concern.[45]

Jesus anointed by a Sinful Woman (Luke 7:36-50)

A sinful woman's response to Jesus surpasses that of a Pharisee

Luke notes a variety of responses to Jesus. Some are ethical responses dealing with horizontal relationships (Luke 19:8), other responses exclusively focus on the praise of God (17:18).[46] In this story a woman and a Pharisee named Simon illustrate two different responses to Jesus. The woman displays deep affection towards him, and her actions are consistent with being forgiven. The implication of the narrative is that she has repented of her sins by accepting the ministry of Jesus. The Pharisee, on the other hand, holds inner attitudes which exclude him from relationship with Jesus and Jesus' people. For this reason the Pharisee does not respond to Jesus with love. The fact that the character who responds positively to Jesus is a woman means that for Luke women are able to respond to Jesus in an appropriate manner without reminder. Love for Jesus is enough for the inclusion of a woman into Jesus' believing circle, and the sinful woman embodies the virtues of humility and love. Jesus also exhibits these qualities and wants his followers to reflect his character. Characteristics such as humility, the integrity of response, and loving devotion to Jesus are key indicators for inclusion in the kingdom of God.[47] Luke often deems women to be righteous before God because of their

---

45. "The Lukan audience might take note of the fact that Jesus showed special concern for a widow. Acts indicates that the early church made special provision for the support of widows (6:1; 9:39). . . . Jesus' compassion for a widow would encourage the Lukan audience to help widows in their community, perhaps imitating the good works of Tabitha, and it would encourage widows to hope in the Lord's compassion, even in difficult times (cf. 18:1-8)." Tannehill, *Luke,* 129.

46. Talbert, *Reading Luke,* 88.

47. Krüger, "La inclusión de las personas excluidas."

humility and concomitant actions. Thus the sinful woman is an example of the possibility of reconciliation with God, for the forgiveness she received is the basis for reconciliation with God and entry into his kingdom.

Furthermore, a woman may embody the right response to Jesus in a manner which is superior to the responses of men. Therefore, in Luke's theology, men are not taken to be ideal believers in every situation. On the other hand, there are situations in which women are ideal followers of Jesus, and may illustrate the best model of love for him.[48] Examples of women as exemplary respondents to Jesus, and their inclusion in the group known as the disciples, follow in the next few chapters.

Women who Support Jesus (Luke 8:1–3)

In this section narrative time speeds up, as Luke summarizes Jesus' preaching ministry throughout the towns and villages of Galilee.[49] The summary recalls Luke 4:43–44 and makes clear to the reader what a careful reading of the narrative implies—that Jesus was an itinerant preacher who was regularly on the move.

It is here that the narrative takes a somewhat unexpected turn. Not only were the twelve traveling with Jesus, but Luke mentions several women who were part of his entourage. It may be a little surprising, and possibly even scandalous,[50] that women, whose cultural location was normally within the home, were part of the entourage of an itinerant charismatic preacher. Furthermore, the identity and social location of at least one of the women is quite extraordinary, as is the role which they are all said to perform.

It is indeed possible to overlook the significance of the summary in Luke 8:1–3 due to its brevity. However, Luke clearly understands it to be programmatic for the ensuing narrative. As Bauckham states, "The lack of other specific references to the women before the passion narrative is not an

---

48. Inyamah, "Contrasting Perspectives.".

49. It is most natural to take κατὰ πόλιν καὶ κώμην to refer to Galilee, as it is not until 9:51 that the journey to Jerusalem begins. Other contextual markers place Jesus in Galilee: the visit by Jesus' mother and brothers (8:19–21), and the calming of the storm on the Sea of Galilee (8:22–25).

50. Corley, *Private Women*, 118; Ricci, *Mary Magdalene*, 53; Witherington, *Women*, 117. Bovon, *Luke*, 1:300, regards it as "unheard of." Reid, *Women*, 131, advocates caution in this respect due to our limited knowledge of Jewish religious practices at the time of Jesus. She points out that all we can say with certainty is that we have no other record of such behavior in first-century Palestinian Judaism. Spencer, *Salty Wives*, 108, points out that the Gospels themselves give evidence of freedom of movement of women in 1st century Palestine. What was considered the "proper place" for women applied more to wealthy aristocratic classes.

indication of their insignificance for Luke, but of the fact that he has highlighted their significance in his general description of the Galilean ministry (8:1-3) and can thereafter take it for granted."[51]

In terms of the structure of the passage, Jesus is the subject of the main verb διώδευεν ("travel through") and its corresponding participles κηρύσσων καὶ εὐαγγελιζόμενος ("preaching and proclaiming the good news"), with the twelve and the women placed in parallel relationship as those following along with him. Nevertheless, the focus falls clearly upon the women because of the details provided about them.[52]

To be sure, Luke is not alone in recognizing that a number of women followed Jesus in Galilee, and from Galilee to Jerusalem. But whereas Matthew (27:55-56) and Mark (15:40-41) only draw attention to this fact at the crucifixion scene, Luke establishes that such women were companions of Jesus from the early stages of his ministry in Galilee.[53] What is more, Mark agrees with Luke's earlier statement that the women provided material assistance to Jesus (see below).[54] By mentioning the women here Luke not only places them in a parallel relationship with the male disciples as those who witnessed Jesus' teaching and mighty deeds, he also prepares for their important role in the passion and resurrection narrative.[55]

In fact the reappearance of the women in passion narrative, and in particular the naming of the first two women who appear here (Luke 24:10), reinforces the point that the women have been constant companions of Jesus throughout his entire ministry. It is further underlined by the words of the angels in the empty tomb who invite the women to recall Jesus' prediction of his passion while he was with them in Galilee (24:6). This must refer to one of the two predictions made in chapter 9, predictions which are made to the disciples (9:18-22, 43-45). The clear implication is that Luke regards the women as disciples.[56]

Three women are named, and it is likely that the reader is meant to note the correspondence between them and the inner three of the male disciples.[57] The three named women are identified as "those who had been cured

---

51. Bauckham, *Gospel Women*, 110. Also Karris, "Women," 9-10.

52. Seim, *Double Message*, 31; Bauckham, *Gospel Women*, 111-12.

53. Bauckham, *Gospel Women*, 112-13.

54. Mark has διηκόνουν αὐτῷ (" they served him"), whereas Luke is more explicit with διηκόνουν αὐτοῖς ἐκ τῶν ὑπαρχόντων αὐταῖς ("they served them from their means")

55. Nolland, *Luke*, 1:366, notes that it is only the women who "are brought into connection with all four stages of the traditional confession preserved in 1 Cor 15:3-5."

56. Bauckham, *Gospel Women*, 113.

57. So Ricci, *Mary Magdalene*, 129; Seim, *Double Message*, 31; Spencer, *Salty Wives*,

of evil spirits and sickness" (τεθεραπευμέναι ἀπὸ πνευμάτων πονηρῶν καὶ ἀσθενειῶν), although Luke does not recount any of these incidents. Mary Magdalene is the only one said to have been afflicted by demons, although this appended information may have been given due to the depths of her affliction. Possibly the other two named, Joanna and Susanna, had been healed of illness. The reference to "many others" (καὶ ἕτεραι πολλαί) is clearly also referring to females, although it is unclear whether we are to regard them all as recipients of exorcism and/or healing.[58]

We will now examine each of the women in turn.

Mary Magdalene

Mary Magdalene first appears in Luke's Gospel here at 8:2. She will also appear in the resurrection narrative along with Joanna and "the other women with them" (24:10). The appended title "who is called Magdalene" references her by her place of origin Magdala. Magdala was a Galilean town located near Tiberias on the western shore of the Sea of Galilee.[59] Titled by location rather than by a named relation—typically a husband—should not, in itself, indicate that Mary was unmarried, although her demonic affliction may point in this direction.[60]

Bauckham considers it possible she was named because she was the most known female disciple of Jesus, rather than being noted for her material contributions as were the other women[61] This prominence of Mary is evident in three ways. First is the number of times she appears in the canonical Gospels. She was present at the crucifixion (Matt 27:56//Mark 15:40//John 19:25), she observed Jesus' body being placed in the tomb (Matt 27:61//Mark 15:47//Luke 23:55), she was one of the group of women who were the first witnesses to the resurrection (Matt 28:1//Mark 16:1; Luke 24:10//John 20:1), and she received an individual resurrection appearance (John 20:11–18). Second is the various named groups of women disciples

---

120; Bovon, *Luke 1*, 300.

58. It is unclear whether ἦσαν τεθεραπευμέναι ἀπὸ πνευμάτων πονηρῶν καὶ ἀσθενειῶν ("who had been cured of evil spirits and diseases") relates only to the three named women, or to the "many others" as well.

59. See Collins, "Mary," 579.

60. Bauckham, *Gospel Women*, 119, 134, who points out that such a woman may well have been divorced by her husband, or rejected by potential husbands.

61. Ibid., 117, n19.

where she is commonly[62] at the head of the list. Third is her prominence in numerous apocryphal Christian texts.[63]

Despite some popular representations, Mary Magdalene is not to be identified with the sinful woman in the immediately preceding narrative (Luke 7:36–50), for nowhere in the narrative is demonic affliction equated with sin.[64] Further, being afflicted by seven demons is not an exercise in status degradation,[65] but is surely a sign of her "grievous condition."[66]

Joanna

As Bauckham notes, the importance of Joanna in Luke's Gospel is more significant than the two references to her might indicate.[67] She is introduced as the wife of Chuza, the ἐπίτροπος of Herod Antipas. The Greek word is used of governors and procurators, but here most likely refers to one who administers a household or estate.[68] Even if Chuza was only one "steward" among many, a high-ranking official is clearly indicated.[69]

The name *Chuza* was quite rare and appears to be Natabean. Given the opposition to mixed marriages in post-exilic Judaism, it is highly likely that he was a convert to Judaism, either prior to or as a pre-requisite for his marriage to Joanna.[70] We are not privy to Joanna's family history, but her

62. The exception is John 19:25, where the relatives of Jesus are mentioned first.

63. The Gospel of Philip (generally regarded as a third-century gnostic work) states "there were three who always walked with the Lord: Mary his mother, and her sister, and Magdalene, the one who was called his companion. His sister and his mother and his companion were each a Mary (59:6–11) Mary is also prominent in other gnostic works such as *Pistis Sophia* and the *Gospel of Mary* (where she is the most loved of all disciples including the male disciples—*Gos. Mary* 18:14–15). See Meyer with deBoer, *The Gospels of Mary*; Ricci, *Mary Magdalene*, 129–55.

64. Contra Grassi, *Hidden Heroes*, 86, who contends that the reference to seven demons "hints that she was a very lively sinner."

65. As Tetlow, *Women and Ministry*, 103. See also Elaine Wainwright, "Some Women who were Healed of Evil Spirits and Imfirmities: Lucan Women Healed," SBL International Meeting Seminar Paper, Singapore, 2005.

66. Nolland, *Luke*, 1:366. The number "seven" may have some symbolic significance with respect to severity. See Rengstorf, *TDNT* 2:630–31.

67. Bauckham, *Gospel Women*, 109.

68. BDAG 385.

69. See Bauckham, *Gospel Women*, 135–38, who discusses the possibilities indicated by the term and the parallels in Jewish literature. He is cautious about the identification of Chuza with the royal official (βασιλικός) mentioned in John 4:46. Nevertheless, it does indicate Jesus' reputation amongst the Herodian elite and would explain Herod's curiosity regarding Jesus (Luke 9:7–9; 23:8).

70. Ibid., 150–61.

marriage to Chuza places her squarely in the higher echelons of Herodian society. We should not therefore minimize "the social gulf she crossed in becoming a follower of Jesus."[71] The circles in which she moved shifted radically from the wealthy elite of Tiberius to the poor and socially marginalized of rural Galilee.[72]

The reason why Luke highlights Joanna's connection with the court of Herod Antipas has been variously construed. It may be to emphasize the source of her wealth,[73] to point out that the influence of Jesus and his message had reached to the upper echelons of society,[74] to provide encouragement and a model to similar wealthy, well-positioned followers of Jesus,[75] or, on the basis that the Herodian court would have "engendered social suspicion and even contempt in the contemporary Jewish context, in other words a kind of dubious 'tax-collector' status," it highlights the diversity of the socially marginalized who attached themselves to Jesus.[76] It is also possible that here Luke indicates the identity of his source material regarding Herod Antipas.[77] Finally, it may be part of Luke's narrative strategy emphasizing that Herod is still in power and creating suspense as to how he will respond to Jesus.[78] The second proposal is probably the most germane. Luke wants us to understand that Jesus did not exclusively focus on the poor and the marginalized of society, but also had positive contact with some sections of the wealthy elite.

Of all the women mentioned in Luke's Gospel, it is the presence of Joanna in his entourage that would likely raise the most eyebrows. It is

71. Bauckham, *Gospel Women*, 145..

72. Ibid., 150, who surmises that Joanna's generosity and allegiance to the ministry of Jesus may have been a deliberate reversal on her part of the oppressive regime of which she had been part.

73. Ibid., 119–21.

74. Corley, *Private Women*, 111; Spencer, *Salty Wives*, 107; Bock, *Luke*, 1:713; Nolland, *Luke*, 1:366; Marshall, *Luke*, 317; Fitzmyer, *Luke*, 1:698. Bauckham, *Gospel Women*, 120, insists that by so doing, Luke is not attempting to confer social legitimacy on the early Christian movement, for such association with Herod would send negative signals to the audience. But this is not necessarily the case, particularly if Theophilus, for example, was a person of high rank in Greco-Roman society. Furthermore, it is possible to conclude from the text that Joanna has severed her involvement in this circle, and is now a follower of Jesus.

75. Esler, *Community and Gospel*, 184.

76. Seim, *Double Message*, 36, raises this possibility, but in the end believes that the reference more serves to emphasize the source of Joanna's wealth.

77. Evans, *St. Luke*, 366; Ricci, *Mary Magdalene*, 155. See also Sawicki, *Crossing Galilee*, 147–53, whose fertile imagination leads her to speculate that Jesus was originally sponsored by the Herodians as an exorcist.

78. Darr, *Character Building*, 160.

possible that she was a widow, although Luke's description of her makes this unlikely. Her husband may also have been a sympathizer, but that cannot be established with certainty. Spencer raises the possibility that she, together with the other women mentioned, may have been intermittent followers of Jesus given his limited movement around lower Galilee.[79] But this is not the impression given by Luke in 23:49 and 24:6.

Susanna

This is the only mention of Susanna in the NT, and nothing else is known of her. She obviously needed no further identification because there was no other Christian disciple with whom to confuse her.[80] In the resurrection narrative where three women are named as part of a larger group, she is replaced by Mary the mother of James. The fact that she is here named alongside Joanna, probably indicates that she was also a woman of means and one of the main contributors to the needs of the wider group.[81]

Narratival Propositions from 8:1-3

The women are disciples of Jesus

Luke 8:1-3, in placing the women in parallel with the twelve disciples of Jesus, invites the reader to journey with the women as well as the men.[82] There are the odd occasions where Jesus and the male disciples, or the inner three of the male disciples, are exclusively present. But where this is not expressly stated, the reader should assume that the women are there as well, listening to his teaching, experiencing the kingdom's power in his healings and exorcisms, and being challenged in their own discipleship.[83]

---

79. Spencer, *Salty Wives*, 111.
80. Bauckham, *Gospel Women*, 118.
81. So ibid., 117,n.19.
82. Seim, *Double Message*, 63, contends that the women are not viewed as disciples, but are given the special function of material support. But as argued above, this flies in the face of the words of the angels in the tomb (24:6-8; cf. 9:21-22, 43).

83 All this opens up the possibility of looking at the text from a female vantage point, a vantage point which can help provide correction to the androcentric perspective that is normally adopted or presented. Bauckham, *Gospel Women*, 199-202, who insists that, for two reasons, such a reading does not run counter to the thrust of the text: (i) the bare-bones stories of the Gospels always invite the reader to flesh out the details, and (ii) various perspectives would have been part and parcel of the numerous

The women are actively involved in kingdom service

The force of the Greek expression αἵτινες διηκόνουν αὐτοῖς ἐκ τῶν ὑπαρχόντων αὐταῖς ("who provided for them from their means") is that the women provided material support for Jesus and his followers.[84] It was not uncommon for Jewish women of means to support religious groups,[85] but Luke's statement here is obviously a generalization. Not all women followers of Jesus were in a position to provide material support, just as not all had been healed of demon possession or illness.[86]

We should not take the expression to mean that the women merely performed traditional roles of cooking, washing, etc.,[87] for they are on the road with Jesus, not in a fixed location. Moreover, the male disciples are later asked by Jesus to provide food, not the women (Luke 9:13; cf. 12:37; 17:7-8).[88] Even if the word διακόνεω does have this connotation, and it probably does not (see below), such service is not placing the women in a subservient role, for service is highly regarded in the kingdom where traditional values are turned on their head and the Master among them is one who serves (22:27). It is also unlikely, given the possessive dative αὐταῖς ("to them" in the sense of "theirs"), that Luke is merely speaking of the women administering the common purse.[89]

As to the sense of διακόνεω, the term can be used of performing household tasks (4:39; 10:40), but it (or the cognate noun διακονία) also has the sense of carrying out a certain ministry such as administering the distribution of food (Acts 6:1-2), or the provision for the poor in Judea (Acts 11:29; cf. Rom 15:25). It is even used in Acts 1:17 with respect to the role of the apostles. Nevertheless, it is the inclusion of ἐκ τῶν ὑπαρχόντων αὐταῖς ("from their

---

oral performances given to the tradition both before and after its encoding in the written Gospels.

84. This assumes the plural reading αὐταῖς. For a defence of the singular αὐτῷ, and its subsequent focus upon Jesus rather than Jesus and the 12, see Karris, "Women," 6-7.

85. See, for example, Jos. *Ant.* 17.2.4; Spencer, *Salty Wives*, 123-24; Reid, *Better Part*, 128 and the material cited in n.19.

86. Sim, "Women Followers," 52; Bauckham, *Gospel Women*, 115.

87. Witherington, *Women*, 118 . He further contends that some of the women would have only been able to give of their time and talents in such duties as meal preparation or the making of garments (195-96). Tannehill, *Narrative Unity*, 1:138, believes it relates to both supplying and preparing food.

88. Reid, *Better Part*, 127.

89. Ibid., 129.

possessions") that indicates that the service should not be construed in terms of menial chores, but of financial backing and provision.[90]

This raises the obvious question as to how women in first-century Palestinian society would have the disposable means to be able to support Jesus and the other disciples to this extent. Bauckham has a helpful discussion on the various ways in which a Jewish women may acquire such resources.[91] Any woman, whether married or unmarried, without male siblings may be the recipient of the family inheritance. She could also be the recipient of a deed of gift. A divorced woman would receive a *ketubba* payment (the part of a Jewish marriage contract where the husband pledges to pay his wife if he divorces her) or the dowry paid by the father to her husband. A widow would receive the same as a divorcee, or her husband's inheritance if there were no other eligible heirs. Any woman could derive an income by working for payment, although a married woman would use it to supplement the family income and would not normally have it at her disposal. With respect to Joanna then, Sim argues that as a married woman, she would not have had the right to dispose of her husband's financial resources.[92] Bauckham, on the other hand, considers the possibility that she was widowed.[93] Further, an aristocratic woman like Joanna, who belonged to a Romanized court circle, likely had greater freedom than many of her Jewish contemporaries.[94]

On the one hand, there are those who regard the women's role in Luke 8:1–3 as radical to the extent that service is provided to a group outside of the family circle. Others regarded it as an attempt by Luke, against the background of expanding roles for women in leadership in the early church, to place women in subservient categories and restrict them from such roles.[95] Neither position shows due sensitivity to the narrative and the way Luke consistently uses women as models of discipleship. Women are indeed often portrayed in a serving capacity, and in that way they are typical of the cultural norm. Yet in a kingdom where service is consistently elevated, and indeed is modelled by Jesus himself, the women represent those who embody the kingdom ideal, and in many ways put the male disciples, who

---

90. Sim, "Women Followers," 56–60 ; Corley, *Private Women*, 111; Seim, *Double Message*, 62; Garland, *Luke*, 341–42. Karris, "Women," 7–9, argues that the forces of the expression is that the women went on mission for Jesus.

91. Bauckham, *Gospel Women*, 121–35. See also Seim, *Double Message*, 64–65.

92. Sim, "Women Followers," 52–55.

93. Bauckham, *Gospel Women*, 117.

94. Ibid., 118.

95. Tetlow, *Women and Ministry*, 103; Schüssler Fiorenza, *In Memory*, 49, 161, 167; Corley, *Women and the Historical Jesus*, 30; Spencer, *Salty Wives*, 118 .

are preoccupied with status, to shame (Luke 22:24–27).[96] It is also important to note that prior to Luke 12, διακονέω ("serve") and διακονία ("service") are only used of women in narrative contexts. Thereafter, the verb begins to be used in didactic passages addressed to the twelve or the wider company of the disciples (12:35; 17:8; 22:24–27).[97] The women therefore function as pre-emptive models for the teaching of Jesus.

Any view that claims that Luke is engaged in deliberate gender differentiation, in the sense that proclamation is assigned to the male disciples, and serving to females, not only fails to appreciate the role of service described above, but is guilty of placing artificial categories on the Lukan text. The male disciples are not ascribed the role of proclamation here, in fact they have yet to have been given any role,[98] and even though they may be so ascribed in Luke 9:1–6, it will be argued in due course that the women are more than likely numbered among the seventy(-two) commissioned in 10:1–11.

In what sense therefore, are the women to be regarded as patrons[99] or benefactors[100] of Jesus and his disciples? Bauckham insists that these are inappropriate categories with which to view the women, given the radical teaching of Jesus regarding the overturning of social honor and prestige. The fact that the women themselves joined Jesus and his disciples also does not sit well with this model. Furthermore, regarding Joanna, the Herodian circle in which she moved could hardly have been given the respect by Galilean peasants normally granted to a patron or benefactor.[101] Seim, however, speaks of a reciprocal benefaction of sorts, where the women become benefactors in response to Jesus' beneficent acts of healing.[102]

The women are thus placed in the larger company of those who support Jesus and later the Christian community (Mary and Martha [Luke 10:38–42], Mary the mother of John [Acts 12:12], Lydia [Acts 16:14–15], Priscilla [Acts 18:26]).[103] In their provision for Jesus and the male disciples in this way, the women reflect appropriate kingdom values and imitate the attitude of Jesus himself (Luke 22:27). With respect to service, the women clearly function as prototypes of the believing community in general,

---

96. Arlandson, *Women*, 165–68.

97. Seim, *Double Message*, 81–83.

98. A point noted by Seim, *Double Message*, 79.

99. So Reid, *Better Part*, 129; Corley, *Private Women*, 119.

100. Spencer, *Salty Wives*, 103, 113; Moxnes, "Patron-Client Relations," 241–68.

101. Bauckham, *Gospel Women*, 163.

102. Seim, *Double Message*, 57–58, although he points out that it does break with the ideal of total reciprocity. Spencer, *Salty Wives*, 144, sees the women repaying Jesus as "grateful clients."

103. Seim, *Double Message*, 64.

and of leadership in particular.[104] A second order narratival proposition arises from this intra-narratival reading: *Women may be involved in serving Jesus and the kingdom.*

The women embody true discipleship regarding the use of wealth and possessions

Although Luke does have a radical strand regarding the total abandonment of wealth (Luke 14:33; 18:18–30; cf. 5:11, 27), he also reflects a more moderate strand whereby wealth is used appropriately for the benefit of others and kingdom advancement (16:10–12; 19:1–10; Acts 12:12–13; 16:15). Although there has been little consensus regarding the reconciliation of these different perspectives, most agree that Luke is not advocating a total renunciation of goods for all followers of Jesus.[105] The women of Luke 8:1–3 thus function as the ideal for those of means (possibly Theophilus?) who would embrace the gospel message and its demands by not selfishly hoarding their wealth but using it for the expansion of the gospel.[106] They also anticipate the believing community in Acts 4:32 where all held their goods (τῶν ὑπαρχόντων) in common.[107] Consequently, a second order narratival proposition would be: *women may embody true discipleship regarding the use of wealth and possessions.*

Anticipating broader narratival and theological themes in Luke-Acts

There are a further two narratival propositions that, while not directly flowing from 8:1–3, emerge from the ensuing narrative in light of what has been stated in 8:1–3.

The women function as a practical example of the "good soil" from the parable of the Sower

---

104. Seim, *Double Message*, 87–88.

105. See Forbes, *God of Old*, 231.

106. Seim, *Double Message*, 78, who mentions Ananias and Sapphira as negative examples. Both Moltmann-Wendel, *Women*, 141, and Sim, "Women Followers," miss the point entirely in arguing that the women could not be wealthy and followers of Jesus because discipleship involved the renunciation of wealth. But surely the point is that, in supporting Jesus and the wider group in this way, they are renouncing their wealth for the sake of the kingdom.

107. Seim, *Double Message*, 79.

Given that the parable of the Sower immediately follows this section, it is hard to avoid the comparison of the women to the good soil. By their deeds of service they are "living embodiments of what happens when the sower sows his seed in soil that can receive and nurture it."[108] Although Reid argues that the women's service is linked more to the healing they had received than any response to the word,[109] this is probably an unnecessary distinction, for Jesus' healing ministry and proclamation of the kingdom went hand-in-hand.

The women are representative of those who forsake family ties for the sake of Jesus and the kingdom

In the hyperbolic statement regarding hating one's family (Luke 14:26), and in the positive affirmation to Peter (18:29–30), Luke's Jesus clearly places loyalty to himself and the kingdom of God above family ties and loyalties. While it is true that we are not informed of the marital status of the women in 8:1–3, it is hard to imagine that all would have been unmarried or widowed. Even if Joanna, who is named by reference to her husband Chuza, was widowed at this time,[110] following Jesus is tantamount to renouncing her ties to Herodian aristocracy. Of course the women are not alone in leaving family, for the male disciples have also left all to follow Jesus (5:11; 18:28). But together with their male counterparts, the women are representative of those who have placed kingdom priorities above those of family. This is consistent with that fact that the kingdom of God breaks down economic and social barriers and incorporates males and females into one believing community.[111] *Thus women can be righteous stewards and servants in the kingdom of God, and have a divine endorsement for sociological flexibility and independence to follow Jesus in the same way as male disciples.*

Jesus' True Family (Luke 8:19–21)

Women are part of the true family of Jesus

This little episode is a condensed version of Mark 3:31–35. We are not told why Jesus' family wished to see him, although the Markan account follows

---

108. Witherington, "On the Road," 243.
109. Reid, *Better Part*, 132.
110. Bauckham, *Gospel Women*, 117, raises the possibility.
111 Witherington, *Women*, 118.

closely on the heels of the episode where his family attempts to restrain him because of his growing public acclaim and accusations of some that he had "lost his mind" (Mark 3:20-21).[112]

Here Jesus redefines kinship not in terms of physical descent, but in terms of openness and response to the word of God (cf. Luke 6:47; 11:28), thus forming a connection with the parable of the sower (8:15).[113] This redefinition would be important for the later Christian communities, where a faith commitment to Jesus often resulted in family antagonism and associated loss of honor. The NT writers consequently work hard at creating fictive kinship among the people of God, with God as father, and believers as brothers and sisters. In this way those who suffer familial estrangement on the one hand, on the other gain membership in a much larger and ultimately more significant family group.[114] Given the mention in 8:1-3 of the women who accompany Jesus and support the itinerant group (see above), women are clearly part of this realigned family grouping.

For the purposes of our study this episode has further significance in that Luke demonstrates that Jesus is prepared to redefine cultural norms and expectations in line with kingdom values and ideals. Consequently a theology of women in Luke must be closely attuned to the narrative context, rather than merely informed, or prejudiced, by a social or cultural context, whether that context is ancient or contemporary.

Raising of Jairus' Daughter and the Healing of the Women with a Hemorrhage (Luke 8:40-56)

The interlocking account[115] of the two healing miracles in this passage is taken directly from Mark. In a narrative sense, the "intercalation fills in time in the narrative and serves to heighten the dramatic tension and the miracle's magnitude."[116] The delay over dealing with the woman with the hemorrhage is in fact integral to the storyline of Jairus' daughter. Taken in conjunction with the surrounding material, the account also serves to underline the point that the compassion of Jesus, and the blessings of the kingdom, are given without discrimination.

---

112. This assumes that οἱ παρ' αὐτοῦ refers to his family. See Stein, *Mark*, 180.
113. Bock, *Luke*, 1:751.
114. See deSilva, *Honor, Patronage, Kinship and Purity*, 157-239.
115. An example of 'sandwiching technique' referred to in chapter 1 on methodology.
116. Garland, *Luke*, 365.

*Jesus has compassion on the daughter of a prominent Jew
and a chronically ill, and therefore unclean, woman*

On returning to Galilee after healing the Gerasene demoniac (Luke 8:26–39), large crowds were waiting for Jesus. Among them was a man named Jairus, a leader of the synagogue, whose "only daughter, about twelve years old, was dying" (8:42). A synagogue ruler was a prominent position in first century Jewish society yet, faced with personal tragedy, the man humbles himself before Jesus and kneels at his feet requesting healing for his daughter. But before Jesus arrives at the house word comes that the girl has died (8:49). The reader feels a certain sadness at this point in the narrative, a pathos heightened by the fact that she is an only daughter.[117] But there is also a sense of expectancy. In the previous chapter Jesus has raised the only son of a widow (7:11–17), now comes the opportunity to raise the only daughter of a man.[118] Clearly the value of a female life is placed on the same level as that of a male, a situation that was not always the norm in the ancient world.[119] Having said this, Luke is not gender indifferent; indeed he is particularly attuned to the specific issues which attend each gender.

From Jesus' perspective the girl "is not dead but sleeping" (8:52), a pronouncement that occasions ironic laughter from those who apparently know better. This is an attitude that is in conflict with Jesus' previous statement "do not fear, only believe, and she will be healed/saved (σωθήσεται)." Those assembled clearly do not believe, but this does not restrict the action of Jesus in this situation. Taking the girl by the hand, Jesus refuses to entertain any notion of contracting ritual impurity by contact with a corpse (Lev 19:11, 13). Rather than her impurity being contagious, it is his wholeness that is contagious (see also below on the haemorrhaging woman). The girl's "spirit" or "breath" (τὸ πνεῦμα αὐτῆς) returns.[120] After she got to her feet, Jesus' concern for her physical well-being is again stressed in the command "give her something to eat." Both actions emphasize her return to normal life.[121]

However, as mentioned above, this healing/resuscitation story contains another healing story within it. On the way to Jairus' house Jesus has an encounter with another woman. The reader is informed that this woman has suffered from hemorrhages for twelve years, and despite spending all

---

117. Garland, *Luke*, 367.

118. On Lukan pairing patterns, see Paffenroth, *Story of Jesus*, 124–26.

119. Reid, *Better Part*, 137.

120. This is more likely a reference to her recommencement of breathing rather than any notion of the spirit having departed (Garland, *Luke*, 369).

121. Garland, *Luke*, 370.

she had on medical treatment,[122] had not been cured. The woman takes the initiative in her healing, and goes one step beyond the centurion who sent friends asking Jesus not trouble himself to come to the house, but simply to "speak the word and let my servant be healed " (Luke 7:7). This woman does not even speak, but appears to consider that a simple touch of Jesus' garment will suffice. The idea that divine power can be transmitted via that which a holy person wears or touches appears to have been widespread (see Acts 19:12; cf. 5:15).[123] The touch does suffice, and she is healed instantly, without a word being spoken to or from Jesus. Jesus is, however, aware that power has gone out from him. His demand to know who had touched him is met with incredulity by Peter, who considers it impossible to sort out one touch from among the thronging crowd. But the woman owns up and comes trembling to the feet of Jesus.[124] It is unclear whether her fear was occasioned by an awareness that she has passed on state of ritual impurity through her touch,[125] or simply being awestruck by the evident power of Jesus.[126] Jesus' response is positive with "Daughter, your faith has made you well/saved you. Go in peace" (Luke 8:48). The appellation of "daughter" may have echoes of covenant membership,[127] although it is a kinship relationship expressed to Jesus, not to Abraham.[128] This is significant for one who was socially marginalized. Further, in the narrative context "daughter" serves as yet another link between the two interlocking episodes (see below).[129] The woman is also commended for her faith, and thereby functions as a contrast with those without faith in the narrative; namely the disciples who consider that they are in mortal peril on the windswept sea of Galilee (8:25), and the parents of the little girl in the narrative in which this episode is embedded (8:53).[130]

122. Assuming the reading in the text, absent from key witnesses such as $\mathfrak{P}^{75}$ B D.

123. Garland, *Luke*, 367.

124. Seim, *Double Message*, 132, believes that the woman's public testimony was required to show that Jesus was right in insisting that someone had touched him.

125. Ricci, *Mary Magdalene*, 29. Dewey, "Jesus' Healings of Women," 127, notes that the woman with the hemorrhage is full of counter-cultural elements: as an unclean woman she should not be in public, let alone touching people by pushing through the crowd. Further, she touches Jesus and then publicly confesses what she has done.

126. Garland, *Luke*, 368. It is hardly the case, as proposed by Reid, *Better Part*, 143, that this an attempt by Luke to place a woman back into a subservient stance by taming her initial boldness.

127. Reid, *Better Part*, 140

128. Dewey, "Jesus' Healings of Women," 127.

129. Talbert, *Reading Luke*, 99.

130. Reid, *Better Part*, 136, believes that the woman's faith functions as a model for the type of faith that Jairus needs in order for his daughter to be healed. But, although he demonstrates initial faith in coming to Jesus it would appear that he was also one

The sandwiching of the two episodes here serves a significant narratival function. This is highlighted by the correspondence in "twelve years," which represents both the age of the girl, and the length of the older woman's illness. The two female characters are both "daughters" and come from opposite ends of the social spectrum. The girl was the daughter of a synagogue ruler, a prominent leadership position in Jewish society, whereas the hemorrhaging woman was considered ritually impure and consequently a social outcast, and economically destitute. These contrasting social positions play out in the way the characters approach Jesus. The synagogue ruler comes to Jesus directly and appeals to his face. The hemorrhaging woman must creep up anonymously from behind.[131] But this sandwiched account, together with the parallel narrative of raising the widow's son at Nain (7:11–17), indicates a second order narratival proposition: *Jesus is interested in and accessible to all, both male and female, old and young, irrespective of their socio-religious status.*[132]

The healed woman is a faithful witness

The woman truthfully announces her experience of the power of Jesus—"she declared before all the people why she had touched him and how she had been immediately healed" (Luke 8:47). In this way she echoes the faithful testimony of Mary and Elizabeth from the infancy narratives, and foreshadows the women as reliable witnesses at the resurrection.[133]

The socially marginalized woman experiences the shalom of God

The final pronouncement "your faith has saved /healed (σέσωκέν) you. Go in peace," mirrors that given to the sinful woman in Luke 7:50. The fact that this full statement is only given in Luke's Gospel to these two women,[134] both of whom would have been considered unclean, gives weight to a second order narratival proposition: *Even women on the margins of society can experience the full shalom of God.*[135]

---

with those who laughed when Jesus indicated that his daughter was only sleeping.

131. Garland, *Luke*, 371.

132. Tannehill, *Narrative Unity*, 1:135–36.

133. Reid, *Better Part*, 140. As the full significance of women as faithful witnesses is brought out in the resurrection narrative, the generalizing role this character plays will be discussed there.

134. In 17:19 and 18:42 the same formula, without the final declaration of peace, is given to the returning leper, and the blind man respectively.

135. Seim, *Double Message*, 89–90; Reid, *Better Part*, 141.

Summary of Narratival Propositions

Jesus is clearly the central character in Luke's Gospel, and his ministry is the ministry of the God of Israel. Jesus is the faithful Israelite, a true and righteous son of Israel who is also the Son of God. He is set apart from other people because God delights in him as his Son and empowers him through his Spirit.

The arrival of Jesus has a determinative impact on all people. He is the promised Spirit-led Messiah who proclaims the good news of the kingdom of God, and who exercises a liberating healing and teaching ministry to all irrespective of age, gender, or social class. This results in full release from demonic and physical affliction through bringing the kingdom to bear in people's lives.

Jesus reconstitutes Israel and thus claims all of Israel has his own. He selects twelve apostles from a larger group of disciples, and his call receives an obedient and proper response from Simon Peter. The character of Judas, however, does not reflect the characteristics that Jesus expects in his disciples.

It is clear from this section that Luke's Jesus has a special focus on women. He shows concern for a marginalized woman's plight, and a sinful woman's response to him surpasses that of a Pharisee. Ultimately, there is no restriction on the inclusion of women amongst God's people aside from forgiveness by Jesus and a response of faith on their behalf. Further, the women followers of Jesus are understood to be true disciples, who exemplify the appropriate use of wealth and possessions and are preemptive models of kingdom service. These women disciples function as a practical example of the "good soil" from the parable of the Sower. They are also representative of those who forsake family ties for the sake of Jesus and the kingdom. In doing so, they form part of the true family of Jesus.

Jesus has compassion on the daughter of a prominent Jew, and a chronically ill, and therefore unclean woman. The latter demonstrates that even women on the margins of society can experience the full shalom of God. Women also faithfully testify to events of which they are a part.

This section of Luke's Gospel highlights that Jesus is interested in and accessible to all, both male and female, old and young, irrespective of their socio-religious status.

Theological Propositions

As can be seen from the narratival propositions above, women are included in Jesus' story in a sometimes socio-religiously atypical manner. These are the narratival outworkings of an undergirding theology. This theology is summarized below. It is by nature broad, which is quite a contrast to its specific and varied out-working in the narrative itself.

Theological propositions to do with Jesus' person

1. God has returned to Israel in the person of Jesus the "Son of God."
2. Jesus is the Son of God in two complimentary manners. As the messianic Son of God, he lived faithfully and righteously as God originally intended for Adam and Israel. As the divine Son of God, Jesus' Lordship corresponds to the Lordship of Yahweh.

Theological propositions to do with Jesus' work

1. God's return to Israel in Jesus reconfigured the nation. This was achieved through Jesus' ministry of bringing about the kingdom of God, expressed in terms of salvation and restoration.
2. As the Spirit-led Messiah, Jesus restored people to God and saved them from afflictions which resulted from distortions in nature, humanity and the demonic realm.

Theological propositions to do with Jesus' people

1. God is just as interested in women as he is in men.
2. God's new community includes both men and women, with no gender restriction on who may be a disciple of Jesus.
3. People are included into the new people of God by virtue of Jesus' forgiveness of their sins as well as their trust and obedience in him.
4. There are no gender restrictions upon the expression of the ideal characteristics which Jesus looks for in his followers.

Anticipating Further Narratival and Theological Themes in Luke-Acts

The sinful women instantiates the characteristics that Jesus embodies and teaches about in future meal scenes

The theme of eating, and scenes which revolve around eating, are employed in the Gospel of Luke in order to communicate several key ideas including wholeness, fellowship, and satisfaction with Jesus' ministry. For example, Jesus provides food for a large crowd in a remote place (Luke 9:10-17). As a result of this miraculous work the people do not have to disperse, but are able to remain with Jesus and with each other. The people eat in groups and are satisfied to the extent that there are leftovers. The meal is an expression of the kingdom of God about which Jesus is teaching. Just as Jesus' teaching is also accompanied by making people whole through healing (9:11), feeding people is another expression of making people whole and restoring their dignity by means of a transition from hunger and need to a situation of satisfaction and liveliness.

The meal scenes in Luke's Gospel reach their peak with meals which are centered on the cross and on covenant theology (the Last Supper in 22:19-27; the Emmaus Meal, 24:30) as well as the future consummation of the kingdom of God (22:29-30; cf. 12:37; 13:28-29; 14:15-24; 22:16, 18). These meals are for the followers of Jesus, so in one sense they bounded to include only those who humbly accept Jesus and his messianic mission. However, although they are 'bounded' meals, there is also a sense that they are profoundly open at the same time, for they included people who might not usually eat at choice feasts.

The surprising inclusion of those who display the characteristics of the kingdom of God receives elaboration in Luke 11:43. Here Jesus rejects Pharisaic pride and elitism: "Woe to you Pharisees, because you love the most important seats in the synagogues and greetings in the marketplaces." The reader is meant to see here a stark contrast between the Pharisees and Jesus. Jesus later describes himself as the one who is not at the banquet table to be served but present as the one who serves (22:27). Thus his actions perfectly mirror his teaching. In addition, the Pharisees are depicted as falling into the same behavioral and perspectival problem as the disciples when they argue over who is the greatest (9:46-48). The great reversal that Jesus' kingdom entails, illustrated by the change in roles in table fellowship, has consequences for many. Jesus seeks to communicate that there are no positions of honor in the kingdom of God. Neither are there people who are the greatest in the kingdom of God, in so far as they attain this designation on the backs of others. God decides who will be honored. The ones who God honors are not the ones who exalts themselves, but rather the ones who humbles themselves (14:11). This leads the reader to ask themselves: who has been humble so far in the narrative? Who have been the prime examples of taking the posture of humility? Furthermore, who has taken this position when they may have had grounds for exalting themselves? Who has served God and Jesus so far?

Further, instances of reversing social expectations used to illustrate the kingdom of God occur in the banquet scenes of chapter 14. In particular, the teaching is an indictment against guests who "chose the places of honor" (14:7). Jesus took the opportunity to propose a new way of understanding inclusion and honor: "When you give a luncheon or a dinner, do not invite your friends, your brothers, or relatives, or your rich neighbors; if you do they might invite you back and so you will be repaid" (14:12). Instead, the banquet host is to "invite the poor, the crippled, the lame, and the blind. And you will be blessed because, although they cannot repay you, you will be repaid at the resurrection of the righteous" (14:13–14). This is consolidated by his parable of a banquet to which the original invitees did not come. Those who were eventually able to partake of the great meal were the "poor, the crippled, the blind and the lame" (14:21). Luke's narrative suggests that many people would feast with Jesus the end time messianic banquet. It would not be a feast for the few who had the ability to make it to the best seats at the table. Jesus' invitation to be with him was cast wide and the response he sought was humility and thankfulness.

The meal settings are also utilized to illustrate the characteristics of those who will enjoy fellowship with God and his people—they are those who need help and are habitually rejected by others. These scenes often involve the reversal of social conventions, a theme common in this gospel and not limited to meal settings. When Jesus upturned social conventions he often proposed a particular virtue as a remedy to the behavior he was rejecting. These virtues are often reflected in women's lives throughout Luke's Gospel.

CHAPTER 5

Travel Narrative (Luke 9:51—19:28)

These chapters of Luke's Gospel make a strong contribution to understanding women as disciples and as persons who exhibit the qualities associated with discipleship. Now Luke fleshes out his picture of discipleship and presents those who trust in Jesus with a higher degree of sophistication. In these chapters Luke also widens the scope of Jesus' ministry by including the twelve and the seventy(-two) in his work.

Sophistication and Paradigms as Narratival Techniques

Before proceeding, an explanatory note regarding one of Luke's narratival techniques is in order. One of his key concerns is to present the reader with a sophisticated view of discipleship. This is achieved through a number of 'sophisticating strategies.' The use of these sophisticating strategies with respect to the disciples plays a stronger role in chapters 10–11 than it has in previous sections of the narrative. For this reason we will discuss this technique here.

By the time the reader/hearer reaches Luke 10–11, they will have formed beliefs regarding discipleship and about those included within the group known as "the disciples." These views have been molded and shaped to various degrees by the narrative. Sophisticating strategies will be employed by Luke in order to augment different aspects of what has been stated, both negatively and positively, with reference to the disciples.[1] This

---

1. Danove, "Narrative Rhetoric," 26–30.

cultivation of beliefs may be achieved by means of word repetition or by aligning certain concepts. This will give rise to "specialized connotation and phrases" which are explained by the narrative itself.[2] For example, in Mark's Gospel the author cultivates a positive regard for the disciples by means of the storied repetition and coordination of "proclaim," "hand over," and "baptize."[3] In the narrative, those who proclaim and are handed over follow the pattern of Jesus and John the Baptist. The pattern of Jesus also includes being baptized.[4] The baptized include Jesus and James and John. Thus the disciples are related to Jesus in that they are baptized like he was, and more specifically, their baptism is like Jesus' in that it opens the possibility of being handed over and killed for the sake of the kingdom which is proclaimed (Mark 10:38-40). Thus the narratival coordination of these three ideas and their repetition "engenders a sophistication of beliefs through the generation of narrative frames linking the disciples' activity and fate to that of Jesus (and John)."[5]

Sophistication may also take place negatively. This is the case when the author employs techniques which portray characters in a negative light. For example, the use of "understand" and its narrative coordination with "discuss" with reference to the disciples in Mark is used to convey the impression that the disciples do not understand Jesus at all times. The strategy imparts information to the end that an increasingly sophisticated evaluation of the disciples is achieved by intensifying the portrayal of their limited understanding.[6]

The process of sophisticating the audience's views of the disciples in Luke 10–11 draws upon chapters 1–9. The questions of who is a disciple and what kind of belief and activity characterize a disciple will receive particular attention.[7] This is achieved by aligning the newer material with earlier ideas, such as hearing the word of God and acting upon it. By means of this word association, and with respect to female disciples, the reader is drawn back to primary female figures and their role in the narrative so far. In addition, the reader is able to develop an increasingly sophisticated view of female disciples in accordance with the progression of the narrative.

2. Ibid., 22.
3. Ibid., 26–27.
4. Baptism is here used metaphorically of suffering and death.
5. Ibid., 28.
6. Ibid., 29–30.

7. This sophistication will continue to the end of Luke's Gospel and through the book of Acts. To anticipate what follows later in the story, the notion of discipleship will receive a strong contribution from the resurrection and Pentecost narratives, and the mission to the Gentiles.

The Mission of the Seventy (Luke 10:1–24)

*The ministry of the seventy missionaries
resulted in joy and success*

The mission of the "seventy others"[8] is unique to Luke's Gospel and contains a number of narrative parallels with the mission of the twelve described in Luke 9:1–6.[9] Both groups are commanded to take nothing for the journey, both are to proclaim the kingdom of God and cure the sick, and both are to shake the dust off their feet as a protest against towns that do not accept them.

On the return of the twelve after the initial mission, Luke informs the reader that "the apostles told Jesus all that they had done" (Luke 9:10). What follows this is an ironic series of incidents which portray both the lack of understanding of the disciples and their lack of faith. They cannot provide food for the five thousand (9:13–14), Peter fails to grasp the significance of the Transfiguration (9:33), the disciples could not cure a demon possessed boy (9:37–43), they fail to understand the passion prediction (9:44–45), they argue over status (9:46–48), they draw restrictive social boundaries and try to exclude those outside the group (9:49–50), and they want to call down fire from heaven on a Samaritan village (9:51–56). This then leads into the mission of the wider group in chapter 10.

Clearly the narrative implies that there is still much for the twelve to learn. In fact, following the failure of the disciples to expel the demon from the boy, Jesus reprimands them "as the prime example of a 'faithless and perverse generation.'"[10] This less-than-ideal behavior of the twelve in chapter 9 means that the inclusion of others in mission comes as no surprise.

At a narrative level, therefore, the mission of the seventy not only seeks to extend the ministry of the twelve, but also to address its shortcomings. At this point the reader cannot help but wonder regarding the success of the former endeavor given the mindset of the twelve. However, the main contrast between these missions lies in the way the author sums up their relative success. The end of first mission is plainly described, whereas the return of the seventy is announced with joy and with success. The presentation of similar events with divergent results, and the contrast between feelings at opposite ends of the emotional range, are deliberate narratival techniques which are

---

8. The manuscript tradition is fairly evenly divided between "seventy" and "seventy two." See Metzger, *Textual Commentary*, 126–27. Tannehill, *Narrative Unity*, 1:232–33, has a helpful discussion on the symbolism involved in both numbers.

9. On the complex issues of sources and historicity, see Bock, *Luke*, 2:986–91.

10. Tannehill, *Luke*, 163.

used to cast judgement on the respective missions. The disciples set apart in the first mission had been unable to set the boy free from demonic oppression (9:39), whereas the disciples in the larger mission could do precisely what the smaller unit failed to do (10:17). Their success brought them joy, and also brought joy to Jesus and to God ("through the Holy Spirit"). The story line thereby gives higher endorsement to the second mission than to the first by means of two factors. First of all, there is a fuller description of the commissioning and sending. Second, the high point of the story is its conclusion with a joyful response of both the seventy and Jesus himself (10:17–24).[11] Hence, in the larger picture of Luke's story "the emphasis falls on the second sending, to which the sending of the twelve is preliminary."[12]

A third technique also highlights the preliminary nature of the mission of the twelve compared to that of the seventy. This technique highlights the cosmic consequences of both missions. Only the work of the seventy leads to Jesus' claim that he saw "Satan fall like lightning from heaven" (10:18). The second mission is the one which is accorded this dramatic consequence for Satan. By means of their inclusion in the second mission, the disciples are intimately involved in Satan's downfall. Their ministry is more than "simply the expulsion of random demons that they may come across in their travels but the beginning of the complete overthrow of Satan's rule."[13] The powerful connection between the ministry of Jesus and the ministry of the seventy is strengthened further on in the narrative when Jesus says that if he "drives out demons by the finger of God, then the kingdom of God has come upon you" (11:20). This echoes the command to the seventy disciples to explain their work with reference to the kingdom of God. He said: "Heal the sick . . . and tell them, 'the kingdom of God has drawn near to you' . . . 'be sure of this: the kingdom of God is near'" (10:9, 11).[14]

Without a doubt, therefore, this second, wider mission is portrayed in a much more positive light and is "a high point in the experience of the disciples."[15] The seventy return with joy, a joy shared by Jesus in his recognition of Satan's fall from heaven (10:18), his thanksgiving in the Holy Spirit (10:21–22), and his pronouncement of blessing on the disciples (10:23–24).

---

11. Ibid, 151.

12. Ibid. Both of these missions are, of course, preliminary to the worldwide mission that Jesus will announce in 24:46–49.

13. Garland, *Luke*, 429.

14. Tannehill, *Narrative Unity*, 1:150.

15. Ibid., 1:232.

The seventy included female as well as male disciples

We have already seen that a group of women—including Mary Magdalene, Joanna, and Susanna—were constant companions of Jesus and were clearly regarded by Luke as part of the wider company of his disciples (Luke 8:1–3). Given their appearance at the crucifixion scene (23:49—"all his acquaintances, including the women who had followed him from Galilee, stood at a distance watching these things") and the words of the angel in the tomb (24:6–7—"remember how he told you while he was still in Galilee, saying that the Son of Man must be delivered up into the hands of sinful men, be crucified and on the third day rise"), it is hard to avoid the conclusion that such women were not merely intermittent followers, but a regular part of his entourage since the early days in Galilee.[16] If this is the case, any basis for regarding the mission of the seventy as a purely male enterprise is external to the text itself. We have already argued that a theology of women in Luke's Gospel must be derived from its narrative context rather than a cultural context (see above on 8:19–21). And on a purely narratival basis, there appears no warrant to exclude the women from this mission.[17] The use of masculine pronouns throughout the account does not prohibit this, for the androcentric nature of the language requires masculine forms for mixed gender groupings.[18] That the disciples were sent out in pairs not only echoes the Jewish requirement for dual testimony (Deut 17:6; 19:15), it also indicates that, if the women were part of this larger company, they would not be traveling alone.

The women were given a proclamatory role in parallel with the male disciples

We need to stress that the women's participation in this larger mission is not an argument from silence; it is predicated on the basis of their ongoing involvement with Jesus, including hearing his words and witnessing his proclamation of the kingdom. Given this, the women share the proclamatory role of the mission together with the male disciples, because their announcing the kingdom of God is an extension of the proclamation of Jesus. From the narrative itself, is inconceivable to draw the conclusion that the proclamatory task was carried out only by the male disciples, with any female disciples

---

16. Contra Spencer, *Salty Wives,* 141–42.

17. Bauckham, *Gospel Women,* 112. Reid, *Better Part,* 42, considers the women's involvement as a possibility.

18. Bauckham, *Gospel Women,* 200.

present merely as passive bystanders. There is no gender-based task allocation to deal with healing the sick (Luke 10:9), neither is it given with respect to proclamation of the kingdom. So, the women are equal participants in the mission at every level. This challenges the stance of numerous scholars who regard Luke as muting the voice of women in the Christian community by assigning them purely to the roles of service and support.[19]

Mary and Martha (Luke 10:38–42)

In another incident unique to the Third Gospel, Jesus lodges at the home of Mary and Martha. Readers familiar with John's Gospel know that the sisters reside with their brother Lazarus in the village of Bethany (John 11:1-2), although Luke does not name the village because it is chronologically out of sequence in his journey to Jerusalem motif.[20] It is also clear from John's Gospel that the family has close ties of friendship with Jesus (John 11:5). This closeness is also evident in Luke's account, where Jesus calls the sisters by name. Martha is likely the older of the two sisters and the householder, as it is she who welcomes Jesus into her home.[21] Read in light of the two mission commissionings (Luke 9:1-6; 10:1-12), Martha contrasts those who oppose the kingdom and thereby do not receive Jesus or his disciples.[22] Seim notes that her name, which means 'sovereign lady' or 'ruling lady,' serves to emphasize her dominant position.[23]

> *Mary is commended by Jesus for listening to his words as her first priority, even at the expense of fulfilling a socially regulated role*

To 'sit at the feet' of a teacher/rabbi was a technical term for receiving instruction as a pupil (Acts 22:3; *m. 'Abot.* 1:4—"let your house be a meeting-house for the Sages and sit amid the dust of their feet and drink in their words with thirst"). Commentators are divided as to whether a woman assuming such a position was forbidden or permitted. This stems from the somewhat ambiguous nature of the rabbinic evidence itself. Although there were some sages who allowed daughters to be taught the law,[24] there are some particularly

---

19. Tetlow, *Women and Ministry*, 103; Schüssler Fiorenza, *In Memory*, 49, 161, 167; Corley, *Women and the Historical Jesus*, 30; Spencer, *Salty Wives*, 118–19.
20. Garland, *Luke*, 450; Nolland, *Luke*, 2:603.
21. Spencer, *Salty Wives*, 166; Witherington, *Women*, 101; Garland, *Luke*, 453.
22. Carter, "Getting Martha out of the Kitchen," 268.
23. Seim, *Double Message*, 98.
24. See *m. Sota* 3.4; cf. *m. Ned.* 4.3.

negative statements to be considered as well, whereby women were discouraged and possibly even forbidden from so doing.[25] Of course, this material dates from a period after Jesus, but there are no compelling reasons to think that attitudes changed significantly in the intervening time.[26] We should also acknowledge that teaching one's daughter the Torah is vastly different from a rabbi going into the house of another woman and teaching her.[27] So we can probably state with some confidence that many would have raised their eyebrows in concern at Mary's posture.[28] As Green states, "To defend this transposition, the word of the Lord is required!"[29]

It is also abundantly clear that social norms dictated that women would be involved in serving and the preparation of food. This expectation is, in fact, reflected in Martha's reproach.[30] Consequently, Mary defied social norms and pressure in at least one, and possibly even two senses.[31] Jesus endorses this departure from the social norm.

We are told that Martha was preoccupied with domestic tasks, probably preparing food for Jesus.[32] She feels put out that her sister has left her to do the work by herself. Her request to Jesus conveys an expectation that he will agree with her and tell Mary to leave her position at his feet and to help her sister.[33] But instead, she is dealt a mild rebuke. Jesus does not insist that Mary help Martha, but views Martha as "worried and distracted by many things" (Luke 10:41). It is not her service that is being questioned, but her anxiety and preoccupation.[34]

It is unclear how we are to take the expression "there is only need of one thing" (10:42—ἑνὸς δέ ἐστιν χρεία).[35] Some have taken this to refer to the need of only one dish, and Martha needs to be content with simple

---

25. "Because it is written, 'And you shall teach them to your sons'—not your daughters" (*b. Kid.* 29b). See also *m. Sota* 3.4; *t. Sota* 21b.

26. See Seim, *Double Message*, 101–3.

27. Witherington, *Women*, 101.

28. Keener, *Acts*, 1:601. Note that the evidence that Reid, *Better Part*, 150–52, cites from the NT regarding Jesus conversing with women is irrelevant to this particular issue, as is the formal education of aristocratic women in the Greco-Roman world.

29. Green, *Gospel of Luke*, 434.

30. Seim, *Double Message*, 103.

31. Tannehill, *Narrative Unity*, 1:136; Garland, *Luke*, 455.

32. We are not told whether any of the disciples are present or not.

33. The Greek particle οὐ expects a positive answer.

34. Seim, *Double Message*, 107; Spencer, *Salty Wives*, 170.

35. For the textual mess at this point, see Metzger, *Textual Commentary*, 129; Seim, *Double Message*, 104. The reading in the text probably has the best claim to originality. For a defence of the longer reading, see Fee, "One Thing is Needful?" 61–75.

preparation.³⁶ More likely, however, it is informed by the following clause "Mary has chosen the better (ἀγαθήν)³⁷ portion," given that this latter expression is introduced by the conjunction γάρ ("for"). This not only coordinates the two clauses, but enables the first to be explained by the second. Thus, the "one thing" is the "better portion," i.e., listening to the teaching of Jesus rather than being engaged in domestic duties. For this she is commended. Of course, this does not mean that domestic duties are irrelevant and can be ignored. Rather, "the shock value provided by such violation of common sense is part of what etches [Jesus'] teaching upon the mind."³⁸

With reference to the previous parable of the Sower, Martha is a living example of the word of God being choked out by the cares of life (8:14).³⁹ Mary on the other hand, is portrayed as the ideal follower of Jesus, a hearer of his words. As Nolland states:

> The episode is concerned to show that even when domestic service has been harnessed to the purposes of the kingdom of God, the danger remains that its concerns will take possession of us. Manifesting as the worries of this life, it will distract from the central necessity of hearing the word of God and choke off the effect of the word that has already been sown.⁴⁰

Jesus' words elsewhere concerning kingdom priorities, and his specific commendation of Mary's behavior suggest a second-order narrative proposition: *The first priority for a female disciple is to listen to the teaching of Jesus. For Jesus, women in God's kingdom are no longer solely defined by socially regulated roles.* The strength of this proposition is clear from the fact that it is not undermined at any point in Luke's two-volume work. As such, it is a key reference point for Luke's characterization of women in that the guidelines for such characterization are established by kingdom parameters not socially regulated norms.

---

36. Corley, *Private Women*, 138; Hutson, "Martha's Choice," 146–47.
37. The adjective is used here in a comparative sense.
38. Nolland, *Luke*, 2:605.
39. Garland, *Luke*, 453.
40. Nolland, *Luke*, 2:605. The point of the story is hardly, as maintained by Schottroff, *Lydia's Inpatient Sisters*, 206–7, that "Jesus (that is to say, Luke's Jesus) expects housework to be done quietly and out of sight."

> *In adopting the position of one who listens to Jesus as her*
> *first priority, Mary is a blessed disciple of Jesus and belongs*
> *to his true family*

Jesus' pronouncement accords with several other statements made in surrounding pericopes concerning hearing and doing the word. By implication, if Mary responds positively to what she hears from Jesus she is part of the blessed company of disciples (Luke 10:23–24; 11:28) and she becomes part of the true family of Jesus (8:19–21).[41]

The final clause "which will not be taken away (ἀφαιρεθήσεται) from her" (Luke 10:42) is quite elusive in meaning. The point appears to be that the teaching of Jesus has eternal value,[42] whereas the performance of domestic chores does not. Alternatively, Jesus may be stressing that in no way will Mary be asked to leave her position to assist Martha.[43]

By means of this story, Luke expands the category of discipleship to include women as well as men. Clearly he is not drawing demarcation lines between male and female disciples in the sense that the women serve and the men are devoted to the word of God.[44] Nor does the narrative allow us to interpret the passage, as do a number of feminist interpreters, not as descriptive of a historical event in the ministry of Jesus, but as prescriptive for leadership roles in the church of Luke's day. For example, Barbara Reid[45] and Kathleen Corley,[46] both following Elisabeth Schlüssler Fiorenza,[47] read the account of Mary and Martha against a subtext of an ongoing squabble regarding women's roles in the early church. In this scenario, Luke, through the words of Jesus, sides with those who wish to keep women in silent passive roles. Mary, in sitting at Jesus' feet, portrays submission to male leadership. Martha, on the other hand, represents those involved in ministerial service, who are 'burdened' by those who are opposed to women's involvement in ministry. Such proposals, however, not only rest on a number of questionable translations,[48] they privilege a hypothetical subtext over Luke's

---

41. Tannehill, *Narrative Unity*, 1:137; Wall, "Martha and Mary," 24–28.
42. Evans, *Saint Luke*, 474; Bock, *Luke*, 2:1042.
43. Nolland, *Luke*, 2:605
44. Seim, *Double Message*, 108.
45. Reid, *Better Part*, 144–62.
46. Corley, *Private Women*, 133–44.
47. Fiorenza, "Martha and Mary."
48. For example, Reid fails to appreciate that: (i) the English prepositions "with" and "concerning" have an overlapping semantic range; (ii) δέχομαι only means "receiving the word" in certain contexts, it is not a meaning inherent in the word itself; (iii) just because διακονία can be used by Luke of ecclesial leadership, does not mean that it is

actual narrative, and questionably employ allegory as an interpretive approach for that narrative. Sadly, these views muzzle the narrative's powerful message about Jesus' regard for women and the nature of their membership in the kingdom of God.

This episode yields a powerful narratival proposition beyond its specific details. The proposal is informed by the convergence of three interests in the narrative. These interests, and the proposition that arises comes together as: *Listening to the words of Jesus, full-fledged discipleship, and membership in his true family provide the coordinates for a new realm of life for women who believe in Jesus.*

The Queen of the South (Luke 11:31)

The Queen of Sheba was attuned to God's work and made right theological judgments with respect to the Lord

Jesus' reference to the "queen of the South" is part of a larger pericope where he castigates his generation as evil and unbelieving: "This generation is evil. It seeks a sign and no sign will be given to it except the sign of Jonah. For just as Jonah became a sign to the Ninevites, so will the Son of Man be to this generation" (Luke 11:29-30). In this context Luke introduces the character of the queen of the South (i.e., queen of Sheba), thus employing another female and male story pairing. "The queen of the South will rise at the judgement with the people of this generation and she will condemn them, because she came from the ends of the earth to hear the wisdom of Solomon, and indeed, something greater than Solomon is here" (11:31).

Jesus' reference to "the queen of the South" invokes the accounts of 1 Kings 10:1-13 and 2 Chronicles 9:1-12. The queen's visit to Solomon represents the highpoint of Israel's influence in the ancient Near East. Israel's vocation to be a light to the nations arguably climaxed at this point. This woman, from the most prominent kingdom in southwest Arabia,

---

always used in this sense, a point typified by the non-technical use of the cognate verb in passages prior to this (4:39; 8:3). Corley makes too much of the semantic difference between τρυβάζω (which appears as a variant reading in vv. 41-42) and θορυβάζω. While it is true that cognates of the latter term appear in Luke-Acts in the context of public uproar and disorder, the passive form of the verb is clearly used of personal distress and alarm in Acts 20:10. Carter, "Getting Martha out of the Kitchen," 264-80, also reads the text against the backdrop of early church ministry. In contrast to the feminist interpreters though, he regards both sisters as positive examples of service. Martha is, however, distracted by ministry duties and is called to listen to the word of the Lord to reorient her vision and focus.

represented the richness of the nations in Israel's region, both in terms of wealth and culture. She would have been either the sole ruler[49] or the "highest level emissary"[50] of her nation. Thus this queen is a person of significant social-political power. Her historical significance is demonstrated by the nature of her visit, and by the fact that she was received into the court of the king. Her journey had both theological and political aims. Theologically, she searched out Solomon's wisdom and its source. From a political and trade point of view, she sought an alliance. Green writes: "The queen came to test Solomon and found that he was indeed an agent of Yahweh, having been placed on the throne by him." This recognition leads to "an alliance . . . signified by mutual gifts."[51]

Interestingly, it is the queen, not Solomon, who holds center stage in the story as recounted in the book of Kings. Her characterization is more developed than Solomon's in the initial story and she is presented favorably. Walsh, writing explicitly about her characterization, describes the high regard of her character as follows:

> In order to investigate rumours about a new maritime power in her sphere of influence, she is willing to undertake an arduous journey. . . . She is sceptical about what she has heard, and she subjects not only Solomon himself but his entire court and administration to careful scrutiny. When he proves even greater than rumour made him, she is also forthright enough to admit her error. Her acclaim of Solomon's glory is unstinting, with no hint of jealousy or envy, and it issues in remarkable and profound praise of Yahweh as ultimate source of the king's blessings as well as of his responsibilities. Her gifts are lavish . . . . In short, the narrator portrays her as a determined, honest, generous, and thoroughly admirable monarch.[52]

For Luke, the queen's theological significance lies in her appropriate understanding of what God was doing through Solomon and Israel. 1 Kings 10:9 records the queen of Sheba praising Solomon's God with the words, "Blessed be Yahweh your God, who has delighted in you and set you on the throne of Israel. Because Yahweh loved Israel forever, he has made you king to execute justice and righteousness." Her understanding is theologically proper, and moreover is properly her own and not the result of Solomon's efforts.[53]

---

49. Walsh and Cotter, *1 Kings*, 126.
50. Kitchen, "Arabia, Arabians," 38.
51. Green, *Gospel of Luke*, 464.
52. Walsh and Cotter, *1 Kings*, 128.
53. Bellis, "Queen of Sheba," 27.

*The queen of Sheba was better able to comprehend the
work of Yahweh than the present generation*

The way in which the queen of Sheba character serves Luke's narratival aim is quite significant. She is an example of an insightful person who is able to recognize the great things God does in history. The gender of the queen of Sheba was not a barrier or limitation to her comprehension of God. Jesus contrasts her with his audience and argues that her insight and response far outweighs that of the crowd. The queen understood the work of Yahweh and responded correctly. The crowd, however, does not recognize the significance of Jesus and their response is superficial at best. Accordingly, they will be judged and condemned for their failure to understand and respond to him. Moreover, not only will they be judged, the queen of the South is one who "will condemn (κατακρινεῖ) them" (Luke 11:31).

In light of this, and the way in which her gender is merely stated, it appears that Luke was as positively disposed towards females as to males when it came to them making theological evaluations. There is no hint in the text that the queen's gender is even a potential stumbling block to her theological judgement and claims about God. It seems that for Luke, the ability to make theological decisions in line with God's actions is not pre-disposed by gender. There is no universal principle at work in Luke's mind whereby women are disqualified from the right interpretation of God's actions.

*The extent of God's inversion of socio-religious
expectations even includes a Gentile woman*

The queen of Sheba was an outsider to Israel; she came from the "ends of the earth" (Luke 11:31). The geographical location of the queen is important to Luke's plotline and to his theology. In terms of the plotline of Luke-Acts, Luke is advancing the argument that God's wisdom is for the world, not merely the preserve of Israel. Theologically, Luke is also making the case that an 'outsider' may make the response which usually corresponds to an 'insider.' The theme of outsiders becoming insiders as a result of a believing response to God and Jesus is consolidated by the immediate and dramatic reference to more outsiders. Jesus draws upon the Ninevites to make his point: "The men of Nineveh will be raised in the judgement with this generation and they will condemn it because they repented at the preaching of Jonah, and, behold, something greater than Jonah is here" (11:32). The earlier reference to the "sign of Jonah" (11:29) thus includes four elements:

(i) preaching judgement, (ii) preaching repentance, (iii) a clear action of divine rescue, and (iv) an openness to outsiders. As Garland states:

> The lesson from Jonah is that God is the God of all and that God's steadfast love is accessible to all. The gospel ends with Jesus teaching the written Scriptures to his disciples—that the Christ is to be raised on the third day and that repentance and forgiveness of sins be preached in his name to the nations.[54]

Together, "the queen of Sheba and the people of Nineveh, Jesus says, will participate in the resurrection and in eschatological judgement, where their status as the people of God will be manifested in their judgement of recalcitrant Israel."[55] The entire episode of Luke 11:29–32 thus serves as an example of Luke's insistence on unexpected reversal. In this instance the reversal, which the queen of Sheba illustrates, is "a pagan approaches the messenger of God and listens to him."[56] This corresponds to a narratival-theological thread aptly described as "the inversion of expectations"[57] that Luke uses in order to argue for two points which are central to his theology. The first is that Jesus is not an important man in the way the Gentile world thought of an important man. He is, rather, God's Son—the Messiah. The second is that followers of Jesus are often unexpected believers. Time and time again, Luke-Acts makes use of a story, teaching, preaching or parable which yields a surprising result. These surprising results are not what the people of Jesus' time expected, nor even what the ideal reader/hearer expects. The foundational point for Luke's theology is that God is responsible for the surprising events.[58]

Jesus' positive reference to the queen of Sheba is especially striking given the context of Second Temple Judaism and Greco-Roman culture. One could argue that a foreign woman may be the prime example that Luke could have chosen in order to illustrate how an outsider to the religious circle of Judaism expresses religious insight. She is presented as a theologically capable and astute woman; a prime model of religious debate and insight. This is an impressive contrast to how the queen of Sheba has been presented in Jewish thought.[59]

---

54. Garland, *Luke*, 486.
55. Green, *Gospel of Luke*, 465.
56. Beale and Carson, *Commentary*, 324.
57. Simons, "La pregunta de María," 63.
58. Ibid.
59. See the references cited in Bellis, "The Queen of Sheba: A Gender-Sensitive Reading."

Anticipating wider themes in Luke-Acts

The author of Luke-Acts is not averse to mentioning the highest expression of female rulership

Acts 8:27 records the encounter between Philip and a man described as "an Ethiopian eunuch, an important official in charge of all the treasury of Candace, queen of the Ethiopians." This verse ends by relating the fact that "this man had gone to Jerusalem to worship." The eunuch would have been excluded from "full participation in Jewish worship (Deut. 23:1; also 1QSa 2.5-6)."[60] However, Philip is able to offer him inclusion in the new people of God. The reference to the queen *Candace* whom the eunuch served is significant. The name itself may have been a designation for a dynastic succession of queens,[61] but whether her name was personal or dynastic, she (not a king) was significant enough to be the reference point of this man and for his high status.[62] The characterization of the woman Candace is very straightforward: she is a powerful woman who is served by appropriate men, one of whom is pious. Candace is an example of a woman who holds, at the very least, one of the highest of ruling offices. The narrator mentions this favorably. The parallel between Candace the queen of Ethiopia and the queen of Sheba should not be missed. Both volumes of Luke's work contain a positive example of a powerful queen. For the author these are facts of history that do not carry any negative connotations in the narrative.

Healing of a Crippled Woman on the Sabbath (Luke 13:10–17)

In the account of the healing of the crippled woman on the Sabbath we have another instance of a Lukan male-female pairing.[63] The corresponding incident occurs in Luke 14:1-6 with the healing of the man with dropsy. Both incidents occur on the Sabbath and both are miracle-controversy stories[64] whereby the religious authorities are silenced by Jesus' action and subsequent rebuke.

---

60. Bock, *Acts*, 340, continues with the hope that was laid before the eunuch: "In the eschaton, eunuchs will be restored to full worship (Isa. 56:3b–5)."

61. Peterson, *Acts of the Apostles*, 293.

62. See the discussion on the possible meanings of the title in Marguerat, *Les Actes Des Apôtres*, 306, n.16.

63. See Seim, *Double Message*, 11–24, for a list and discussion of these pairings.

64. Form critics normally classify the account as a miracle/pronouncement story.

Chapter 13 commences with a call to repent or perish (Luke 13:1-5), followed by the parable of the Barren Fig Tree (13:6-9) as a graphic illustration of the fate that awaits those who do not repent and bear fruit. This follows warnings regarding discerning the nature of the times and the need for watchfulness (12:35-48, 54-56). Here in 13:10-17, the indignation of the ruler of the synagogue is typical of those who lack such discernment and who are not bearing fruit and need to repent of their myopic vision. Given the outcome that "all those who opposed him were put to shame" (13:17) clearly implies the synagogue ruler was not alone in his antagonism, he thus functions as a representative of the Jewish leadership who need a dramatic change of perspective.[65]

A crippled woman was the equal beneficiary of God's compassion expressed through Jesus' kingdom ministry and healing power

The reader is informed that the woman had "a spirit of infirmity" (Luke 13:11—πνεῦμα ἀσθενίας). It is unclear whether we are meant to understand this as a physical disability occasioned by some form of demonic oppression,[66] or whether "spirit" is being used in an idiomatic sense of a debilitating condition.[67] The fact that Jesus does not perform any exorcism tends to favor the latter interpretation, although his later reference that "Satan had bound her for eighteen years" (13:16) may indicate the former. At the very least it is a demonstration of the ongoing conflict between Jesus/God and Satan.[68]

The woman was "bent over double and unable to straighten completely" (13:11). Here the Greek is ambiguous with εἰς τὸ παντελές belonging either with μὴ δυναμένη giving "she was completely unable to straighten," or with the infinitive ἀνακύψαι giving "she was unable to straighten completely." Either way, the severity of her complaint is underlined, a complaint which in contemporary medical terms is probably *spondylitis ankylopoietica*, a fusion of the spinal bones.[69]

Jesus takes the initiative to heal the woman upon seeing her dire need. In a culture where women were often shunned by men in public, Luke once

See Bock, *Luke*, 2:1213.

65. The Mishnah tractate *Sabbat* discusses rabbinic teaching concerning various forms of "work" on the Sabbath.

66. So most commentators—e.g., Bock, *Luke*, 2:1215; Talbert, *Reading Luke*, 163; Tannehill, *Narrative Unity*, 1:65..

67. Nolland, *Luke*, 2:724.

68. Bock, *Luke*, 2:1214.

69. Ibid., 2:1215.

more demonstrates that the compassion of God cannot be limited by cultural forms and practices.[70] Such compassion is accentuated by the physical touch of Jesus that accompanies the healing. The woman is a passive character, whose only direct action is that following her healing she "began to glorify God" (13:13), thus typifying the gracious response of those who are beneficiaries of Jesus' kingdom power and ministry (4:15; 5:25–26; 7:16; 17:15; 18:43). The fact that Luke pairs this account with that of the man with dropsy in the following chapter is a clear indication that he wants to convey the general point that *both men and women are equal beneficiaries of God's compassion and blessing.*

> *The crippled woman is an equal participant in the covenant community of God's people regardless of her gender and social status*

In order to convey to his antagonists the right of the woman to be healed on the Sabbath, Jesus labels her "this daughter of Abraham" (Luke 13:16), not a common designation in Jewish literature.[71] This statement is striking in its emphatic position in the Greek sentence. It is clearly a covenant description, parallel to "son of Abraham" in 19:9. It is also instructive that both of these terms are applied to those who are socially marginalized.[72] This serves to highlight the status of such people as equal participants in God's covenant community. The implication of this for the crippled women is that as a participant of that community, she is surely to be the recipient of its privileges and blessings. More than this, it serves to facilitate an *a fortiori* argument whereby "daughter of Abraham" is contrasted with "ox or donkey" in order to highlight the misguided sense of priorities shared by Jesus' opponents.[73] The contrast is further made by a play on words with "untie (λύει) the donkey or ox," and the daughter of Abraham to be "freed" (λυθῆναι) from her bond. The greater importance of the latter is further highlighted by the statement of divine necessity (ἔδει). This statement of divine necessity is employed to stress the importance of this daughter of Abraham. She has intrinsic value in God's eyes despite her social status. Jesus rejects any notion of her social status, or indeed for that matter any legal accretions of Second Temple Judaism, being an impediment to her full rights as a member of

---

70. Ibid., 2:1216. It is extremely hard to agree with the contention of Reid, *Better Part*, 167, that the incident portrays the woman as the victim dependent upon the male Jesus for healing.

71. The idea occurs in a couple of places in 4 Maccabees, and in later rabbinic literature For a discussion, see Seim, *Double Message*, 43–49.

72. Witherington, *Women*, 70.

73. Bock, *Luke*, 2:1218.

God's covenant people. *Women who are participants in God's covenant community are entitled to the full blessings that derive from it.*

The Parable of the Lost Coin (Luke 15:7–10)

*Jesus depicts his own kingdom ministry
in terms of a diligent housewife*

The parable of the Lost Coin forms another male-female pair with the parable of the Lost Sheep. However, the introductory formula is slightly different with the omission of ἐξ ὑμῶν ("of you"). Thus Jesus is not inviting his audience to place themselves in the position of the woman as he does with the shepherd. This, amongst other factors, leads Susan Durber to contend that the parables of Luke 15 reinforce sexist values by portraying women as domestic housewives and prostitutes. The text assumes a male reader, with the poor housewife compared to the man "who roams the open land with his substantial property."[74] However, Durber fails to appreciate that a shepherd was also a despised profession at the time, and she does not take into account that he was unlikely to be the owner of the sheep.

More to the point, Kenneth Bailey points out that such a pairing of male-female imagery is almost non-existent in Middle Eastern sacred literature.[75] He proposes that Jesus used this example as a deliberate critique of a culture that devalued the role of women to the extent that a pious male Jew would regularly thank God that he had not been born female.[76] Luke's Jesus thereby stresses the importance of women in God's kingdom. Furthermore the female analogy would resonate more specifically with women disciples.[77]

Given the context of the parable, where Jesus responds to the criticism of the religious authorities concerning his association with tax collectors and sinners (Luke 15:1–3), the referent for the woman in the parable is clearly God/Jesus.[78] The search by the woman for the coin corresponds to the search by God/Jesus for the lost. Consequently, this parable is consistent

---

74. Durber, "Parables of the Lost," 59–78 (esp. 62).

75. There is a similar rabbinic parable concerning ten coins, although the subject is a man not a woman, and the lost coin represents the words of the Torah (*Cant. R.* 1.9).

76. See the prayer preserved in *The Authorized Daily Prayer Book of the United Hebrew Congregations of the British Empire*, 7.

77. Bailey, *Lost*, 93–100. Also Witherington, *Women*, 34.

78. Plummer, *Saint Luke*, 370, obviously reluctant to seek God portrayed by a woman, asserts that the woman represents the church.

with other passages in Scripture where the character and mission of God/ Jesus, often in the context of searching for his people, is depicted by the use of a female/feminine analogy.[79]

The Parable of the Judge and the Widow (Luke 18:1–8)

The parable of the Judge and the Widow is a further example of the positive use of a woman in an analogy. Unlike the parable of the Lost Coin, here the woman does not function as a referent for Jesus/God, but is a positive example of the persistence required of believers in prayer. Thus she is more closely allied with discipleship and reinforces other uses of women as models of discipleship throughout Luke's Gospel.

There are some similarities between the parable and Sirach 35:15–19, where God responds to the cries of the widow and dispenses swift vengeance on the oppressor. But the differences between the accounts tend to indicate that rather than a conscious borrowing, the parable draws on the widow as a common OT symbol of oppression. This combined with the propensity of Palestinian judges in NT times to be less than honorable,[80] provides the setting for the parable.[81]

The judge is introduced as one who, by his own admission, neither fears God nor respects his fellow human beings. The covenant demanded special protection and consideration for widows,[82] although it is clear that they were still being exploited at the time of Jesus (Mark 12:40). This woman sought justice from the uncaring judge, with the iterative imperfect ἤρχετο ("kept coming"—Luke 18:3) capturing her repeated attempts to persuade him.[83] But her efforts initially made no impact on this obdurate character. In fact, the condensed nature and structure of the narrative actually leads the reader to view the judge as the opponent of the woman.[84] However, the reader is prepared for a change of heart by the use of ἐπὶ χρόνον "for some

---

79. See Deut 32:18; Isa 42:13–14; 49:13–15; 66:7–9, 13; Jer 31:20; Hos 11:1–4; Luke 13:34.

80. Bailey, *Peasant Eyes*, 131.

81. In small towns or local villages, people of prominence were appointed to the judicial role as required. See Jeremias, *Parables*, 153. Spencer, *Salty Wives*, 277–78, believes that the judge's uncaring character tends to indicate a local Roman magistrate rather than a Jewish magistrate.

82. Exod 22:21–24; Deut 10:18; 27:19; Ps 68:5; Isa 1:17, 23; Mal 3:5.

83. Spencer, *Salty Wives*, 264–76, has a discussion of the legal difficulties encountered by women in Jewish society and possible scenarios behind the story here.

84. Scott, *Hear Then the Parable*, 183.

time" (18:4). The change of heart comes not due to a re-evaluation of his own attitudes, but because he wants to be rid of the woman's constant pestering.[85]

The parable is applied by means of a rhetorical question that argues in an *afortiori* manner. An emphatic negative οὐ μή (18:7) is also employed to accentuate the situation. If a selfish uncaring judge will eventually grant justice to a persistent widow, how much more will God grant justice to his people who consistently petition him.

The woman functions as a model for
discipleship with respect to prayer

The woman is aggressive and assertive. Contrary to cultural norms and expectations, she has no legal counsel and represents herself before the judge. She does not address the judge in respectful terms, merely and blatantly requesting justice. Moreover, like the housewife who sweeps the floor until she finds the lost coin, this widow persists at the task until she is awarded justice.[86]

Most feminist writers read the story as a positive comment on women's affirmative action.[87] Reid is one exception, contending that the woman is domesticated by the parable into a docile model of prayer.[88] However, the widow functions as a model for persistent prayer for both male and female believers. She is not domesticated into anything; her assertive behavior stands as an example. This is emphasized both by the Lukan introduction in 18:1, and the application in verses 6–8.

For Luke, believers are exhorted to faithfulness in prayer for two reasons: to be vindicated by God (Luke 18:7–8a), and to be found faithful (18:8b). Consequently the woman functions as a model of both persistence and faithfulness. This parabolic instance serves to reinforce other real-life examples of women throughout Luke's Gospel who function as positive models of discipleship in its various aspects.

The woman functions as a model for
seeking justice in an unjust world

Spencer is critical of Reid and other feminist interpreters who insist that the widow has been domesticated and tamed by Luke from an active pursuit of justice to a purely contemplative act of prayer. He rightly points out that this misconstrues the function of prayer in Luke-Acts. He states:

---

85. The interpretation of ὑποπιάζω is an interpretive crux at this point in the story. See Forbes, *God of Old*, 203–5.

86. Spencer, *Salty Wives*, 277–83.

87. See, for example, Schottroff, *Lydia's Impatient Sisters*, 101–18.

88. Reid, *Better Part*, 194.

> More to the point, however, prayer in Luke is by no means purely passive, pensive, and apolitical. Mary's Magnificat, as a song of praise, blends together prophecy, prayer, and psalm in a political tour de force (1:46–55). . . . . Anna's praise and prophecy are of a piece with her praying—and all focus on the "redemption of Jerusalem," a thoroughly justice-centered, political, eschatological, revolutionary concept, especially when the Holy City is under Herodian-Roman control.[89]

The eschatological nature of things means that God will act finally and decisively to bring ultimate justice and overthrow all evil at the End. In the meantime, however, he works through human agents to give small glimpses of this ultimate justice. Prayer is a crucial component of this divine-human partnership, where God's will for justice and righteousness is mediated through and extended to sinful human beings. Seen in this light prayer is anything but passive. Rather, it is a purposeful, vibrant component of active engagement with God and his cause/will.[90] This is reflected briefly in the Lukan version of the Lord's Prayer (Luke 11:2), and comes to concrete expression in the prayer of the disciples after being warned by the Sanhedrin to no longer proclaim the name of Jesus (Acts 4:23–31).

Consequently, the widow in our parable is both a model for prayer, and a model of those who, through active partnership with God in prayer, struggle resolutely and persistently for justice in the world. This interpretation is given supporting weight by the final pronouncement in Luke 18:8b: "Nevertheless, when the Son of Man comes will he find faith on the earth?"[91] In context, "faith" relates primarily to faithfulness in prayer. However, faith is clearly a virtue that is more encompassing than prayer, and involves alignment and commitment to God's values and will. Spencer again is insightful:

> The parable's widow then supremely typifies that rare and special faith God seeks, which, driven by the hope of God's ultimate reign of justice, moves with brisk dispatch and bold determination to bring God's justice on earth.[92]

---

89. Spencer, *Salty Wives*, 305.

90. Ibid., 305–11.

91. Commentators have consistently wrestled with this difficult pronouncement, and its relationship to the larger parable. For a discussion, see Forbes, *God of Old*, 208.

92. Spencer, *Salty Wives*, 313.

Summary of Narratival Propositions

The ministry of the seventy, which included men and women, resulted in joy and success. In this mission, female disciples of Jesus were given a proclamatory role together with the male disciples.

Mary is commended by Jesus for listening to his words as her first priority, even at the expense of fulfilling a socially regulated role. Indeed, for Jesus, women in God's kingdom are no longer solely defined by socially regulated roles. In terms of Luke 8:21, in adopting the position of one who listens to Jesus as her first priority Mary is a blessed disciple of Jesus and belongs to his true family. Thus, the first priority for a female disciple is to listen to the teaching of Jesus. Further, listening to the words of Jesus, full-fledged discipleship, and membership in his true family provide the coordinates for a new realm of life for women who believe in Jesus.

The Queen of Sheba was attuned to God's work and made right theological judgments with respect to the Lord. In fact, she was better able to comprehend the work of Yahweh than the present generation. Here we see that the extent of God's inversion of socio-religious expectations even includes a Gentile woman.

A crippled woman was the beneficiary of God's compassion expressed through Jesus' kingdom ministry and healing power. She was also an equal participant in the covenant community of God's people regardless of her gender and social status. It is clear from Luke's Gospel that both men and women are equal beneficiaries of God's compassion and blessing, and that women who are participants in God's covenant community are entitled to the full blessings that derive from it.

Jesus depicts his own kingdom ministry in terms of a diligent housewife, and the persistent widow functions as a model for both discipleship with respect to prayer, and for seeking justice in an unjust world.

One feature of this section of the narrative which we have been exploring is that Luke's positive characterization of women is seen not only in living encounters between women and Jesus, but also in parables whose central character is a woman. Luke's overall portrayal of women is thereby becoming rich and diversified. In addition to this, there is a developing tendency to present women in a way that is not bound by the strictures of Second Temple Judaism. These factors produce a certain narrative pressure through which the texts' inherent theological judgments emerge.[93]

---

93. For the notion of narratival pressure, see Rowe, "Biblical Pressure and Trinitarian Hermeneutics," 295–313.

Theological Propositions

The theological propositions with respect to women that emerge from the Travel Narrative are:

1. God's kingdom is a theo-social reality in which men and women may equally receive his compassion.
2. The kingdom of God is the new and ultimate context for life and ministry which may reconfigure a female believer's native socio-cultural background.
3. The ideal human response to God's revelation is to listen to his words and reflect his character to other people.
4. God authorizes women to hear, teach and confirm Jesus' words through signs, prayer, and living justly.
5. God's mission includes women through whom he speaks and works to establish his kingdom despite Satanic and socio-cultural adversity.

CHAPTER 6

Jerusalem Narrative (Luke 19:29—24:53)

The Widow's Offering (Luke 21:1-4)

THE ACCOUNT OF THE widow's offering follows immediately on from the denunciation of the scribes who "devour widow's houses" (Luke 20:45-47).[1] Here the offering of a poor widow, whether poor due to the unjust actions of others or simply life circumstance we are not told, is used as the final installment with respect to Luke's ubiquitous theme of wealth and possessions.

The poor widow models discipleship with
respect to wealth and possessions

In the literary context the widow serves as a double contrast.[2] On the one hand, her true piety is contrasted implicitly and ironically with the religious elite who act piously but in reality oppress those like her (Luke 20:45-47). On the other hand, there is an explicit contrast between her offering and the

---

1. This enigmatic expression has been interpreted in different ways. For a discussion, see Nolland, *Luke*, 3:976.
2. Seim, *Double Message*, 95.

offerings of the rich. The rich placed their presumably large gifts[3] into the temple treasury,[4] but the "needy" (πενιχράν) widow gave "two *lepta*."[5]

The *lepta* was the smallest coin in circulation in Palestine, and was a minute fraction (1/100th) of a day laborer's daily wage.[6] So this was, on the surface of things, a totally insignificant offering and one that would contribute in no substantial way to the temple coffers. But once more Jesus is concerned not with outward appearance but inner motives. The rich gave "out of their abundance," whereas the widow gave "from her lack" (21:4). The latter expression is qualified as "she gave all that she had" (πάντα τὸν βίον ὃν εἶχεν ἔβαλεν). Jesus does not denigrate the offerings of the rich,[7] but is concerned to stress the higher value of sacrificial giving. The true value of the gift is not determined by its size, but what it costs the giver. Thus, the widow functions as a model of sacrificial giving and hence a model of discipleship with respect to wealth and possessions. This recalls the provision of the women who accompany Jesus in 8:1-3. But whereas they are examples of the more moderate strand in Luke's Gospel regarding a proper use of possessions, the widow is an example of the more radical strand of total renunciation.[8] Once again, Jesus (and Luke) is not averse to using women as examples and models of kingdom living and discipleship.

Peter's Denial and the Astute Servant Girl (Luke 22:54-62)

Luke's characterization of those closest to Jesus takes a somewhat negative turn in chapter 22. This chapter describes a number of failures of character and judgment by those in his most intimate circle: Judas betrays Jesus (Luke 22:1-6, 47-48), an argument about who is the greatest breaks out amongst the disciples immediately following Jesus' declaration of a new covenant in his blood (22:24-30), the disciples fall asleep instead of praying that they do not fall into temptation (22:39-46), and Peter publicly renounces Jesus

---

3. Luke omits Mark's reference to the rich donating "much" (πολλά).

4. The γαζοφυλάκιον is here most likely referring to a series of (thirteen) horn-shaped receptacles that were used for the placement of offerings. The narrow opening and wide lower section was designed to prevent theft (see *m. Shekalim* 2.1; 6.1, 5).

5. For a discussion of the financial means and social status of widows in Judaism and early Christianity, see Seim, *Double Message*, 228-48.

6. Garland, *Luke*, 818.

7. Contra Nolland, *Luke*, 3:980.

8. On these two strands regarding wealth and possessions in Luke, and their potential reconciliation, see Forbes, *God of Old*, 228-33.

three times (22:54-62). In this chapter, and in chapter 23, Jesus' behavior is a strong contrast to that of the disciples in that he stays true to his Father and his mission. The dramatic actions by which he does so include his acceptance of the titles of the Son of God (22:70-71) and of king of the Jews (23:3b) whilst fully aware of the consequences of these actions. Jesus is not alone in providing a contrast to the failure of some of his disciples. Some of the stories which Luke includes in the latter portion of his narrative make a significant contribution to his characterization of women by means of contrast with Jesus' more prominent male disciples.

A servant girl is keenly insightful with respect to people and their significance

Women are mostly absent from Luke's trial scenes. However, when a female character is present she plays a decisive key role. After Jesus' arrest, Peter follows at a distance and eventually warms himself by a fire. Here he is approached by an insightful woman. She is a "servant girl,"[9] and she has a role to play which distinguishes her from other people in the background narrative. In fact, her distinctive actions set off a chain of events. She watched Peter carefully: "seeing him in the firelight and looking intently at him" (Luke 22:56). Her conclusion about his identity was based on thoughtful observation. She is the first to identify Peter as one of Jesus' associates. Before any male is able to publicly identify Peter, she said: "This man was with him too." An unidentified man points out Peter's association with Jesus only after a period of time ("a little later") elapses following the woman's recognition of Peter. The narrative explicitly notes that a third person recognizes Peter "after about an hour had passed" (22:58, 59). This descriptive account portrays an insightful woman. It is not proposing that women are more insightful than men at all times. However, the reader who follows the train of the narrative is led to understand that women may be insightful with respect to persons and their significance.

The servant girl's insight is consistent with the insight demonstrated by Mary, Elizabeth, and Anna in the infancy narratives. They also came to astute conclusions based upon events occurring around them. Their judgments were based upon their unique insights and were accurate. There is no story in Luke which negatively portrays the theological judgment of a female follower of Jesus.[10] Furthermore, there are no stories in Luke's

---

9. This servant "announces her suspicions to the gathered company that he [Peter] was with Jesus. According to John 18:16 she was the doorkeeper. What gives him away, she does not say, but Peter, the rock, begins to crack." Garland, *Luke*, 891.

10. Though Martha may have made an error in judgment relating to hospitality and

Gospel that undermine the value of women as witnesses and reporters. Consequently a second order narratival proposition emerges: *Women may be keenly insightful with respect to people and their significance.* The story of the girl who rightly identifies Peter complements the author's portrayal of women as witnesses and so paves the way for them as insightful interpreters and valid reporters of the resurrection of Jesus.

On the Way to the Cross (Luke 23:26–31)

*Jesus is mindful of the plight of women
even on the way to the cross*

Jesus' route to be crucified takes a couple of unforeseen turns. First, Simon of Cyrene is compelled to carry Jesus' cross. Second, Jesus is able to interact with women who were "mourning and lamenting him" (Luke 23:27). Jesus "turned" in order to speak to them (23:28). This detail is interesting given that Simon of Cyrene had been made to carry Jesus' cross, presumably because Jesus was no longer physically able to do so. The fact that Jesus turned to give his attention to the women despite his excoriation and death sentence reveals a strong deliberateness about this action. The mere fact that he says something to the women is thus as significant as it is surprising. Jesus took the attention off his own immediate predicament and focused on their plight. He said to the women:

> Daughters of Jerusalem, do not weep for me; weep for yourselves and for your children. For indeed the days are coming when they will say, "Blessed are the barren women, the wombs that never bore and the breasts that never nursed!" Then they will say to the mountains: "Fall on us! And to the hills: Cover us!" For if they do these things when the tree is green, what will happen when it is dry? (23:31).[11]

---

household duties, it was not a theological error.

11. "Daughters of Jerusalem" is "not intended to present them as symbolic representatives of Jerusalem or Israel. . . . Mothers, and their children, will be innocent victims like him." Garland, *Luke,* 919. Green believes the women represent the population of Jerusalem and therefore by implication there is nothing particular about the gender of the women. This view fails to notice the immediate words of Jesus are to people whose gender is such that they may have barren wombs and breast feed babies. Therefore, to our mind, Jesus is speaking to women. If this group of women has a representative function, and this may be the case, then they represent the *women* of Jerusalem. Green, *Gospel of Luke,* 815–16.

These words anticipate a future disaster. In addition, they are words of concern as Jesus laments the suffering that is to come upon women of this region. This is not to say that Jesus is not concerned about men. However, the mourning of the women gives rise to the opportunity for Jesus to make a prophetic announcement about the fate of Jerusalem. Further, the gender of the women is apparently no barrier to his surprising and purposeful interaction with them.

The Death of Jesus (Luke 23:44–49)

*The women from Galilee were faithful to Jesus,
even to the devastating end of his life*

Luke's crucifixion scene is horrific. Jesus has been treated with extreme brutality. He is surrounded by criminals, as well as being mocked by oppressors and former followers alike. He is also apparently defeated by liars and the enemies of God. Nature itself compounds this awful scene: "and darkness fell over the whole land until the ninth hour" (Luke 23:44). This should not be construed purely as a metaphor, for Luke clarifies that "the sun was obscured" (23:45).[12] For the author, nature's darkness was appropriate to the death that was taking place, for this is indicative of a situation when darkness is allowed to reign. At his arrest Jesus had designated the entire episode of his judgment and rejection as "your hour and the power of darkness" (22:53).[13] In Luke and Acts light and darkness are also employed symbolically, with light representing God's presence and the availability of God's salvation (Luke 1:78–79; 2:32; Acts 13:47; 26:18, 23), and darkness representing human lostness and the power of evil (Luke 1:17; Acts 26:18). However, God responds to this darkness by tearing the temple curtain which symbolically extends the impact of Jesus beyond the Jewish people. In an immediate sense this is reflected in the confession of the centurion.[14] From a human perspective, the broader impact of Jesus beyond his death is

---

12. On the potential symbolism attached to the darkness, see Forbes, "Darkness over all the Land."

13. Tannehill, *Luke*, 344.

14. "The 'power of darkness' is particularly formidable, but does not nullify the presence of God, who responds to the escalation of hostility against his Son by rending the curtain of the temple. . . . [T]he Evangelist reports the effects of Jesus' death on the centurion. . . . Luke has begun to demonstrate that rejection of Jesus by Jewish leadership, in alliance with diabolic power (22:53), leads not to the squelching of the divine purpose but to the widening of the mission to embrace others." Green, *Luke*, 824.

contingent upon the faithfulness of his female disciples. Women will play key roles in the broader functional extension of God's work through Jesus.

After Jesus' death the multitude divides into two portions. The "crowds" ultimately "returned home" (Luke 23:48). These people, who had come to see "the spectacle" leave the scene when a carcass is all that is left of Jesus. Those "who knew him, including the women who had accompanied him from Galilee" do not leave the scene of the crucifixion so quickly (23:49). They were "standing at a distance, observing these things" (23:49). It is interesting to note that those who ultimately were not followers of Jesus—the crowds—are given a single designation. On the other hand, Luke includes the detail that women as well as men were present as those who remained attentive to Jesus at the crucifixion. It is also noteworthy that the male disciples are no longer referred to as 'disciples' at this point, for they had not been behaving as disciples of Jesus since the departure of the group for the Mount of Olives (23:39).[15]

The women are supremely faithful to Jesus in his darkest hour. There is no indication that the women were less faithful than the male disciples, in fact the opposite appears to be the case. The narrative makes this clear. The "women who had accompanied him from Galilee" (23:49), are named shortly thereafter in 24:10. Read in conjunction with 8:1–3, these women are those who had been a constant part of his ministry entourage. "They ventured with him to Jerusalem and stuck with him to the end. . . . Their presence reveals that they had not only received the word with joy; they are deeply rooted and in a time of testing do not fall away (8:13)."[16] The enduring faithfulness of the women is a stark contrast to the number of male disciples who had not been faithful to Jesus in multiple episodes which immediately precede this story: the male disciples fall asleep during Jesus' despair in the Garden of Gethsemane (22:39–46), Judas betrays Jesus (22:47–53), and Peter denies any relationship with him (22:54–62).

The Resurrection of Jesus (Luke 24:1–12)

Here we see an example of the resolution of a narrative knot *par excellence*. Not only was Jesus abandoned by his male disciples, but his fate effectively meant the death of the Messiah of Israel, and the victory of the religious leaders and the Roman authorities. This problematic knot is further complicated by the empty tomb. The resolution of this knot is achieved by the women disciples in three ways, all of which highlight their steadfastness:

15. Tannehill, *Luke*, 346.
16. Garland, *Luke*, 930.

carrying out culturally expected tasks, remembering Jesus' words in light of the angelic declaration, and their announcement to the male disciples in the face of skepticism.

The women are sufficient witnesses to the empty tomb

The women from Galilee knew where Jesus had been buried (Luke 23:55), and returned to that place "on the first day of the week, at early dawn" (24:1). The narrative does not break its consistent reference to this group of women: the "they" throughout the resurrection narrative are the same "women who had accompanied him [Jesus] from Galilee" (23:49, 55). There is no mention of the addition of men to this group, nor would it be a reasonable inference that men were present to treat the body of Jesus with the spices that the women had prepared (24:1). Thus, the women from Galilee approach the rock-hewn tomb without the company of men. So begins a key-turning point in Luke's story. The narrative will confirm Jesus as the Messiah who, contrary to social expectations, fulfilled the Jewish socio-religious expectations of salvation. Further, his ministry, death and resurrection will be established as the sole basis for the forgiveness of sins and salvation for all people.

The women approached the tomb with a common task at hand. They were carrying "spices they had prepared" (Luke 24:1). There is nothing to suggest that they were concerned about anything other than attending to the corpse of Jesus. However, they found that the entrance stone no longer blocked the way into (and out of) the tomb. The women entered the tomb but "they did not find the body of the Lord Jesus" (24:3). The body was gone; the tomb was surprisingly and strangely empty. The women alone are witnesses of this peculiar phenomenon. Moreover, the witness of the women was sufficient to ascertain that Jesus' body was missing and the tomb was empty. Their record of the events that took place did not require validation by any other authority—neither an institutional nor a gender authority figure.

The narrative gives the impression that the witness of the women as the first observers of the empty tomb is unproblematic. This occurs against the cultural and legal background of a woman's testimony being considered invalid. Josephus wrote with respect to the legal testimony of women: "But do not let a single witness testify; but three, or two at the least, and those whose testimony is confirmed by their good lives. But do not let the testimony of women be admitted, on account of the trivial and rash nature of their gender."[17] Interestingly, Josephus is commenting on the Pentateuch, in which there is no specific claim regarding the inappropriateness of a woman

---

17. Josephus, *Ant.* 4.8.15/4.219.

as a witness. Josephus, therefore, has gone beyond the injunctions of Torah and interpreted the Pentateuch through the traditions of Judaism which were contemporaneous to the writing of Luke's Gospel. Clearly, Luke has not adopted the interpretive position of some of his contemporaries regarding women as witnesses, for his characterization of women includes the fact that they are trustworthy.

What is important for Luke, however, is that in line with Deuteronomy 19:15, there were multiple witnesses to the empty tomb. In the same way that multiple women observed the empty tomb, the two angels function as heavenly witnesses to the fact that Jesus is alive. Luke's narrative thus operates in line with Pentateuchal thought when it repeatedly stresses the importance of witness. Yet clearly the gender of the witness is not an issue.

> *The role the women play in the resurrection narrative is predicated on their longstanding inclusion in the group of Jesus' disciples*

The narrative records that after Jesus' death, "all his acquaintances and the women who had accompanied him from Galilee were standing at a distance, observing these things" (Luke 23:49). That is, the women were a subgroup within "the multitude of disciples" who were with Jesus as late as 19:37. In fact, the women from Galilee are a very important 'corporate character' in the burial and the resurrection narrative. They followed Joseph of Arimathea when he laid the body of Jesus in the rocky tomb, and these same women returned after preparing spices and perfumes for Jesus' body (23:55–56). The identity of some of these women is specified during the resurrection account: "they were Mary Magdalene and Joanna and Mary the mother of James . . . as well as the other women with them" (24:10). The naming of the women is intended to "reflect how extraordinarily important, for the whole story of Jesus, were the events of which they are the sole witnesses."[18]

18. Bauckham, *Gospel Women*, 297–98. Bauckham concludes that based upon the names given to the women in the various Gospel accounts of the resurrection, seven women were involved as the first witnesses to the resurrection. He writes that "in all, there are five named women (Mary Magdalene, Mary the mother of James and Joses, Salome, Joanna, and Mary of Clopas), together with two anonymous but specified women: the mother of the sons of Zebedee and the mother of Jesus." Ibid., 299. Bauckham believes that Joanna (who is unique to Luke's Gospel) is named in the resurrection narrative because she was his particular eyewitness source for the story about the empty tomb. (In the same way, he believes that Cleopas is the eyewitness from whom the Emmaus story was sourced. Ibid., 301.) Garland suggests that this may be the case because she appears to be at the center of a chiastic structure in 24:9–10 and Luke appears to be working independently from Mark 16:1–8 and John at this point. Therefore, argues Garland, the source for his empty tomb account is likely to be Joanna. Garland, *Luke*, 942.

The designation "from Galilee" is obviously a geographical pointer. Yet it is also a temporal marker, indicating how long these woman had been part of Jesus' circle of disciples.[19] For the author, the crucial role of women as witnesses and heralds of the empty tomb is based upon their longstanding inclusion in the group of Jesus' disciples. Their understanding of the resurrection is predicated on the fact that they had been with Jesus as his disciples and heard him speak in Galilee.[20] Thus the author anchors the credibility of their witness as those who are thankful participants in Jesus' work.[21]

When the women find the tomb empty they are also met by two men (angels) in dazzling clothing who ask a simple question: "Why do you seek the living among the dead"? This is followed by a statement of fact that Jesus "is not here, but he has risen" (24:5b-6a). Significantly, the only way by which the angels enable the women's interpretation and understanding of the empty tomb is by means of encouraging the recall of the words of Jesus. That is, the previously spoken words of Jesus are the key to understanding what has taken place after his death: "Remember how he spoke to you while he was with you in Galilee" (24:6b). Therefore the women must have been with Jesus in Galilee to hear his words so that they would later understand how the empty tomb relates to the larger story of Jesus.[22] What Jesus had said to them in Galilee was "that the Son of Man must be delivered into the hands of sinful men, and be crucified, and on the third day rise again" (24:7). The author reports that "they remembered his words and returned from the tomb and reported all these things to the eleven and to all the rest" (24:8-9).[23]

> *The women have the ability to rightly interpret*
> *Jesus' words concerning his resurrection*

After Jesus' death, the majority of Jesus' disciples awaited an uncertain future in Jerusalem. Meanwhile, outside the rock-hewn tomb, the women

---

19. This has been addressed in our discussion of the women in Luke 8 and 10.

20. "The women are addressed as persons who had themselves received Jesus' teaching in Galilee." Green, *Luke*, 838.

21. Ibid., 839.

22. The summary of Jesus' message by the angels (24:7) is "a composite of phrases from the major passion and resurrection prophesies of Jesus in 9:22, 44; 18:32-33. . . . According to verse 8, the women remembered Jesus' words. . . . [T]he apostles and other companions are still where they were in 9:45 and 18:34, unable to understand or accept these events. Progress will require not only a personal encounter with the risen Messiah but also instruction from him about how God has been working in the world." Tannehill, *Luke*, 350-51.

23. "Like Mary at the beginning of the gospel (1:38), these women respond with faith." Garland, *Luke*, 942.

from Galilee became the first to understand Jesus and his ministry in a new way (Luke 24:8–9). What separated their understanding of Jesus from that of the other disciples was their interpretation of the empty tomb in the light of Jesus' words about his resurrection on the third day.

Once they were directed to the words of Jesus, the women had the internal resources to recollect these words. This is described very simply, in a matter-of-fact manner: "and they remembered his words" (24:8). The women must have heard these words themselves as part of Jesus group of disciples (9:18–22). Jesus' words alone were sufficient to enable the women to rightly interpret the event; they did not introduce any error to their interpretation, nor did they leave off any aspect of what had occurred. They got it right. There is nothing in the resurrection narrative to cast doubt on the ability of women to rightly interpret the words of Jesus. Therefore, the gender of the women from Galilee did not disable their ability to properly interpret the empty tomb through the previous words of Jesus. Indeed, throughout Luke's Gospel women have been astute witnesses and interpreters of divinely initiated events.

The comprehension of the women is also a significant contrast to the other disciples. Whereas the male disciples were unable to make the connection with Jesus' previous words about his death and resurrection based on the testimony of the women, the women were immediately able to make this connection based simply on the words of the angels.

The women correctly applied the words of Jesus to the situation of the empty tomb. The next step they took was to interpret the words as they related to themselves and to the other disciples: "They returned from the tomb and announced all this to the eleven and to all the rest" (Luke 24:9). There is a direct link between the women's "remembering" and "returning" to the other disciples. The correct interpretation of Jesus' words immediately compels them to tell others that Jesus was not dead but alive. The activity of remembering leads to telling, for the correct interpretation of Jesus' words is not complete without this activity of announcement. A narrative technique is in play here, by which the placement of scenes next to each other establishes the causation of one event by another (not merely correlation).[24] The women announce their new realization to others. Hence, the strength of insight and witness which is exemplified by women reaches its apex precisely at the climax of the narrative.

---

24. Green, *Luke*, 823.

The women are appropriate heralds of the resurrection of Jesus

According to Luke's narrative, the witness of the women from Galilee is the first step in transforming the other disciples' theological beliefs about Jesus.[25] This is because Jesus' prophecy about his resurrection is actualized when the women believe and announce the angelic message to the other disciples. What was once Jesus' prophecy for his people, is now a reality which forms the basis of the new life of his people.[26] Furthermore, what had been spoken in the Scriptures about God's plan has been fulfilled in the hearing of the women.[27]

The angels are God's agents who pass on special revelation to the women. The women are then, in turn, the next bearers of special revelation in the events which comprise the proclamation of the resurrection of Jesus. "No other visitor to the tomb, not even a male disciple, could reproduce it. Hence the Gospel stories of the empty tomb perpetuate the women's witness: all readers of them are confronted with *their* distinctive witness."[28] The witness of the women was a unique and unrivalled step in the progress of Easter faith.

As far as the author of the Third Gospel is concerned, women were sufficiently qualified for the task of announcing both the empty tomb and the angelic claim that Jesus was alive. There is nothing in the narrative that discredits them from adequately carrying out this role. This attitude was not shared by the eleven and the others with them (which may have included other women). The report by Mary Magdalena, Joanna, Mary the mother of James and the other women was met by nothing but resistance. The women's "words appeared to them as nonsense, and they did not believe them" (Luke 24:11).[29] According to the thrust of the story the disciples should have believed the women; there is no reason which is native to the Gospel of Luke which provides grounds for not believing them.[30]

---

25. Grundman, *Das Evangelium nach Lukas*, 3:441.

26. Agua Pérez, Agustín del, "El testimonio narrativo de la resurrección de Cristo," 255.

27. Ibid.

28. Italics are Bauckham's. Bauckham, *Gospel Women*, 276.

29. "Their reaction seems to be the precursor of Celsus' mockery that only half-frantic women have seen the resurrected Jesus in their crazed imaginations (Origen, Cels. 2.55)." Garland, *Luke*, 943.

30. In the second general audience of his pontificate, on April 3, 2013, Pope Francis noted the contrast between men and women in the Gospel narratives about Jesus' resurrection and the women's proclamation of this event. He said that Jesus' apostles and disciples "find it harder to believe in the risen Christ. . . . Peter runs to the tomb, but stops before the empty tomb. Thomas has to touch the wounds of the body of Jesus with

The disciples' disbelief continues despite the women's claims and the background of Jesus' life, works, and words about the resurrection. Despite this, there is no indication that the women from Galilee either denied or adjusted their report under such pressure. The women remain steadfast in their theological interpretation of the empty tomb. This is consistent with Luke's earlier portrayal of Mary and Elizabeth as being faithful to God, and also his portrayal of the steadfast presence of female disciples with Jesus until his death on the cross.[31]

The resistance which meets the women from Galilee highlights the fact that they were sufficient to the task. Luke makes it clear that the disbelief of the others occurs despite the fact that once they had received the witness of the women, this larger group of people also now had access to the same events and interpretation by the angels and the women. Luke has established a strong contrast between the women of Galilee and the other followers of Jesus. Peter proves a case in point. After rising and running to the tomb, he bent down to look in and saw the linen cloths by themselves. The result is that "Peter is 'amazed' (θαυμάζων) but this is not yet a believing comprehension."[32]

The author again overturns any cultural resistance to the reception of special revelation by women with the story of the travelers on the road to Emmaus.[33] In this episode, the travelers tell Jesus that some of their women had "amazed" them with a report of Jesus' missing body and a vision of angels who claimed Jesus was alive (24:22–23). The travellers appear unconvinced about the truth of this claim. For this reason they are rebuked by Jesus: "Oh, how foolish you are, and slow of heart to believe all that the prophets have declared!" (24:25). These travellers should have done what the women were able to do, namely draw together the fact that the tomb was empty along with the special revelation the women had received. Both the travelers and the women had the same information; but whereas the women believed, the travelers were puzzled.[34]

---

his own hands." For Francis, the women behave differently in that "they are driven by love and they know to accept this proclamation [of the Resurrection] with faith." Moreover, "they believe and immediately transmit it; they do not keep it for themselves." *National Catholic Reporter*, April 12–15, 2013, 8.

31. Bauckham concurs: "Female recipients of divine revelation should not come as a surprise to readers of Luke's Gospel. All three women in his strongly gynocentric birth and infancy narratives are such." Bauckham, *Gospel Women*, 276.

32. Tannehill, *Luke*, 351.

33. We have labelled this as 'cultural' as there is no *prima facie* theological basis for this resistance in the OT.

34. "The joyful expectations for the redemption of Israel in the infancy narrative have been passed on and are expressed again by the disciples on the Emmaus road. But

Jesus' interpretation of himself through the Scriptures in Luke 24:25–27, 44–47 provides a parallel to the opening of Luke's Gospel. Just as the infancy narratives provide the announcement of salvation from God supported by the witness of the OT, so Jesus announces his resurrection through the lens of various OT Scriptures. Given the role of women in the infancy narratives and in the resurrection narrative, it can be observed that the Lukan message of God's new work in Jesus was prophesied in Scripture, uniquely attested to by women and confirmed by Jesus.

There may have been a tension between the author's point of view and the early perspective of the other disciples with respect to the validity of women as appropriate witnesses to the empty tomb. It is probable that this resistance was not solely related to the claim that the tomb was empty. As indicated above, the gender of the women would have been problematic for their status as valid witnesses. Thus Luke has something new and distinctive to say about women as witnesses to the empty tomb: *women may be the first witnesses to God's works, they are fit to interpret what they witness, and to herald these things to others.*

The second order narratival proposition above is fleshed out through a number of narrative and theological points in Acts. In his second volume Luke makes it clear that it is the words of Jesus and the words about Jesus which are the authoritative and powerful means of God's communication to the world. Hence, gender is not causally related to the success or failure of the proclamation of the resurrection of Jesus. In addition, the power and authority of the message does not reside in the herald *per se*. The ministry of the Holy Spirit ensures that God's special revelation is active and powerful in the midst of the diverse ministries of the early Christian movement. It is the Holy Spirit who primarily enables the continuing memory of Jesus and the proclamation of the theological significance of his life and ministry. Jesus' own words, their Old Testament background, and special revelation received by the early church are the source of such a message. In view of these factors (amongst others—such as the specific use of characters) Acts promotes a new anthropology in which gender is not a stand-alone factor

---

now they speak of a past hope that has been disappointed. Reliable interpreters of God's purpose in Luke 1–2 (angels and inspired prophets) spoke of Jesus as the Messiah who would redeem Israel from oppression. The disciples on the road to Emmaus were right to share this hope, but they, like the other disciples, did not reckon with Jesus' rejection in Jerusalem." Ibid., 354. He continues: "The references to the prophets in verse 25 and to Moses and the prophets in verse 27 make it clear that the disciples should have been able to recognize from scripture the necessity of the Messiah passing through suffering to glory[:] . . . first century Jews, whether they believed in Jesus or not, did not approach scripture as a document whose meaning was limited by the original historical context of the words." Ibid., 355.

which dictated whether or not a person could be a courier and herald in the service of such a message.[35]

The women are amongst those commissioned to proclaim forgiveness in the name of Jesus to the world

After the episode on the road to Emmaus, Jesus appeared to those who received the report from the travelers on the road (Luke 24:36). These were "the eleven gathered together and those who were there with them" (24:33). This group included the female disciples of Jesus.[36] Jesus settled their minds with the proof that he was alive again and that they were not seeing his ghost. Once he ate the fish in their presence, Jesus explained that his past and present ministry was grounded in, and the fulfilment of, the "Law of Moses and the Prophets and the Psalms" (24:44). The OT refers to more than the Messiah's death and resurrection. Moses, the Prophets and the Psalms also anticipated the ministry of Jesus' followers: "repentance for forgiveness of sins would be proclaimed in his [Christ's] name to all nations" (24:47).

Those people who proclaim forgiveness in the name of Jesus are the same people to whom Jesus had appeared. This was because they are "witnesses to these things" (24:48). The disciples thus have a new identity and mission conferred on them: they are Jesus' "witnesses." This leads to a transition in Jesus' mission. He now shifts his focus from the work he has already accomplished to the work he will accomplish through the apostles and their companions. In this near future, the "eleven and their companions will have a central role[:] . . . Jesus commissions his hearers as his witnesses, giving them a task and a promise."[37] Thus, the commission as witnesses and the promise of the Holy Spirit make the proclamation of repentance and forgiveness of sins the mission and responsibility of the disciples.[38]

In Acts, Jesus' mission continues by the power of the Spirit who is the gift of the Father. The ministry of proclamation cannot be carried out by drawing upon the strength of nationality, gender or educational background. The Spirit will empower those gathered around their devotion to Jesus to carry out a ministry that is so powerful and far reaching that it is

---

35. This draws upon the contrast between the fragility of people and enduring power of the word of God which is set out in Isaiah 40–55. This is particularly encapsulated in Isaiah 40:6–8. Pao, *Acts and the Isaianic New Exodus*, 147–80.

36. "The 'eleven and their companions' refers to the circle of the apostles sans Judas -presumably women and men (vv. 9–10), those gathered in the opening chapter of Acts (Acts 1:12–26)." Green, *Luke*, 850.

37. Tannehill, *Luke*, 360.

38. Ibid., 361.

beyond the particular socio-cultural and innate attributes and distinctives of any individual or group. The significance of the commission and promise of Jesus also lies in the fact that "Jesus is handing over a task that was central to the missions of both John the Baptist and himself."[39] The mission of Jesus will continue through the eleven and their companions once their minds are able to understand Scripture.[40] In a sense this understanding has been foreshadowed by the women in their recollection of his passion predictions. The commission and gift are given with the assumption that the eleven and their companions will work together and not in isolation.[41] He blesses them as a group and thus approves them as co-workers for his sake.

Early on in his Gospel, Luke recorded Simeon's words that Jesus' ministry would have a salvific effect on the Gentiles (Luke 2:32). This work is not complete at the time of Jesus' resurrection, thus a "narrative need" is unmet.[42] It will be met through the ministry of the apostles and their companions. The mission conferred upon Jesus' people is of such a magnitude that all the nations would hear about the risen Messiah. This is the lens through which Luke's Gospel sets up Christian ministry for the new community of Jesus. This perspective will be complementary to that which is provided at the opening of Acts. As the Gospel of Luke comes to a close, the hearer/reader notices that the narrative leaves them with characters who are in a similar posture to those who opened the Gospel story: "The opening scenes of Luke are filled with waiting people: Zechariah and Elizabeth, Mary, and Simeon and Anna. The Gospel ends with waiting disciples, but the waiting is only to be temporary...."[43]

Summary of Narratival Propositions

Women continue to function, via the example of the poor widow, as models of discipleship with respect to wealth and possessions.

Women, as typified by the servant-girl, may be keenly insightful with respect to events, and people and their significance.

Jesus is mindful of the plight of women even on the way to the cross.

The role the women play in the resurrection narrative is predicated on their longstanding inclusion in the group of Jesus' disciples. These women from Galilee were faithful to Jesus, even to the devastating end of his life.

39. Ibid.
40. Ibid., 362.
41. Garland, *Luke*, 968.
42. Green, *Luke*, 853.
43. Garland, *Luke*, 968.

Moreover, they were sufficient witnesses to the empty tomb. The women had the ability to rightly interpret Jesus' words concerning his resurrection and they were appropriate heralds of the resurrection. They were also amongst those commissioned to proclaim forgiveness in the name of Jesus to the world. This demonstrates that women may be the first witnesses to God's works, they are fit to interpret what they witness, and to herald these things to others.

Theological Propositions

The following theological propositions arise from the passion and resurrection narrative with respect to women who are disciples of Jesus:

1. God's character is clearly reflected by female believers in instances of generosity and faithfulness.
2. God includes women within his new people as full-orbed disciples of Jesus.
3. God's words may be rightly interpreted and contextually applied by women.
4. Women may rightly announce the resurrection of Jesus to male and female disciples.
5. Women are included in God's mission to the extent that they may announce the good news of his salvation.

CHAPTER 7

The Purpose and Structure of Acts

Luke's Portrayal of Women in Acts

As WE MOVE FROM the Gospel to Acts we are immediately struck by the background role that women take in Luke's second volume. As Keener notes:

> This interest in women appears in both the Gospel and Acts but is more obvious in the former. . . . [T]he greater emphasis in the Gospel is not surprising. Many marginalized groups in the Gospel of Luke appear never or rarely in Acts [the poor, prisoners, lepers]; women fare better but also are affected by the shift in focus between the Gospel and Acts. This shift may reflect the nature of Luke's material; in the former work he has many traditions about Jesus and, in the latter, a tighter focus on the Gentile mission.[1]

Luke's portrayal of women in Acts was potentially affected by a number of factors, none of which are mutually exclusive. These can be identified as the available source material, literary conventions, the purpose of Acts, its narratival structure, and the selective inclusion of characters. At the most basic level is the source material available to the author. If Luke is generally faithful to his sources, a fact that can be demonstrated by the way he handles the Markan and Q material in the Gospel, then he would have been somewhat constrained by the "general historical reality" of these

---

1. Keener, *Acts,* 1:600–601.

sources.² Of course, we can only speak of sources for Acts in a general sense, for any reconstruction of source material must remain speculative. But the argument regarding sources actually works in two ways. In one sense, one could argue that Luke's depiction of women is constrained by a limited presentation of the involvement of women in the early church represented by an "androcentric bias"³ in his source material. On the other hand, "Luke's sources may also reflect a pre-Lukan interest in gender egalitarianism that emerged in the earliest decades of the Christian movement."⁴ Yet, if the latter is the case, it is likely that perspective was one with which Luke himself was sympathetic.

In terms of literary conventions, if Acts is to be aligned in some way with Hellenistic historiography, and most would say that it is, then the concern to portray historical facts would also have been a limiting factor on Luke's presentation of women. Although there remains a skeptical end of scholarship in this respect, where it is argued that Luke's concern for good theology is often presented at the expense of historical accuracy, cogent arguments remain that Luke has presented his theology in a way that does not compromise history.⁵ If this is the case, then Luke would have also been constrained by "the historical realities of his day rather than his own bias."⁶ So if, according to cultural expectations and constraints, there were limited opportunities for women to speak in public, fewer opportunities for leadership in the early church, and if most of the traveling missionaries were male, then Luke is not attempting to suppress women's involvement in the early church,⁷ but merely echoing the cultural and historical actualities of the day.⁸ Having said this, however, there is still bias at work, but it is bias constrained by source data and concerns about historicity.

The purpose of Acts, its narratival structure, as well as its selective inclusion of characters all determine the range of material which Luke presents to the reader. Consequently, this has a bearing on the narratival and theological propositions which emerge from the narrative. This selectivity

2. Ibid., 1:603.

3. Ibid., 1:601.

4. Ibid., 1:599.

5. See the excellent up-to-date discussion in Keener, *Acts*, 1:90–220. Alexander, *Acts in Its Ancient Literary Context*, 133–62, examines whether Acts, with respect to wider Greco-Roman literature, should be viewed as fact or fiction. She concludes that Acts breaks the bounds of both categories.

6. Keener, *Acts*, 1:603.

7. As in Tetlow, *Women and Ministry*, 103; Schüssler Fiorenza, *In Memory*, 49, 161, 167; Corley, *Women and the Historical Jesus*, 30; Spencer, *Salty Wives*, 118–19.

8. Keener, *Acts*, 1:602–3.

was also at play in the Third Gospel. This means that in both volumes, Luke's presentation of female disciples of Jesus will only surface primarily as it is oriented toward the purposes of the book, its structure and specific characters, who in turn serve this larger purpose and structure. We would expect, therefore, that Luke's characterization of women in Acts will not be fully orbed. He presents only a partial characterization of female disciples of Jesus to the extent that they serve the larger narratival and theological agenda.

Drawing on the above considerations, two points need to be made with respect to our study. First, in discussing a Lukan theology of women, we need to bear in mind that we do not have access to this theology beyond the narrative that conveys it. This limits the scope of the theological claims that can be drawn with respect to women in Lukan theology. Second, the narrative may be silent, or at least minimal, on some issues which interest contemporary readers such as the kind and extent of the roles played by women in the early church. This limits the ability of the Lukan narrative to prescribe for us the particulars of female discipleship and roles in the church today.

The Purposes of Acts: Theological and Apologetic

The internal evidence suggests that Luke and Acts are both written by the same author (Luke 1:1-4; Acts 1:1-5).[9] It appears that both volumes are part of a single project with a common goal,[10] although it remains unclear whether Luke envisaged a two-volume work at the outset.[11] But what was Luke's particular purpose with respect to Acts, and to what extent does this overlap or differ with respect to the purpose of the Third Gospel?[12] It is

---

9. For the relationship of the preface to Acts to the preface of Luke's Gospel, and the relationship of both to prefaces in Hellenistic historiography and technical prose, see Alexander, *Acts in Its Ancient Literary Context*, 21-42.

10. Peterson, *Acts of the Apostles*, 36; Maddox, *Purpose of Luke-Acts*, 3-6, demonstrates how unity of purpose can be seen in the conforming of the twin prefaces to Greco-Roman literary conventions, as well as the structural components that link both volumes. Marguerat believes that common authorship can be established by pointing to the literary homogeneity between the two documents (Luke and Acts). This homogeneity is due in large part to the common vocabulary (which includes distinctive Lukan features), and authorial idiosyncrasies which these documents share. The single authorship suggested by these features is consistent with the explicit authorial statement which claims authorship of Luke and Acts (Acts 1:1). Marguerat, *Les Actes Des Apotres (1–12)*, 17-18.

11. See Alexander, *Acts in its Ancient Literary Context*, 23-29.

12. In addition to the options discussed below, Johnson, *Gospel of Luke*, 3-10, suggests that Luke-Acts was written as a 'theodicy.' Squires, *Plan of God*, 191-94, contends

important to establish this for, as mentioned above, purpose drives the narrative, and the inclusion of characters and their portrayal.

In terms of theological focus, Luke clearly writes to show that in Jesus and his followers the Jewish hope of salvation has come to realization. Thompson argues for such continuity as follows:

> Luke's stated purpose in the preface to his Gospel, the language and style of his writing as "biblical narrative" and his explicit links between the OT, Luke's Gospel and Acts all indicate that Luke is writing for a Christian audience familiar with the promises and language of the OT in order to provide assurance concerning the continued outworking of God's saving purposes.[13]

Bock also highlights the continuity of God's actions in history in Luke's purpose for the book of Acts: "In a sense, the theme of Acts is that salvation is for all because Jesus is Lord of all, a view that has its roots in a program God set forth through the sacred promises. The Spirit's arrival is the indication that promises have moved from being made to being realized, as the speech in Acts 2 shows."[14]

Seen within this larger schema, and at the risk of oversimplification, the Gospel deals more with Christian origins, whereas Acts writes about particular aspects of the development and progression of the fledgling Christian movement. Bock writes similarly: "Whereas Luke's Gospel outlines his [Jesus'] ministry, the book of Acts shows how the risen Lord continued to be active and how the new community preached Jesus as central to God's plan."[15]

It is also possible to view the theological purpose of Acts with reference to the motif of the kingdom of God. In Acts, the kingdom of God is mentioned at both the very beginning (1:3) and its end (28:23, 31).[16] This *inclusio* suggests that the kingdom of God is the theological framework for the book and has a significant bearing on its overall purpose. Acts is, in fact, about the outworking of the kingdom of God in post-ascension history. Here we see a common theological thread between Jesus' teaching about the kingdom of God in the Third Gospel and the purpose of Acts. But whereas in Luke's Gospel the kingdom of God is bound up with the presence of Jesus, in Acts it is focused on God having raised Jesus from

---

that it was penned as a 'mission tool' to either assist Christians in the task of promoting the gospel.

13. Thompson, *Acts of the Risen Lord Jesus*, 19.
14. Bock, *Acts*, 24.
15. Ibid., 7.
16. The phrase also occurs in Acts 8:12; 14:22; 19:8.

the dead and sending the Spirit in such a way that a new people of God is established.[17] These people will serve God's universal mission of salvation, and Luke is concerned to present an account of key aspects of that mission and its historical development.

Central to the above is the continuing existence of Jesus as ascended Lord of all (Acts 1:9–11; 2:33–35; 3:21). As Rowe observes, this is theologically and sociologically decisive, for the resurrection and sending of the Spirit is the basis for a new human reality. His life

> transcends the normal human realm, that overcomes, as it were, the limitedness inherent to human situatedness and finitude . . . a kind of space in which the Lord stands outside of the system over which he presides or even creates a "zone" . . . in which the legal and political elements of human life are suspended and from which they are created and legitimized.[18]

This new "zone" of life as Rowe labels it, is basically the kingdom of God on earth. Much of Acts will be preoccupied with establishing what this new "zone" of life looks like. It is a powerful and subversive zone that turns life "right side up." With respect to the focus of our current study, it will be seen that women will be powerfully impacted and decisively reinterpreted by the new cultural realities which the ascended Lord creates.

In addition to Luke's overt theological purpose in writing Acts, it also appears that he has a certain apologetic intent. Having said this, there is a natural interplay between the theological purposes of Acts and its apologetic concerns.[19] But what is the focus of the apologetic? We need to examine this first of all because the direction of Luke's apologetic may shape his presentation of women, and second it provides the religio-cultural backdrop against which his presentation of women may reveal its distinctiveness.

Whereas it is relatively clear that Luke seeks "to legitimise the claims of the new movement,"[20] to whom he seeks to provide that legitimation is less clear. Alexander lists five main possibilities that have been proposed for the apologetic focus: (1) an inter-church apologetic that seeks to defend Paul against "rival theological interests"; (2) a sectarian apologetic seeking to defend Christianity to the non-Christian Jewish community; (3) an apolo-

---

17. On the resurrection of Jesus as the focus of Lukan soteriology, see Anderson, *The Theology of Jesus' Resurrection in Luke-Acts*.

18. This is consistent with the "lordship Christology" which is found in Acts. Acts 1 presumes the continuing activity of Jesus, it is about what Jesus "began to do and teach" (1:1) and continued to do Acts 2:33. Rowe, *World Upside Down*, 110.

19. As clearly demonstrated in C. Kavin Rowe's work, below.

20. Bock, *Acts*, 24.

getic addressed to the secular Greek world, more evangelistic in orientation; (4) a political apologetic—to defend Christianity before the Roman state. This may be quite general, or more specific in relation to a defence brief of sorts for Paul at his impending trial; (5) an apology addressed to Christians to enable them to better understand their faith and identity, and to empower them to give an appropriate defence of the faith when required.[21]

Alexander contends that the fact that so many plausible options exist regarding the direction of the apologetic indicates that either the apologetic intent is not consistently maintained, or that "Luke has failed in his task."[22] Moreover, unlike more overtly targeted apologetic works, the narrator never reinforces and takes up the apologetic intent; it is all done within the narrative. This serves to keep the apologetic focus muted. But it is in the latter speeches of Paul, where the terms ἀπολογία and ἀπολέγομαι feature prominently,[23] that we gain the most clues to Luke's apologetic intention. For even when Roman officials are present, the majority of the content of the speech is addressed to Jews and is presented as an intra-Jewish debate.[24] Moreover, in the final two chapters where Paul is on his way to Rome to give his defence before Caesar, we do not have any hearing or ἀπολογία before a Roman tribunal, but a defence of the gospel before Jewish community leaders who are divided in their response.[25]

It is in this final scene of Acts that Alexander notes an important narrative connection with the opening four chapters of Luke's Gospel. Following the nationalistic flavor of the infancy narratives, with the focus on the realization of the promises made to Israel, we then find an attack on Israel's doctrine of election both by John the Baptist (Luke 3:7–9), and less overtly by Jesus in the Nazareth sermon (4:18–30). In the concluding scene of Acts, the response to Paul's preaching to the Jews in Rome is at best ambivalent, and here Luke has Paul cite a full quote of Isaiah 6:9–10 as a final indictment. Alexander contends that Luke only included an abbreviated quote of this text in Luke 8:10 in order to hold over the full citation until the end of Acts so as to facilitate his apologetic intent. This narrative link between the Gospel and Acts not only gives narrative unity to Luke-Acts as a whole, it also helps explain why Acts ends where it does.[26]

---

21. Alexander, *Acts in Its Ancient Literary Context*, 184–87.

22. Ibid., 190.

23. Acts 22:1; 24:10; 25:8, 16; 26: 1,2, 24.

24. Even in his defence before Festus, Paul's speech is actually directed to King Agrippa.

25. Alexander, *Acts In Its Ancient Literary Context*, 217.

26. Ibid., 207–29.

Consequently, Luke is concerned to (1) show how God has been faithful to his promises to Israel and has worked out those promises in the life, death, and resurrection of Jesus; (2) explain why Jews have, to a large extent, rejected the gospel; and (3) validate the ongoing proclamation of the gospel (to the Gentiles) despite Jewish rejection. On this basis, Alexander concludes that Acts is largely an apology directed to a (Diaspora) Jewish context.[27]

Alexander's argument is compelling at several levels, however we are hesitant to totally dismiss the idea of any apologetic intent focused, even indirectly, on Rome. Although it is true that Luke does not always present Roman officials in a favorable light, it is hard to avoid the perception that he does present Christianity not only as the legitimate fulfilment of Judaism (*a religio licita*), but as a movement that is not politically subversive. Keener, for instance, favors an apology directed to Rome. Luke is concerned to demonstrate that the Christian movement is no threat to the political stability of the empire, and should be tolerated due to its continuity with Jewish biblical history.[28]

Rowe takes a more nuanced approach. Acts' theological vision of God in Christ creates a distinctive people who live a qualitatively different life to their non-Christian contemporaries. Thus the book of Acts aims "at nothing less than the construction of an alternative total way of life—a comprehensive pattern of being—one that runs counter to the life-patterns of the Graeco-Roman world. His literary work is . . . a culture forming narrative."[29] For Rowe, the author's hope is that the thoughtful reader of Acts will be convinced that accepting "the theological vision of the Christian gospel simultaneously creates a new cultural reality."[30] Acts also makes it clear that this decision leads to a collision of cultures and destabilization: "this process of revelation and formation inherently destabilizes essential assumptions and practice of Mediterranean culture . . . ."[31] However, at the same time, the author of Acts depicts the birth of the Christian movement in such a way that it is not presented as a threat to Rome.

> [Luke] narrates the threat of the Christian mission in such a way as to eliminate the possibility of conceiving it as in direct competition with the Roman state. Of all forms of sedition and treason . . . Christianity is innocent. Paul may well engender

---

27. Ibid., 204–6.
28. Keener, *Acts*, 436–58.
29. Rowe, *World Upside Down*, 4.
30. Ibid.
31. This emerges pragmatically in the scenes in Lystra, Philippi, and Ephesus (Acts 14, 16, 17, and 19 respectively). Ibid., 4–5.

considerable upheaval as a part of his mission, but repeatedly . . . the political authorities reject the accusations of his opponents: Paul is *dikaios*.[32]

Herein lies a tension: Christ sets up a new culture within a polytheistic world, but not a coup against the state.[33]

An assessment of the role of women in Acts must necessarily take account of Luke's purpose and apologetic intent, for the theological foci of Acts as well as its apologetic concerns shape how Luke characterizes female disciples of Jesus. Following Alexander's view of the apologetic focus, the narratival propositions regarding women that emerge from the narrative must be considered in the light and context of Hellenistic Judaism. Yet here, Keener's comments are also apt: "Conforming to norms in their milieu, Jewish women in the Greek Diaspora were regulated by Greek, rather than Judean, practices."[34] Consequently, we will need to draw on the material presented in chapter 2, above, regarding the roles of women in Judaism and the wider Greco-Roman world.

The apologetic directed towards Rome also has bearing here. For even if, as Rowe maintains, there would have been a cultural collision and destabilization with respect to the roles of women in that religio-social community occasioned by the gospel, Luke is not wanting to start a social revolution. Consequently, his portrayal of women may well be shaped to conform to varying regional-cultural expectations in order to achieve this apologetic aim. This is not to say that the author will shy away from presenting Christian women as they are caught up in the "world right side up." But he will not present women in such a way that they are a threat to Rome.

The Structure of Acts

Luke's theological and apologetic purposes are expressed through a narratival (literary) agenda. It is structured according to the progression outlined in Acts 1:8. This structure, drawing in part on Isa 49:6, is clear: "But you will receive power when the Holy Spirit has come upon you; and you will be my witnesses in Jerusalem, in all Judea and Samaria, and to the ends of the earth." This is the programmatic statement of the book, and governs its literary progression.[35] Having said this, however, the progression from Jerusalem to Judea to

---

32. Ibid., 5.

33. "New culture, yes—coup, no. The tension is set." Ibid.

34. Keener, *Acts*, 1:614.

35. Dunn, *Acts of the Apostles*, 9, correctly recognizes that 1:8 also responds in a corrective way to the misapprehension of 1:6–7.

Samaria to the ends of the earth is not always neat. For example, the Ethiopian eunuch (8:26-40) and Cornelius (10:1-48) each in their own way anticipate the gospel progressing to "the ends of the earth." Nor can we say that the mission is completed by the end of Acts, for Rome is not the ends of the earth[36] but only a stopping point along the way.[37] As Tannehill observes, "Acts 1:8 does not outline the actual course of Acts beyond Samaria.... It is an outline of the mission, but only in part an outline of Acts."[38]

The geographical extension which Luke records is also very selective. Luke concentrates his narrative on the Middle East, Asia Minor, Greece and Italy. He does not leave a record of Egyptian nor Western Imperial Christianity. In addition, the Johannine communities remain outside his purview.[39] The select nature of the narrative serves an illustrative principle. Luke illustrates the universal expansion of the Christian movement along two select vectors, the Petrine and the Pauline missions. These vectors themselves are only partially described; we do not have the entire picture of either mission.[40] Rowe writes that "Luke himself does not offer as much concrete description of early Christian communities as we might wish. What he offers instead is a vision, a pattern of lived thought that displays something of the main interconnections that make up Christian existence in the Mediterranean world."[41] Hence, there clearly are "sociological gaps in the story's detail."[42]

It is also apparent that not only is the larger narrative driven by Acts 1:8, but character deployment within the narrative is also governed by this agenda. Acts features only the leading players, and those with whom they interact, in the movement of the gospel out from Jerusalem. Given the focus on the eleven (soon to be twelve) apostles in the opening eleven verses, we would expect them all to be the leading characters in the narrative. But only a small selection of the twelve actually play any part. Peter plays the pre-eminent role, accompanied in the early chapters by John. James is mentioned only with reference to his martyrdom (12:1-2), while the Philip who dominates chapter 8 is likely not one of the twelve but one of the seven

---

36. Although "the ends of the earth" does likely appear as a designation for Rome in *Psalms of Solomon* 8:15.

37. Tannehill, *Narrative Unity*, 2:17-18.

38. Ibid., 2:18.

39. Marguerat, *Les Actes Des Apotres (1-12)*, 26.

40. Ibid., 27.

41. Rowe, "Reading World Upside Down: A Response to Matthew Sleeman and John Barclay," 336.

42. Ibid., 336.

mentioned in 6:5 as appointed by the twelve to "wait on tables."[43] Not only is the sparse treatment of the activities of the twelve apostles surprising, others outside the twelve such as Stephen, Philip, James the brother of Jesus, and Saul/Paul play a leading role. So it would appear that the role of a character in the narrative is determined not by their apostolic status, but by their participation in the geographical extension of the gospel. Nevertheless, despite (1) the selective nature of Luke's presentation in order to achieve his theological and apologetic purposes, and (2) the shift away from a portrayal of the marginalized of society found in Luke's Gospel, women play a number of key roles in the emerging patterns of life in the early church.

---

43 Most commentators (e.g. Peterson, *Acts*, 235; Bruce, *Acts of the Apostles*, 184; Bock, *Acts*, 261) believe that the Philip depicted in chapter 8 is not the apostle, but the one appointed to a serving role in 6:5. There are a couple of points to note here. First, it is reasonably clear that the Philip of 6:5 is not Philip the apostle, given that the 12 explicitly appoint the 7 so as they can continue the ministry of the word (6:2). Second, although Stephen was one of those appointed to the serving function, he clearly also is involved in evangelistic activity (6:8–15). This then, does not rule out the Philip mentioned in 6:5 from engaging in the activity narrated in chapter 8. Third, the reader is informed in 8:1 that all except the apostles were scattered throughout Judea and Samaria. This would tend to favour the majority opinion that the Philip spoken of in chapter 8 was not Philip the apostle.

CHAPTER 8

The Birth of the Church (Acts 1–2)

Acts 1

*In Acts, the women remain part of
the inner circle of Jesus' followers*

As mentioned in the previous chapter, the initial focus in chapter 1 is on "the apostles whom he had chosen" (Acts 1:2)—reminding the reader of the choosing of the twelve in Luke 6:12–16. The eleven are named in Acts 1:13—Judas having suffered his ignominious fate (1:16–20)—and they alone appear to witness the ascension. Matthias is added to the eleven after the divinely supervised lottery (1:21–26).[1] Nevertheless, in the upper room are a wider group of disciples including "the women" (1:14). Who are these women? Although there is lexical ambiguity with the term γυναιξίν, we should dismiss the idea that these are the wives of the male disciples,[2] for women disciples have featured prominently in Luke's Gospel. Here they provide "a line of continuity and also an example of consistent faithfulness not found with the male apostles."[3]

---

1. Dunn, *Acts of the Apostles*, 18, notes that "the overall impression given by the account is often uncertainty, awkwardness and powerlessness—just what is needed to be remedied by the coming of the Spirit at Pentecost."

2. As represented in Codex Bezae (D) which adds και τεκνοις ("and children"). For a refutation, see Gaventa, *Acts*, 68.

3. Keener, *Acts*, 1:746.

Only Mary the mother of Jesus is mentioned explicitly, and here she appears for the final time in Luke-Acts. But here there is an interesting parallel with the opening of Luke's Gospel. There, Mary had a unique experience of the Spirit with the miraculous conception of Jesus. Here, along with the other women, she is about to have an experience of the Spirit at Pentecost that will be a catalyst for the proclamation and spread of the gospel of Jesus. So in both Luke and Acts, Mary functions as a paradigm of sorts. As discussed in chapter 3, Mary appears in the infancy narratives as a valid interpreter and communicator of salvation history and the mighty deeds of God (Luke 1:46–56). Here in Acts she is about to become a communicator of God's further deeds of power (Acts 2:11).

Regarding the other women, the reader is expected to draw on the previous narrative in Luke's Gospel, for several women have been named previously—Mary Magdalene, Joanna, Susanna (Luke 8:1–3), and Mary the mother of James (Luke 24:10). The first three women are explicitly named as part of Jesus' entourage in Galilee where they provided material support for Jesus and the wider group. Mary Magdalene, Joanna, and Mary the mother of James were also the first witnesses to the resurrection. To these names we must add the numerous other women not named but mentioned in both the above contexts. So it is clear that the women are not sustained in the group only by Jesus' presence but by the fact that they are legitimate disciples of Jesus. There is never any question of whether or not they are accepted by the male disciples as part of the wider followers. Their presence and membership in the new community is noted as a matter of course, even though it "could continue a potential for scandal found in Luke 8:2–3, where women travelled with Jesus."[4]

The women participated in the decision-making process of the early church

Standing up before the assembled group, which we are told amounted to approximately one hundred twenty believers, Peter speaks of the need to replace Judas (Acts 1:15–26). Peter has now become an interpreter of Scripture, taking over that role from Jesus and obviously equipped to do so by Jesus "opening their minds to understand the scriptures" (Luke 24:45).[5] In this sense his role as an interpreter of scripture parallels that of Mary in the infancy narratives.

---

4. Ibid., 1:604.
5. Tannehill, *Narrative Unity*, 2:20.

The rationale for Judas' replacement is provided in the citation of Psalm 109:8 (LXX) in light of Psalm 69:25, which leads to the statement of necessity (δεῖ). Beyond this it is reasonable to conjecture that the filling of the twelfth position is bound up with restoration eschatology. The twelve apostles are representative of a new or reconstituted Israel which will be birthed very shortly in the outpouring of the Holy Spirit. The twelve represent the claim that the risen Jesus has over all Israel.[6] Following this, those who die (e.g., James the brother of John in Acts 12:1–5) are not replaced, so it appears as though the number twelve had a representative and symbolic function rather than indicating a perpetual role.[7]

It is clear that the women were numbered among the one hundred twenty believers who "devoted themselves to prayer" (Acts 1:14–15). So clearly they constituted part of the addressees of Peter's speech. If it be objected that Peter only addresses the males in the crowd with ἄνδρες ἀδελφοί ("men, brothers"—Acts 1:16), then we must recognize that ἄνδρες is not always a precise designation of gender. In Acts 17:34 a woman called Damaris is included in a three-fold group labelled as ἄνδρες.[8] Following Peter's speech, we are told that "they put forward two men" (1:23) who qualified for the position. In question here is the identity of the third person plural "they."[9] Between the introduction of the one hundred twenty and this particular statement, there is no intervening subject of a third person verb that would give any warrant for understanding the "they" as a subset of the larger group. Consequently, the most obvious sense is that the entire body of believers, including the women, were part of this decision-making progress.

We may question why, even though some of the women would have met the stated qualification of traveling with Jesus from the outset of his ministry until his death and resurrection, one of them was not nominated as Judas' replacement. Here Keener's comments are apt:

> In the cultures most relevant to both Peter and Luke's audience, male testimony was nearly always accepted most highly, a point relevant to the issue of "witnesses" here. Further, ... too much cross-gender association among leaders could play into hostile accusations.[10]

---

6. Ibid., 2:22.

7. Peterson, *Acts of the Apostles*, 126; Keener, *Acts*, 1:774–76.

8. Bock, *Acts*, 81; Bruce, *Acts of the Apostles*, 108; Peterson, *Acts of the Apostles*, 122; Keener, *Acts*, 1:757.

9. Although Codex Bezae has the third person singular "he" (referring to Peter), the text has overwhelming support in ℵ A B C E Ψ *Byz* etc.

10. Keener, *Acts*, 1:768.

Given this, it may be premature to make maleness a necessary condition for apostleship in all given situations.[11]

The inclusion of women alongside men is an essential mark of the early church in Jerusalem

Why does Luke mention the women in his description of the earliest group of believers in Acts? They play no overt part in the ensuing proclamation of gospel, and indeed are not named again in the Acts narrative. But then, we might say the same for the other apostles named in 1:13, who then drift off into narratival oblivion. Yet we should not assume that the apostles not mentioned in the ensuing narrative play no part in the proclamation of the gospel,[12] and the same assumption should not be made regarding the women. Luke is obviously being selective in the events he recounts. Not only would it be outside of his agenda to include accounts of all those actively involved in missionary endeavor, it would be impractical. Nevertheless, the mention of the women at this early stage serves a twofold purpose. First of all, it enables the reader to understand the broader composition of the early Christian group. Second, Luke is setting the scene for the coming of the Holy Spirit at Pentecost in chapter 2.

The point about the gender composition of the group is vital to Luke's view of early Christian ecclesiology. Acts 1:14 is Luke's first "summary of the book of Acts."[13] It is also a "miniature portrait" which provides the "permanent traits" of what Luke regards as the ideal Christian community.[14] Marguerat sums the marks of the original church as "unity, constancy, prayer, and the presence of men and women."[15] The female believers are just as integral to the community and to the devotional practices as were the men. Together they wait for the gift of the Holy Spirit.[16]

---

11. Though Luke-Acts is silent on this matter it does not preclude further investigation. Junia (Rom 16:7) is a case in point. Those who argue that this is a female name and she is to be numbered among the apostles have the better of the argument. See Bauckham, *Gospel Women*, 165–86. In fact, one could argue that Luke's narrative silence on this issue is filled by Paul with whom he travelled and about whom he wrote.

12. Contra Dunn, *Acts of the Apostles*, 20, who contends that those in the apostolic group are not in themselves missionaries, but only mentioned in chapter 1 to act as "guarantors of the continuity and the teaching of Jesus."

13. Other such summaries occur at points such as Acts 2:42–47; 4:32–35; 5:12–16, 42; 6:7; 8:1b–4). Marguerat, *Les Actes Des Apôtres (1–12)*, 50.

14. Ibid.

15. Ibid.

16. The continuity between the earthly ministry of Jesus and his ministry via the Holy Spirit is not solely determined by the eleven male apostles. Rather, it is determined

Acts chapter 1 opens by aligning Jesus' preaching about the kingdom of God and the anticipation of the coming of the Holy Spirit (Acts 1:1–5). Jesus ascends to heaven and the angels assure the witnesses that he will return (1:10–11). In the time between Jesus' ascension and return, the Spirit will come upon the witnesses in such a way that they will participate in the expansion of the kingdom of God. Because the women are named as part of the wider group in 1:14, the narrative suggests that the women will be equally caught up in this new powerful work of God.

Acts 2

*The women disciples were present at Pentecost
and received the power of the Holy Spirit*

Chapter 2 commences with both a temporal and spatial marker: "When the day of Pentecost had come,[17] they were all together in one place." The "all" denotes those mentioned in Acts 1:12–14—the now twelve apostles, certain women including Mary the mother of Jesus, and his brothers.[18] Indeed the reader has been informed that the crowd of believers that Peter had previously addressed "numbered about one hundred twenty persons" (Acts 1:15). The "all together in one place" has a twofold narrative function. First of all, at a practical level, the Spirit falls upon the entire group at once. Second, it highlights the sense of unity and solidarity amongst the believers that Luke is keen to portray (see 2:43–47; 4:32–37). Though the apostles may be the nucleus of the larger group, the theological point is that all the one hundred twenty have been beneficiaries of the resurrection of Jesus.[19]

The tongues of fire "rested on each one of them" and "all of them" were filled with the Holy Spirit (2:3–4). The "all of them" clearly relates to 2:1; those who were "all together in one place." This most obviously refers to the one hundred twenty mentioned in 1:15, and includes the women disciples. The "each one of them" (ἕνα ἕκαστον αὐτῶν), together with the distributive

---

by Jesus' promise for those who awaited the Holy Spirit in Jerusalem (Acts 1:4, 8).

17. Literally "fulfilled" (συμπληροῦσθαι), which helps convey a salvation-historical sense to the arrival of the Feast. See Peterson, *Acts of the Apostles*, 131.

18. This is obviously meant in a literal sense as the apostles have just been mentioned by name. Jesus' siblings only feature in Luke's Gospel at 8:19–21 (Mark 3:31–35), and also appear in John 7:1–5 as antagonists. They are named in Mark 6:3 as James, Joses, Judas, and Simon. Only James is mentioned further in Acts, after he ascends to leadership of the Jerusalem church. It would appear that the resurrection was the occasion for a dramatic change of heart in his brothers (cf. 1 Cor 15:7).

19. Marguerat, *Les Actes Des Apotres (1–12)*, 72.

compound verb διαμεριζόμεναι, emphasizes that none of the assembled disciples were excluded from this supernatural empowering.

*The women are empowered by the Spirit to
share the gospel in foreign languages*

Here the narratival thread of women as mouthpieces of God is resumed. Given that women participated in the Pentecost event, then they too were among those who declared "God's deeds of power" in foreign languages (Acts 2:11). Indeed, this is endorsed by the Joel citation that follows in 2:17–18, where the prophet speaks of the promise of the Spirit and the accompanying gift of prophecy for "your sons and your daughters." This forms an interesting correspondence with the opening of Luke's Gospel, where Spirit inspired women—Elizabeth, Mary, and Anna[20]—prophesy regarding the role of the baby Jesus in the fulfilment of God's plan of redemption. Here, in the opening chapters of Acts, Spirit-empowered women form part of the group that testifies to God's deeds of power, most obviously to what he has done through Jesus.[21] So the OT precedent of particular heroines (Miriam, Deborah, Hannah) endowed with the gift of prophecy has now been widened, in line with the Joel citation, to include all in the believing community irrespective of gender, age, or class.[22] This represents the "absolute democratization" of the gift of the Spirit.[23] Therefore, with Joel's oracle as its theological background, Pentecost is the advent of a new "prophetic-people"[24] that includes all believing men and women who receive the Spirit. That Luke understands Pentecost as paradigmatic with respect to the gender-inclusive gift of prophecy "should be beyond dispute, since he illustrates it in his narratives (with respect to Anna and Phillip's four daughters)."[25]

---

20. Anna's prophetic activity is not explicitly linked with the Spirit, but given the link between the Spirit and prophecy throughout Luke-Acts it should be so understood.

21. Bock, *Acts*, 104.

22. Ibid., 113–14. This is not to say that all had the ongoing gift of prophecy (cf. Acts 21:9), but (i) all prophesied on this particular occasion, and (ii) none would be excluded from the gift of prophecy on the basis of gender, age, or class (although the words "and they shall prophesy" which follows "even upon my slaves, both men and women" is a Lukan addition to the Joel text. It is also important to note that the Joel citation should not be limited with respect to the initial Pentecost experience, but as "a divine promise that is realized progressively, but only partially, in Acts as a whole" (Tannehill, *Narrative Unity*, 2:30).

23. Marguerat, *Les Actes Des Apôtres (1–12)*, 88. Also Keener, *Acts*, 1:603.

24. Marguerat, *Les Actes Des Apôtres (1–12)*, 88.

25. Keener, *Acts*, 1:637.

The Pentecost empowerment and proclamation must also be understood in terms of the commission to witness to the ends of the earth in Acts 1:8. Even though directed initially to the apostles, this commission takes on a wider purview as the Acts narrative progresses.[26] All those involved in "testifying to God's deeds of power" are of course witnesses, and the "devout Jews from every nation under heaven" (2:5) can be seen as representatives of sorts from "the ends of the earth." Consequently, the women disciples are part of the development of the 1:8 commission, even though they play a limited role in the subsequent narrative that depicts it.

The women continue to form part of the group of disciples and are understood to be present when the entire group is mentioned

Luke is obviously concerned to stress the unity of the early church.[27] He does this initially through two passages in the early chapters that stress the unity of mind, common purse, and shared purpose in mission (Acts 2:43–47; 4:32–37). The group is designated as "all the believers" (2:44) and "the whole group of those who believed" (4:32). This includes the women disciples, a point made clear by the Ananias and Sapphira account in 5:1–11. Consequently, we should understand the women disciples to be present when the entire group is mentioned in one way or another.

Summary of Narratival Propositions

The group of Christian disciples who trusted Jesus' words about remaining in Jerusalem and awaiting the gift of the Spirit included women. These women are identified as believers in Jesus without qualification, and they continued as an essential part of the early church in Jerusalem. As part of the group of disciples they are understood to be present when the entire group is mentioned.

The women in the upper room participated in the decision making process regarding the replacement of Judas, and in devotion which was consistent with the group's beliefs about Jesus. Together with men, women received the Spirit as members of God's new 'prophecy-people.' They were empowered by the Spirit to share the gospel in foreign languages.

---

26. Ibid., 1:603.

27. This need not be understood, as per the Tübingen School, as an artificial smoothing of ongoing tensions between a conservative Jewish Christianity (represented by James and Peter), and a law-free and growing Gentile party (represented by Paul).

Theological Propositions

Several theological propositions to do with women who are disciples of Jesus arise from Acts 1–2. They mostly concern the status of women as believers and their active membership in the new people of God as enabled by the Spirit.

1. There is no discrimination between men and women as recipients of salvation.
2. Women are as intrinsic to the constituency of the new people of God as are men.
3. God is present by his Spirit in the lives of female disciples of Jesus.
4. Women participate by the Spirit in the new people of God in fulfilment of his end-time promises.
5. Being a disciple of Jesus does not deny the gender of the disciple.
6. God's presence in the lives of female believers by his Spirit empowers women for the same range of service as men in working for end-time kingdom expansion.
7. There is no discrimination between men and women as agents of God's salvation and ongoing care.

CHAPTER 9

The Church in Jerusalem (Acts 3-12)

Ananias and Sapphira (5:1-11)

*Ananias and Sapphira lie to the Spirit who is the guarantor
of the existence, unity and purity of the early church*

ANANIAS AND SAPPHIRA ARE introduced into the narrative after Luke's second summary of the virtues of the early Christian community (Acts 4:32–35). These verses restate many of the Lukan marks of the eschatological community of salvation which Luke calls the ἐκκλησία (church),[1] including unity of heart and soul, a common purse, and powerful testimony and witness. In the context of Acts 2–5, the narrative suggests that the Holy Spirit is the guarantor of these virtues. This is made clear by the community-forming event of Pentecost and the Holy Spirit's ongoing work in and through the church, including the marks of the church which are noted in the two descriptive summaries (Acts 2:42–47; 4:32).[2] The ideal of generosity is one of these marks.

The ideal of generosity in the church is embodied by Joseph Barnabas. He sold a field which belonged to him, and brought the money and laid it at the feet of the apostles (4:37). Luke sets up a contrast between Barnabas on the one hand, and Ananias and Sapphira on the other, by linking the two accounts. Ananias and Sapphira are introduced as a married couple involved

1. Marguerat, *Les Actes Des Apôtres (1-12)*, 177.
2. Marc, "Ananie et Saphire (Ac 5,1-11)," 150-51.

in the crime of deceit. It should be stated at the outset that the crime of the pair was not choosing to keep part of the proceeds for themselves. In fact, it was their decision whether or not to sell the property. Peter made this clear to Ananias in his indictment (5:4). But it is possible to detect here a measure of pressure to conform to the practices of the wider group. Rather than admit that they had kept some of the proceeds for themselves, they lie about the sale price apparently to measure up to what they see as the group ideal.[3]

The story of Ananias and Sapphira is shocking not only because it is the first story of internal conflict in the early church, but because Ananias and Sapphira tested the Spirit who enabled the existence of the church and who was the basis of unanimity and generosity.[4] Indeed, Peter's responses to both Ananias (5:4) and Sapphira (5:9) express incredulity that they would do such a thing. Marc captures the essence of the problem in stating that lying to the Spirit is the "opposite of what was practiced by the Christian community."[5] Thus, "'lying to the Holy Spirit'—drives the story's plot and theme."[6] The theological points that Luke wishes to communicate to his readers through the episode concern the purity required of the church and the power of God.[7] From a narratival perspective this story is significant because the reader is alerted to the fact that Luke is not writing an idealized ahistorical account of the church. Tannehill notes: "it is significant that there *are* problems in the internal life of even the earliest church. The portrait is not so idealized as to deny the necessity of clearly facing problems in order to preserve and restore the life to which the church has been called."[8]

This story's intent is to highlight the role of the Spirit in the new ideal Christian community as well as the fallibility of those who are expected live holy lives. The story also serves to illustrate the fact that the original sin of Adam and Eve is paralleled in God's newly created community. Even though it is a work of new creation, the church is, like the first creation, open

---

3. Peterson, *Acts of the Apostles*, 210.
4. Marc, "Ananie et Saphire (Ac 5,1–11)," 151.
5. This is our translation. Ibid., 153.
6. Harrill, "Divine Judgment against Ananias and Sapphira (Acts 5:1–11)," 353.
7. "From the perspective of Luke's narrative, the deaths of Ananias and Sapphira are not tragic. Rather, the scene encourages the audience to have confidence that the church (ἡ εκκλησία) is blameless of impiety (ασέβεια) and that promises about its deity are true. The positive resolution thus matches the form or structure of a comedy. The author of Luke-Acts engages the notions of ritual and religious identity in his contemporary culture. He distinguishes the piety of his early Christian heroes by the deaths of Ananias and Sapphira, who scorn the keeping of oaths that God demands." Ibid., 369.
8. Italics are Tannehill's. Tannehill, *Narrative Unity*, 2:79.

to the threat of sin and its consequences.[9] Ananias and Sapphira's "double death clearly emphasizes the seriousness of . . . a threat of a particular kind, one that arises from inside, is deceptive, and attacks a central aspect of the church's life, as presented by the narrator: the heartfelt devotion to others demonstrated in the community of goods."[10]

The significance of the above with respect to the characterization of women in Acts is that this story is not primarily about female sinfulness. The character of Sapphira does not function to suggest a universal principle that women are more susceptible to sin than men. Nor is she illustrative of a supposed danger of female spirituality or decision-making. Sapphira's sin is paired with the sin of her husband. She is not sinning as an independent woman, but within the usual social structures for a woman in both the church and society.

The book of Acts records innumerable sins committed by men. The horrific death of a treacherous apostle is one of the opening stories (Acts 1:16–20). The graphic nature of his death anticipates different kinds of brutal, and at times deadly, persecution of the church by Romans, Greeks and Jews. Due to the historical realities in which this story is set, all of these reported crimes against God and his church were committed by men. By way of contrast, Sapphira is the only female protagonist in Luke-Acts who is portrayed negatively. What does this mean for Luke's portrayal of women? We need to be wary of making much from silence, however we can say that in Acts women disciples, apart from Sapphira, are not portrayed negatively as either instigators nor as agents of antagonism against the church nor sinners within it.

The story of Judas darkens the mood of the opening chapter of Acts. Judas was a turncoat, an apostle "who was a guide to those who arrested Jesus" (Acts 1:16). The scandal about Judas largely lay in the fact that, as Peter says, "he was numbered among us, and was apportioned his share in this ministry" (1:17). His sin resulted in financial gain; with it, he "bought a field with the reward of his wickedness" (1:18). Judas comes to a dreadful end. His death is described in detail, suggesting that his fate was a powerful memory in the early church. The narrative highlights the fact that his actions are diametrically opposed to those of Barnabas with respect to money and the field. Whereas Judas attempted to halt Jesus' mission, Barnabas enables it. Whereas Barnabas entrusts the money from the sale of a field to the apostles, Judas severs his relationship to the group and buys a field for himself (1:18–19).

---

9. Marc, "Ananie et Saphire (Ac 5,1–11)," 160.
10. Tannehill, *Narrative Unity*, 2:79.

Ananias and Sapphira parallel the Judas story in many respects. All three characters find themselves in a situation in which they mishandle money. This reveals a failure to appropriate one of the main themes of Jesus' teaching in Luke's Gospel—the stewardship of wealth and possessions. The three characters also betray God, Judas by treason and Ananias and Sapphira by deceit. Finally, all characters die dramatic and public deaths.

With respect to Luke's portrayal of women, this story alerts the reader to the fact that women can sin as grievously, and may suffer for it, as dramatically as men. This leads to the conclusion that Luke does not have such an idealistic view of women that it prevents him from mentioning internal conflict to do with female believers. Therefore we can say that Luke's ideology of women is not biased to the extent that he glosses over instances of women committing sin, especially such a deadly sin as lying to the Holy Spirit. Thus, the Sapphira story is significant because it prevents the charge of blind bias being levelled at Luke's presentation of women. Luke clearly does not hold a perfectionist ideal with respect to female disciples of Jesus. *Women may be involved in the worst kinds of sinful acts against God and his new people.*

The Seven who Serve (Acts 6:1–7)

Luke again avoids idealizing the church when he mentions the difficulties concerning food distribution in the burgeoning Christian community. This event is one of a series of crisis stories which serve to demonstrate how the early church overcame both internal and external threats. The internal threat of sin was powerfully dealt with by the Holy Spirit through Peter (Acts 5:1–11); the external threat of persecution (5:17–42) was also overcome by God's powerful work through Gamaliel's wise counsel, and the boldness given to the apostles. Despite these challenges the church continued to expand numerically across cultural barriers—from Judean Jews to Hellenistic Jews and to Gentiles. The present story deals with the internal threat posed by administrative and cultural issues. This event surrounding the selection of the seven who serve reveals something about Luke's theology of gender, the work of the Spirit, and criteria for various forms of service in God's new community.

The narrative locates the challenge of food distribution as "in those days when the number of disciples was increasing." There had been an unintentional neglect of some needy people: "the Hellenists complained against the Hebrews because their widows were being neglected in the daily distribution of food" (Acts 6:1). The mention of widows in the narrative reminds the reader of the positive portrayal they have received throughout Luke's Gospel. Hence the reader is predisposed to see them in a positive light.[11]

Rather than taking this complaint as an affront, as would have been customary when the actions of leaders were challenged, the twelve kept the welfare of the community at the center of their concerns.[12] They recognized that an addition to their own role was not the best solution for their quickly changing situation: "And the twelve summoned the whole group of the disciples and said: 'It is not right that we should neglect the word of God to serve tables'" (Acts 6:2). Their solution was to call a public meeting and ask the body of believers to "select from among you seven men of good repute, full of the Spirit and of wisdom, whom we will appoint to this task" (6:3). The group of believers who selected the seven would have included women as well as men.[13]

For their part, the apostles resolve to devote themselves "to prayer and to the ministry of the word" (6:4). The response to their proposal "pleased the whole group." The result was twofold: the election of the seven and the continued growth of the community. Three narratival proposals concerning women arise from the larger picture provided by this story.

The seven take on a role which was usually carried out by women

The ministry of table serving meant that the men may have found themselves in roles traditionally given to women. Women would have carried out this function as it fell within the domain of the home. This may suggest that gender was not the driving criterion for participation in a serving ministry in the early church. This suggests the more general proposition that *gender may not be the driving criterion for participation in a ministry of service in the church at large.*

The whole community, including men and women, elected the seven

11. In Luke's narrative "some widows receive notable blessings: the earlier widow of Zarephath, a model of God's favor through a prophet (Luke 4:25–26); the widow of Nain (7:12); also those widows blessed through Dorcas and whose entreaties to Peter are answered with Dorcas' resuscitation (Acts 9:39–41). A widow becomes a parabolic model for insistent prayer (Luke 1:3–5). Nor are widows only on the receiving end of blessing: Anna the prophetess bears witness to Jesus as an infant (2:37); a poor widow in the temple becomes a model for sacrificial giving (21:2–3)." Keener, *Acts*, 2:1264.

12. Ibid., 2:1249.

13. See above on the selection of Judas' replacement. Even a conservative scholar such as Peterson, notes that it was the "whole church" who chose the Seven. Peterson, *Acts of the Apostles*, 233.

The presence of women in the church of Acts is one of the distinctive features of the narrative. In selecting the seven, "the twelve summoned the whole group of the disciples" (Acts 6:2), which obviously included the women. This participation of the women in the election of Judas' replacement (see chapter 8, above) and the seven is not insignificant. The cumulative force of these two incidents suggests that the degree of the women's participation in the community matched their presence. Although this full participation in decision-making would appear to transcend cultural expectations of the day, particularly with respect to Palestinian Judaism, it comes as no surprise given Luke's consistent depiction of women's involvement in Jesus' mission to this point. This then leads to the more general proposition that *women may participate fully in the decision making processes of the church.*

Spirit-formed character was a primary characteristic of being set aside for a ministry of service in the early church

From the narrative it is clear that maleness alone is not a sufficient criterion for Christian service and leadership. These roles require Spirit empowerment and its attendant wisdom. These men were "full of the Spirit and wisdom" (Acts 6:3). Stephen fulfilled these criteria perfectly; he was "full of grace and power" (6:8) and his opponents "were not able to resist the wisdom and Spirit by which he spoke" (6:10).[14] This is consistent with the hermeneutic which Acts 2 provides: the Spirit will empower and enable all believers in diverse ways. In the case of the seven, men are chosen for a task which was usually a woman's domain . This demonstrates that this form of service is not gender-specific. Hence, the narrative suggests that the audience view Christian work as "Spirit-specific" rather than gender specific.

But the fact remains that men, not women, were chosen for this task. Might not this be taken as warrant for the exclusion of women from certain tasks in the early church, an exclusion that Luke supports? Not necessarily. As far as the biblical material is concerned, the delegation of duties goes back to Jethro's advice to Moses regarding the appointment of able men to act as judges (Exod 18:21–22). This practice was later enshrined in Deuteronomic law (Deut 16:18). That this Deuteronomic tradition was still well

14. The Greek expression τῇ σοφίᾳ καὶ τῷ πνεύματι ᾧ ἐλάλει is ambiguous. Spirit may be capitalized or not. If capitalized, the dative is likely construed as instrumental of means ("the wisdom and the Spirit by which he spoke"—so NKJ), or if uncapitalized, instrumental of manner ("the wisdom and the spirit with which he spoke"). Most EVV merge the two options, having "the wisdom and the Spirit with which he spoke" (so ESV, NAS, NET, NLT, NRSV). In light of the requirements stated in 6:3, the balance of probability is that Luke intended the reference here to be the Holy Spirit. Consequently, in our translation we have taken the dative to be instrumental of means.

regarded in the first century A.D. is evident by the actions of Josephus, who replicated this in his own leadership of the resistance forces in Galilee. He appointed seventy leading men as rulers of Galilee, and seven judges in every city to preside over minor disputes (Jos. *War* 2.571). While the numbers seventy and seven are not prescribed in the Mosaic legislation, they do have clear biblical usage and precedent. Thus it is possible that the early church was following this legal and cultural tradition in appointing the seven men. This is made even more likely given that the care of widows was an ancient tradition within Israel itself, and so the need to continue this concern may have prompted reflection on related traditions. It would be therefore unwise to regard this episode in Acts as making a definitive statement regarding gender prerequisites for a particular role.[15]

Beyond these three narrative propositions, the details of the story contribute to significant narratival threads which have a bearing on how women are portrayed in Acts. These are (1) Luke's portrayal of women and women in Christian service, and (2) the word of God as it is related to Christian ministry and gender. These two narratival threads will be explored in turn below.

Luke's Portrayal of Women and Women in Christian Service

The Spirit empowers Stephen, a man outside the twelve, to prophesy and preach in addition to his diaconal role

In our discussion of Mary and Martha in Luke 10:38-42, we argued that the thrust of the narrative is that roles other than serving tables are open to women. Here in Acts 6 Luke makes it clear that the role of serving at tables is open to men. Thus, Luke's reversal theology works bilaterally: it applies to both men and women and this often includes reversing social expectations of service and honor.

Διακονία, the generic word for "ministry" or "service" occurs eight times in Acts (1:17, 25; 6:1, 4; 11:29; 12:25; 20:24; 21:19). At certain points in Acts, particularly in 6:1-2, it may carry undertones of being onerous. The apostles decided that it was not right under God for them to carry out

---

15. See Witherington, *Acts of the Apostles*, 249; Schnabel, *Acts*, 332. Peterson, *Acts of the Apostles*, 232, notes the continuing significance of the OT and the models it provided for the early church. He writes that the "earliest Christians were concerned to maintain their own pattern of care and thus fulfil the injunctions of Scripture, especially as they related to widows and others in need (e.g., Ex. 22:22-24; Dt. 14:2-29; Ps. 146:9; cf. 1 Tim. 5:3-16). This was an important indication of their faithfulness to the God of Israel and of his Spirit's work in their midst."

this kind of ministry, and thus they selected others to do the task. By their choice to refuse this particular διακονία they were able to focus on preaching and prayer. This may appear to present the reader with a false antithesis whereby serving (the seven) and preaching/praying (the twelve) are conceived as normatively distinct ministries to be carried out at the exclusion of the other. By means of the stories of Stephen and Philip that follow, the narrative disallows this notion.

Stephen's ministry beyond waiting on tables was due to the fact that he was a man full of grace and power and spoke with wisdom energized by the Spirit (6:8, 10). These two references are narrative expressions of the previously stated requirements for the seven which included being "full of the Spirit and wisdom" (6:3). The use of "grace" in 6:8 does not refer to Stephen's charm, but to divine enablement.[16] This divine enablement occurs under the rubric provided by Joel 2:2–29 in Peter's sermon in Acts 2 where, as discussed above, the Spirit of prophecy is given to all disciples. Stephen's prophetic role is therefore the new normal for the early Christian community; God may enable anyone to speak prophetically. Thus it is not surprising that we find two of the seven, Stephen and Philip, portrayed in the ensuing narrative as prophetic proclaimers of the word.[17] Positively speaking, the Lordship of Christ provides a religio-social "zone" in which a prophesying ministry or work could be carried out by any person who was so empowered by God.[18] This contrasts, and possibly even challenged, Hellenistic practices which restricted prophesying to certain persons and roles. Furthermore, Stephen is a heroic and lively demonstration of the fact that diaconal service may be carried out in tandem with a ministry of prophecy and proclamation. Hence, *a diaconal form of ministry does not preclude prophesying and preaching.*

*Service is a positive mark for any disciple,
not for those of female gender alone*

The service of the seven who wait on tables is portrayed positively. Luke records the selection, the names of the seven, and their appointment by prayer and the laying on of hands. The narrative immediately passes positive judgment on this sequence of events "so the word of God spread. The number of

16. Bock, *Acts*, 269.
17. Ibid., 233.
18. God's choice of Stephen for this work may be recorded as a witness to the universal expansion of the gospel. Stephen is a "Hellenist with the enablement that apostles have displayed. God will work through the various ethnic wings of his church." Ibid., 270.

disciples in Jerusalem multiplied greatly, and a large number of priests became obedient to the faith" (Acts 6:7). This suggests that table service is not demeaning work in Luke's eyes. A Lukan view of service and its relationship to honor should also be contrasted with the honor system which dominated Greco-Roman society. Under the Greco-Roman system, those of inferior status served those of a noble or more honored status. Luke has told his story in such a way that the widows (of inferior service) are served by those who have been deemed to have the noblest virtues (in terms of character and Spirit empowerment). Through stories such as these Luke applies to the early church Jesus' teaching about humility and places of honor in hospitality settings. Such application only serves to reinforce Luke's strong theology of service in the minds of his audience.

The significance of this for Luke's view of women is that gender alone is not directly correlated with particular types of service. Luke's high view of service means that the divide or demarcation of service roles along gender lines, as was generally the case in Jewish and Greco-Roman society, may not be seen in the early church. We see here that Luke is reordering, where appropriate, the prevailing norms and cultural expectations of gender roles and relationships. The most important point about this reordering is that it is realized according to the mission and values of the kingdom of God.

This reordering first appears in the ministry of Jesus with his attitude to women. In the early chapters of Acts this continues as the believing community is shaped by the Spirit. In the chapters after Pentecost, Luke shows that under the power of the Spirit, Christians will serve the Lord, each other, and the world in a unique manner. This manner reflects the way in which the kingdom is to play itself out in the world. This has already been suggested in Jesus' life and teaching, where the kingdom is subversive with respect to the ways of the world, but is life-giving as it shapes existence according to the intentions of God. As a consequence of this, *women and men who participate in the kingdom of God will not necessarily be channelled into stereotypical roles which correspond to expectations in wider society.*[19]

The work of the Spirit in a given context is the impetus for Christian ministries and ministry designations

---

19. For instance, a Galilean fisherman is called to leave his nets and the social order in which his occupation places him, into a previously unknown role—a fisher of men. This profound change continues after Pentecost where Peter's dominant occupation and relationships center on a people who worship the risen Lord Jesus. This example suggests that serving Jesus may lead to breaks from societal patterns to do with service and gender.

In Luke's Gospel, the Spirit clearly directs Jesus' ministry. The Spirit incarnates, anoints, empowers, and even leads Jesus into the wilderness in order to be tempted. In Acts, the Spirit has a powerful and directive ministry with respect to the followers of Jesus. From Pentecost onwards, the Spirit forms communities in response to the proclamation of Jesus as Lord of all, and empowers and directs those communities in sometimes surprising ways.

Philip serves as a case in point for the various ways in which a person may be led to a wide range of ministries according to local needs concerning proclamation of the word and community formation. Luke describes Philip and his ministry in several ways: Philip is one of the seven (Acts 6:5); he is also an interpreter of Scripture who teaches the Ethiopian eunuch (8:26-40). In Acts 21:8 he is described as an evangelist. His ministry is clearly driven by the Spirit.

Though Philip "waits on tables," this designation does not follow Philip as the primary descriptor of who he is as a servant of Christ. Neither do other titles such as 'evangelist' follow Phillip throughout the narrative. This suggests that the roles people play in Christian ministry in Acts are not carried out according to designated offices or titles but according to the Spirit's leading and enabling in given situations. This is not to say that Philip was not always held in good standing by his community as a leader, or that he was not known for a range of good works. Rather, that for the narrator, those who serve Jesus in their context do so by the enabling of the Spirit and that this may entail a variety of roles.[20] At a practical level, the missionary situation of the early church meant that ministries were understood to function in parallel with one another and not to be held as separate entities.[21] However, the deeper theological underpinning of this united perspective on ministries is rooted in the fact that the church continues the ministry of Jesus through the Holy Spirit.[22]

The significance of this for women is that we would expect that *the ministries of women would be Spirit led, and the tasks entailed by these ministries may vary according to different ministry contexts.* This potentially calls for a certain fluidity with respect to role descriptors for women in their service in the kingdom of God.

---

20. Marguerat, *Les Actes Des Apôtres* 1:210.
21. Gebauer, "Mission und Zeugnis," 72.
22. Kremer, "Weltweites Zeugnis für Christus," 147–49, 51 ff. .

The Word of God as it is Related to Christian Ministry and Gender

The word of God is personified in the book of Acts

The word of God is one of the controlling themes of Acts and draws substantially on Isaiah 40–55.[23] The function of the term the "word of God" and its role in Acts is instructive for, as Bovon has noted, Acts can be understood as the narration of the "diffusion of the Word."[24] This emphasis is borne out by the fact that Luke's Gospel only uses the phrase ὁ λόγος τοῦ θεοῦ four times whereas Acts, on the other hand, employs ὁ λόγος τοῦ θεοῦ eleven times in addition to ὁ λόγος τοῦ κυρίου eight times. Other closely related terms such as ὁ λόγος τῆς σωτηρίας ("the word of salvation"—13:26), τῷ λόγῳ τῆς χάριτος αὐτοῦ ("the word of his grace"—14:3; 20:32) and τὸν λόγον τοῦ εὐαγγελίου ("the message of good news"—Acts 15:7) also appear. Significantly, these phrases are employed together with the wide diffusion of the absolute use of λόγος in Acts 1–20.[25]

The first instance of "the word" to refer to the Christian message in Acts is found in 4:4, where the proclaimed word is foundational to the very existence of the nascent church: those who believe the word become part of the community of faith.[26] Pao notes that at times the advance of the word is stated in military terminology, echoing OT language of conquest. Hence, the advancement of the λόγος in the face of persecution is a victorious advance.[27] Regarding Acts 6:7, Marguerat states:

---

23. Pao, *Acts and the Isaianic New Exodus*, 111, contends that the theological agenda and narrative of both Isaiah and Acts are controlled by four themes. These are "the restoration of Israel, the word of God, the anti-idol polemic, and the salvation offered to the nations/Gentiles." Hence the advance of the word of God parallels the advance of God's kingdom in history.

24. Bovon, *Luke the Theologian*, 283.

25. Pao, *Acts and the Isaianic New Exodus*: 147–48. Pao notes that Luke's use of λόγος is different to that of ῥῆμα which is used of particular words spoken, and not in the singular (as is λόγος) as a technical term for the gospel itself.

26. "[T]here is a statement concerning the massive growth of the community; and members of this group are those who believed the word . . . ." Pao, *Acts and the Isaianic New Exodus*, 150.

27 "Significantly, this statement appears in the midst of persecution from the leaders of the Jews . . . the report of the number that constitute the community is important in that in Israelite traditions numbering 'men' (that amounts to thousands) most often appears in military contexts where thousands of 'men' were involved. In Acts 4, therefore, the formation of the community as well as the victory (with its militaristic overtones) over the opposing force are important themes related to the term λόγος." Pao, *Acts and the Isaianic New Exodus*, 150–51.

> [T]he narrator speaks not only of the multiplication of the disciples but also of the growth of the word of God. These are two ways of speaking of the same development, but the narrator directs attention first of all not to the church but to the creative force behind its growth, the word of God. . . . [T]his metaphor (which appears in 12:24; 19:20) shows the continuing influence in Acts of Jesus' parable in Luke 8:4–15, where the sower's growing seed represents the word of God. This metaphor becomes a vehicle for understanding the word of God as an active force in the world, full of its own vitality.[28]

Luke's use of the metaphor of a growing organism in order to speak of the word of God serves to heighten its personalization (cf. 1 Pet 1:24). On this basis Marguerat is correct to argue that for Luke the church is "the visible manifestation of the word of God."[29] This personalization of the word of God has a number of implications which deconstruct the potential for a narrow over-identification between apostleship on one hand and authoritative proclamation on the other.

The personalized word of God advances independently of apostolic ministry

The strength of the personalization of the word of God is such that it appears to have an itinerary and will of its own in the narrative.[30] This means the word and its growth is not tied to the apostles. Tannehill's narrative analysis brings this out effectively, and his comments merit extended quotation. Regarding Acts 6:7 he states:

> This reference to the word's growth without reference to a human speaker separates the appointment of Stephen to care for the widows from the report of his mission, involving wonders and powerful speech. At this point there is a shift in Stephen's role for which we were not prepared by 6:1–6. The twelve draw a clear distinction between two types of service, serving tables . . . and the service of the word. . . . Because they believe that the former is now interfering with the latter, the twelve propose a division of labor. . . . However, the growing word has its own

---

28. Tannehill, *Narrative Unity*, 2:82.
29. Marguerat, *Les Actes Des Apôtres*, 1:213.
30. Pao has noticed the connection between the "word" and conquest language such that "the word conquers in the midst of opposition and . . . the word never visits a geographical location twice during its journey." Pao, *Acts and the Isaianic New Exodus*, 150.

ways.... So much for human plans as to how the mission should proceed! Philip's ministry will show the same surprising shift. Appointed to serve in the distribution of charity, he becomes a missionary who takes a bold new step in fulfilling part of the apostles' commission before they are ready to do so.[31]

If Luke understood the advance of the word of God as being inextricably linked to the proclamation of the apostles, then one would expect that the narrative would privilege the speech of the apostles in terms of length and frequency. However, Stephen's speech is the longest recorded by Luke.[32]

Tannehill's attention to the flow of the narrative and its inclusion of strong exceptions to the division of labor suggested by the apostles counters the idea of a unique relationship between the apostles and the word of God. Bock states, "The word is described in personified terms here, as the word directs its own growth. This depicts God sending forth the word through the apostolic preaching, with the word much like seed growing into fruit or a harvest."[33] This is correct, as long as we understand the term 'apostolic preaching' to relate to the content of the message but not necessarily descriptive of those who deliver it. So, the narrative sequence disallows an exclusive correspondence between the apostles and the growth of the word of God.

The significance of this is that Luke's presentation of the word of God deconstructs assumptions to do with communication in antiquity. Assumptions held by Hellenistic Jews and Greco-Roman pagans often tied the success of communication to the designated communicator. The personification of the word of God in Acts makes it clear that it is not tied to particular persons, even apostles. This embodies one of the many cultural breaks which the early church makes with its Israelite, Hellenistic and pagan background. Furthermore, the advancement of the word of God is not limited by the demarcations of labor in the early church. Thus, *the personalization of the word of God and its advancement resist it being necessary linked to apostolic ministry*

Because the narrative does not understand the word of God and apostolic ministry to be coterminous, the advance of the word of God may include the participation of people across the gender and social spectrum. This creates a narrative space in which women could potentially participate in the advancement of the word of God. And in fact they do, as we will shortly see with Priscilla.

---

31. Tannehill, *Narrative Unity*, 2:82–83.

32. "the longest in a book full of speeches . . ." Witherington, *Acts of the Apostles*, 251.

33. Bock, *Acts*, 264.

*The apostles and the seven serve the
word of the Lord, not vice versa*

Acts 6:7 recounts the bold advance of the word of God: "And the word of God increased; and the number of the disciples in Jerusalem multiplied greatly, and a great many priests became obedient to the faith." The increase in the word of God is the result of God's work through the miraculous signs that occurred through John, Peter, and Stephen, their bold preaching, and the diaconal ministry of the seven. This phrase serves as a narratival marker that indicates the outcome of what has occurred in the story so far. This provides a clue to Luke's understanding of the relationship between God, the word of God and God's servants.

The first point is that *God* is responsible for the spread of his word. The word spreads due to the fact that God stands behind it. The authority and power of the word belong to God and thus the word of God is not tied to the ability or gender of the apostles nor to the purity of the church. Keener writes:

> The "word of the Lord"—that is, the prophetic message of the apostolic witnesses (cf. 1:1)—was spreading. As is presumably the case here, Luke elsewhere uses summary statements to chart the gospel's expansion (9:31; 12:24; 16:5; 19:20).... [T]he summary in 6:7 is simply another sign pointing to God's securing the spread of the gospel through and sometimes despite the church. By God's intervention, obstacles produce growth; growth leads to more persecution, but even this does not stop the spreading of God's message.[34]

Second, the narrative indicates that the word of God is the authoritative basis for proclamation. Given this, the gender of the proclaimer is not a prerequisite for the advancement of the word of God and its impact.

Given this theological underpinning regarding God's authority and his word as the basis for proclamation, together with the cumulative force of Luke's narrative concerning women's involvement in proclamation (mission of the seventy, women as heralds of the resurrection, Pentecost) it is difficult to resist the general narrative proposition that *a woman's gender does not disable her from authoritatively and effectively proclaiming the word of God.*

---

34. Keener, *Acts*, 2:1291.

Tabitha—also known as Dorcas (Acts 9:36-42)

After the dramatic account of Saul's conversion (Acts 9:1-31), the narrative of Acts returns to stories about Peter and the conversion of Gentiles.[35] This transition is achieved by means of a characteristic Lukan pairing of male/female miracle stories. At the outset of the Gospel of Luke the author works with male/female pairings such as Zacharias and Elizabeth, Mary and Joseph, Simeon and Anna, and the centurion and the widow of Nain. This symmetry continues throughout the narrative in such a way that women are always in view at key moments in Luke's story. This has the effect of depicting women in various significant roles and situations.[36] In Acts, the same pattern is also common as women appear in many roles across the religious and societal spectrum. For example, Luke records pairings such as the eleven apostles and the women (1:13-14), prophets and prophetesses (2:17-18), male and female converts (5:14), Ananias and Sapphira (5:1-11), Denys the Aeropagite and Damaris (17:34), Aquila and Priscilla (18:1-28), Felix and Drusilla (24:1-27), and Agrippa and Berenice (25:23-27).[37] Here in the Tabitha story (9:36-43) the narrative thread of God's compassion for women is resumed.

> *Tabitha's story is paired with the story of Aeneas in such a way that she emerges as the more commendable character of the two*

The two miracle stories in Acts 9 also play a larger narratival role in that they further legitimate Peter as God's agent.[38] This in turn will legitimate his forthcoming ministry to the gentiles.[39] The first story is about the healing of Aeneas (9:32-35) whereas the second concerns the revivification of Tabitha (9:36-42). These parallel the stories of Jesus healing of the paralytic (Luke 5:1-26) and the raising of Jairus' daughter (Luke 8:40-56).[40] However, the story to do with Tabitha is far more extensive than the male story in this

---

35. The interweaving of the Peter and Paul stories, and in particular Peter's mission to the Gentile Cornelius, serves to legitimize Paul's upcoming Gentile mission.

36. For a comprehensive list see Marguerat, *Les Actes Des Apôtres (1-12)*, 348, n.2.

37. Ibid.

38. Though the narrative leads the reader/listener to understand that Jesus continues to work through his disciples (Acts 1:8). Ibid.

39. Keener, *Acts,* 2:1704.

40. The OT precedents for this are most probably found in miracle stories involving Elijah and Elisha (1 Kgs 17:17-24; 2 Kgs 4:32-37). There may also be a parallel with Luke's pairing of stories involving Jesus healing a paralysed man and the son of a widow in Luke 7:11-16.

pairing. Whereas the Aeneas story is quite short, the Tabitha episode is more detailed. Based on this narratival difference, the story about Tabitha is "considerably more substantial and impressive than the Aeneas story."[41] The reason why Luke has given this story more attention is that it is one of the most powerful miracle stories in Acts.[42]

The pairing between Tabitha and Aeneas is a form of deliberate gradation, an example of 'parallel spotlight' technique.[43] The details of the gradation, whereby the Aeneas story sets up a greater character (Tabitha) in the story that follows, will be apparent as we proceed. In the first instance, Tabitha's significance as a "disciple" is confirmed via the literary technique of contrast. In the immediately preceding story of Aeneas, he is merely referred to as "a certain man" (Acts 9:33). By means of this contrast the narrative honors Tabitha as a more prominent character than Aeneas.[44] A further contrast between the stories is that ultimately Tabitha and the widows supplant Peter at the center of the second story.[45]

Tabitha's life is strong within the social memory of the Christians of her region

The story begins with a geographical marker: Joppa. Scholars have noted that Luke's geographical knowledge is particularly accurate when he writes about the coastal plain rather than when he writes about other parts of Palestine. Keener suggests that this indicates that Luke had travelled through these areas on the way from Caesarea to Jerusalem (Acts 21:15–17) and the level of detail in the stories suggests that they were very powerful memories in the earliest Christian communities.[46] This would indicate that the

---

41. Witherington, *Acts of the Apostles*, 330.

42. "This woman is the object of one of the most astounding miracle stories in Acts. Luke introduces her with great care." Schnabel, *Acts*, 468.

43. See chapter 1, under methodology.

44. Keener, *Acts*, 2:1715.

45. Ibid.

46. The narrative notes a number of details which are not necessary to the story, but are included nonetheless. For example, after Peter "got down on his knees and prayed" in the room where the dead woman lay, Luke records that immediately after "he turned toward the dead woman" (9:40b) and then commanded her to rise up (9:40c). Keener, *Acts*, 2:1704. This passage is the only place in the NT where the female term for disciple (μαθήτρια) is used. Of course this does not mean that the concept of female discipleship was foreign to the author of the Third Gospel or Acts as we have previously demonstrated. Keener states that Luke's use of the female term for disciple indicates what is "indicated for a male disciple: an adherent of the Jesus movement and Jesus tradition whose faith was demonstrated by good works." Furthermore, he notes that Tabitha was

memory of Tabitha was one of the strongest in the region, even more significant because of Joppa's religious milieu in which there were a number of syncretistic religions competing for people's allegiance.[47] Importantly, the fact that Luke was familiar with her Aramaic name from a local tradition lends credibility to her continuing renown in the area.[48] Furthermore, that Tabitha is introduced by both her Jewish and Hellenistic names probably serves to highlight her ministry and renown to both groups within early Christianity. From a narrative perspective, the inclusion of both her Jewish and Greek names also serves as a transition to the dramatic story of the conversion of Cornelius' Gentile household in the next chapter.

Tabitha is a female disciple whose gender is not a barrier to discipleship, and neither is her discipleship a barrier to the expression of her gender

Tabitha is introduced by a unique NT designation: she is a μαθήτρια "female disciple" (Acts 9:36a). Her designation as a female disciple means that at some stage this woman of Jewish heritage would have overcome religious barriers to understand Jesus as the Messiah, as well as the social challenges which would have accompanied conversion to Christianity.[49] Her designation as a female disciple positions her as Acts' character equivalent to Luke's Mary the sister of Martha (Luke 10:39–42). The parallel lies in terms of an ideal response to God's particular actions in salvation history. However, Tabitha represents a later stage of discipleship than Mary as Tabitha belongs to the post-resurrection Christian community. Interestingly, both the group of Jesus' early followers and the early church include women who are presented as ideal. So, both Mary and Tabitha are ideal disciples at different stages of salvation history; Mary is the ideal inquirer and Tabitha is the ideal convert.[50]

The story of Tabitha contributes to Luke's broader understanding of female discipleship. Luke-Acts leaves no doubt in the reader's mind that believing women are full members of Jesus' community and are rightly designated as disciples. This view is predicated upon the women's continual presence in the narrative as disciples, by Jesus' words and actions, by the nature of the kingdom of God and the coming of the Holy Spirit. Given the

---

taken to be a model for Christians by historical luminaries such as John Chrysostom. Keener, *Acts*, 2:1715.

47. Erischen-Wendt, "Tabitha," 71–74.
48. Ibid., 75.
49. Tannehill, "'Cornelius' and 'Tabitha' Encounter Luke's Jesus," 350.
50. North, "Text, Subtext and Context," 13.

numerous examples of women being ideal disciples, ideal discipleship is not compromised by being female. Therefore, *female believers may be disciples in the fullest sense.* A corollary of this, which Tabitha exemplifies, is that female disciples may continue to carry out culturally appropriate gender interests which align with their temperament without compromise to their discipleship. In other words, *being a female disciple does not mean the suppression of gender expression.*

Tabitha's ministry takes the form of active service for the sake of the needy

Tabitha's activity is outstanding. Her designation as a disciple of Jesus was due to her loyalty to him, a loyalty expressed in activity.[51] She is described as "always doing good and helping the poor" (Acts 9:36b). This may suggest that in Luke's mind she was following Jesus' ministry model, which is described in Acts as good works and liberation from oppression: Jesus was "travelling around doing good and healing all who were oppressed by the devil" (10:38). Tabitha was doing good works which liberated widows from their socio-economic affliction. The relationship between Tabitha's life as a disciple and the extent of her activity is aptly drawn together in Erischen-Wendt's description of Tabitha as living an "active Christian existence."[52] This strenuous and functional faith is further suggested by the fact that Dorcas was the Greek term for "gazelle." It was not uncommon for people to be described according to desirable characteristics seen in animals. A gazelle in particular was at times associated with service, vitality, speed, and nimbleness.[53] It is not too much of a stretch to see how these personal characteristics would be exhibited by the kind of person who "always doing good and helping the poor" (9:36b) and would have nimbly made "robes and other clothing" presumably for the widows (9:39b).

Eckhard Schnabel is probably correct in suggesting that Tabitha had been carrying out this ministry in the medium term rather than carrying out a short-term ministry. If this is the case she may have been "a prosperous woman" as well as "an indispensable pillar of the congregation."[54] Interestingly, this ministry is carried out by Tabitha without reference to a male helper or male oversight. Tabitha's unique role in her community

---

51. Rather than because she personally knew Jesus before his ascension. Erischen-Wendt, "Tabitha," 75.

52. "ihre tätige Existenz als Christin." Ibid.

53. The author cites Keller's *Die Antike Tierwelt,* and Zahlhaas' *Aus Noahs Arche,* for her evidence. Ibid., 76.

54. Schnabel, *Acts,* 468.

contributes to several aspects of the story. Luke includes the detail that after her death "her body was washed and placed in an upstairs room" (9:37). Laying out Tabitha's body suggests that those around her did not want to proceed with the funeral without asking for Peter's help to bring her back to life. This alerts the reader to the high regard in which both Tabitha and Peter were held. Tabitha's community clearly wanted her to continue to minister amongst them.

A key area of discontinuity between Aeneas and Tabitha concerns the effect that their ill health has on their respective communities. Tabitha's absence from the Joppa community after her death was a source of massive distress whereas no such statement is made regarding the community impact of Aeneas' long-term disability. By preserving this detail of the wailing of the widows in his story, Luke points out the communal suffering which Tabitha's death involved. This emphasizes Tabitha's centrality to her community.

The weightiness of Tabitha's life is again underscored by the fact that two disciples are sent to Peter to implore him to "please come at once" (9:38). When Peter is taken to the room where her body lay, "all the widows stood around him, weeping and showing the robes and clothing that Dorcas had made while she was still with them" (9:39). The fact that the widows are "weeping" shows the high regard and affection that the community had for Tabitha.[55] Luke's record of them "showing the robes and clothing" may be intended to generate emotion in the audience. This narratival technique was apparently used to sway people over to one particular side of an argument.[56] In this story, the pathos has the effect of moving the emotions of the reader/hearer to the effect that they would want to emulate Tabitha's good works. The story about Tabitha also suggests that *a woman may be the central figure in a Christian ministry of service.*

Mary mother of John, and Rhoda (Acts 12:12-17)

Mary hosted regular Christian gatherings in her home

---

55. Ibid., 469. Peter sent the mourners out of the room, as Jesus had done with the Markan account of the revivification of Jairus' daughter (Mark 5:40). This detail is not included in the Lukan parallel (Luke 8:49–55). There is some archaeological and iconographic work which portrays prostitutes working in textile making (Erischen-Wendt, "Tabitha," 78). If there is an association between textile making and prostitution, then the fact that Tabitha would be prepared to be mistaken as a prostitute and undertake menial textile handiworks is remarkable. This is all the more so if she indeed was a wealthy woman. The servant nature of her discipleship has few parallels in Luke-Acts.

56. Keener, *Acts*, 2:1720.

The plot of Acts contains a number of narrative knots which must be overcome. One is Peter's imprisonment and subsequent angelic liberation. What will Peter do now? Surely he needs to communicate the news of his escape and then find refuge. The problem of communicating with his associates is resolved by means of a meeting house which the early Christians frequented; a house run by a woman. After realizing that an angel had liberated him from prison, the apostle Peter "went to the house of Mary the mother of John, also called Mark, where many people had gathered and were praying" (Acts 12:12b, c). Peter probably chose the house of Mary because he knew that believers were likely to be there.[57] This suggests that Mary's house was a hub for the early Christians in that part of Jerusalem, or for Jerusalem as a whole.[58] This conforms to the ideal pattern set out in Acts 2:42–44, whereby the believers were continually together and were devoted to the Lord and each other. Hence the pattern is implicitly approved according to the narratival standards set by the author.[59]

"The reference to 'many' meeting in the household suggests a house of considerable size, as does the reference to a courtyard gate and a female gatekeeper."[60] The fact that Rhoda later recognizes Peter's voice also intimates that he was a frequent visitor to the house in which she served.[61] Mary is one of six characters so named in the NT.[62] She was a wealthy woman (the house had an outer gate) who presented her home as a meeting place for the believers in Jerusalem. The fact that a woman is the head of the house is noteworthy, and it is most likely that she was widowed. At a broader narratival level this anticipates the later story of Lydia (16:11–15).[63] Once Peter departs, the reader assumes that the assembly of Christians will continue to meet at Mary's house and she will continue to be the patron and convenor of the Christians that meet there. This would leave her in the role of organizing all the daily details and events that would occur in these gatherings in line with Acts 2:42–47.[64]

---

57. Peterson argues for a number of houses in use in the Jerusalem church. Commenting on Mary's house, he writes: "There were probably other such houses in Jerusalem where large numbers of Christians could also meet, since growing opposition from unbelieving Jews would have made it impossible for them to meet in the temple courts (cf. 2:46)." Peterson, *Acts of the Apostles*: 365.

58. Schnabel, *Acts*, 539.

59. Reimer, *Frauen in der Apostelgeschichte des Lukas*, 247.

60. Witherington, *Acts of the Apostles*, 386.

61. Peterson, *Acts of the Apostles*, 365.

62. Schnabel, *Acts*, 539, n.14.

63. For example, Witherington, *Acts of the Apostles*, 386.

64. Reimer, *Frauen in der Apostelgeschichte des Lukas*, 248.

> *By virtue of her inclusion in the Christian community, Rhoda operates beyond the sociological expectations of her gender and class*

"Peter knocked at the outer entrance, and a servant girl called Rhoda came to answer the door" (Acts 12:13). As a female slave (παιδίσκη), Rhoda was at the near-bottom of the social strata and open to double standards and abuse, such as sexual abuse by male masters and their associates.[65] Given that characters in Greco-Roman narrative literature were not often developed but were mostly left one-dimensional, the first-time reader would assume that a slave girl would follow the stereotypes for such a character in literature.[66] Slave girls were often presented with low regard. Keener describes common depictions regarding their reporting of events in particular:

> [S]laves could be associated with the insane, but more often moral connotations were attached to their reports. Ancient literature regularly portrays them as flatterers, liars, and twisters of the truth to ingratiate themselves with their slaveholders (Char. *Chaer.* 6.5.5). Novels portrayed them as unafraid to lie under oath (Apul. *Metam.* 10.7), even under torture (10.10). Masters taught them to deceive by the servile behavior for which they rewarded them.[67]

Luke's story surely would have surprised first-time hearers/readers as far as his characterization of Rhoda was concerned. Given that Rhoda had to go to the gate to answer Peter, this suggests that she was not present at the gate when he first knocked. Given the context of the passage, the narrative does not prohibit her presence and participation in the prayer meeting that was the focus of the household at the time. This inclusive possibility has been anticipated in Acts 1, and thus does not come as a surprise to the reader/hearer. In 1:14 the eleven apostles "all joined together constantly in prayer, along with the women and Mary the mother of Jesus, and his brothers." Not only were males and females meeting for prayer, but the Joel

---

65. See the well-documented excuses on "woman slaves" and "sexual abuse" in Keener, *Acts*, 2:1928–42.

66. "Ancient characterisation in Greco-Roman literature tended to portray stylized characters who were unchanging and predictable. Characters were not developed psychologically and showed little inclination to introspection, . . . the outward actions and words of a person reflected what was inside a person's mind or heart. . . . Ancient type-characters tend not to change a great deal." Rhoads, Dewey, and Michie, *Mark as Story*, 100–101.

67. Keener, *Acts*, 2: 1944.

citation in 2:18 records God's promise that female as well as male servants will prophesy after they receive God's Spirit.

The story provides a number of strong clues that Rhoda was a believer in Jesus. First, when she heard Peter's voice, she recognized him. Second, upon recognizing him she experienced a powerful emotional reaction. Luke tells us that "she was so overjoyed that she ran back without opening the gate and exclaimed that Peter was standing at the gate" (12:14).

In fact her response to Peter is as comedic as it is emotional. In this sense she does live up to some expectations with respect to slave girls being foolish. However, this comedic twist is felt more strongly with respect to the others in the house. The real laugh is had at the expense of those who believe Rhoda is lying or hallucinating and then proceed to tell her to be quiet. The comedic thread ultimately serves to enhance Rhoda's character and witness in the eyes of the audience. This is achieved because Luke subverts the character conventions which would have Rhoda say ludicrous (but funny) things. She speaks the truth whilst others deride her. Thus the role of the 'fool' is played by the Christian community gathered in the house, not Rhoda.[68]

Rhoda's witness and strength of character in the face of opposition are ultimately successful. By means of these the narrative establishes her as the lead female protagonist with reference to the house. Rhoda had to assert herself in an uncustomary manner. She did not lecture her patron, but did assert her conviction over and against that of all the others in the house, including Mary. As the story progresses she moves from being portrayed as a mere servant to the character upon whom the narrative focuses.[69] This episode, and other stories of female characters in Luke-Acts, work cumulatively to direct the audience to Luke's view that *the Christian faith not only allows women to operate within the sphere of the kingdom of God, but even to serve God and others beyond what their social circumstances would usually prescribe.* Keener writes: "Because Rhoda has the higher role than her mistress here, Luke is able to hint at his larger portrayal of good news as transcending class as well as gender (cf. Luke 4:1–19; esp. 1:4, 51–53)."[70]

Rhoda's announcement meets incredulous resistance as did the women's proclamation of Jesus' resurrection

---

68. Ibid., 1947.

69. This overruling of social norms is theologically consistent with Paul's words in Galatians 3:28: " There is neither Jew nor Greek, slave nor free, male or female, if you are all one in Christ Jesus." Richter Reimer, *Frauen in der Apostelgeschichte des Lukas*, 248.

70. Keener, *Acts*, 2:1945.

Rhoda's character begins with a significant disadvantage with respect to truthful witnessing to an event. Her character must overcome deep social and literary expectations:

> Rhoda's gender and slave status together conspire against her credibility with others in the narrative world; Josephus, perhaps our best extant reflection of what some Hellenists in the Upper City would have thought, warns against trusting women's testimony because of their instability and that of slaves because they lack virtue (*Ant.* 4.219).[71]

Given the first-century context of the stories in Acts, it is not surprising that Rhoda's initial report about Peter is met with "You are out of your mind!" (Acts 12:15a). However, Rhoda does not conform to stereotypical depictions of females or female slaves. She brings a faithful, if somewhat surprising, witness to the Christian group. Indeed, Rhoda's truthful claim is contrasted with theological confusion: "When she kept insisting that it was so, they said, 'It must be his angel'" (12:15).[72] Rhoda's depiction in the narrative as far as her witness is concerned is positive. This would be surprising to the first readers and hearers of Acts. However, it would not be as surprising to those in the audience who had heard or read the Third Gospel.

The climax of that Gospel arrives on the lips of women who conveyed the news about Jesus' resurrection to more notable characters who did not believe them. Moreover, the disbelief occurred in the context of joyful news. To the apostles and those gathered with them in the upper room, the news of the resurrection which was brought to them by the women was deemed to be "nonsense" (Luke 24:11). This mistake is repeated and condemned by the narrative in the Rhoda story; Luke suggests that those who reject good news based on the gender or status of the carrier are fools.[73]

Rhoda's announcement is confirmed as true witness

Rhoda's words are ultimately vindicated. "But Peter kept on knocking, and when they opened the door and saw him, they were astonished" (Acts 12:16). Rhoda's message and character are vindicated by the fact that Peter was indeed knocking at the outer entrance. Rhoda had perceived clearly—Peter

---

71. Ibid., 1944.

72. Wright, *Resurrection*, 131–40, shows how the designation of "angel" was a Jewish term for the intermediate state—a dead person awaiting resurrection.

73. Their foolishness is heightened by the possibility that they were praying for Peter yet did not believe that their prayers would be answered positively or so immediately!

was there. Rhoda had also demonstrated the strength to persistently point to the truth in the face of resistance.

This is the second servant girl story in Luke-Acts in which a servant girl has spoken rightly about Peter in the context of a wealthy home and in the face of denial. In Luke 22:56, a servant girl recognized Peter for who he was "in the middle of the courtyard" (22:55), however he denies her claim is true. In this story Rhoda recognized Peter at the outer gate of the courtyard, yet her claim is denied by those inside the house. The parallels are such that careful craftsmanship is evident in affirming the witness of a lower-class woman over and against the denials of others.

The Christian gathering in Mary's home played a pivotal role in the transition of leadership from Peter to James

This story is told at a time when there was transition in the Jerusalem church leadership. Once Peter is surrounded by the larger group of believers, he "motioned with his hand for them to be quiet and described how the Lord had brought him out of the prison. He said, 'Tell James and the believers about this,' and then departed for another place" (Acts 12:17).[74] This verse functions as a transition from Peter's leadership role in the Jerusalem church to its leadership under James. Witherington writes: "this narrative intimates that Peter will no longer be the leading authority figure in Jerusalem, and that James is *already at this time* the one to whom this report must especially go."[75]

There are two reasons to suggest that the gathering in Mary's house played a pivotal role in this transition of leadership. First, is Peter's awareness that there would be a gathering of trustworthy Christian people at this house. Second, it appears that they alone were entrusted with the important task of conveying the news concerning Peter's escape.

Mary embodies the qualities of hospitality and generosity

The narrative presents certain character qualities which enable Mary to play a leading role in the early Jerusalem church. She is hospitable and possesses a disposition of generosity towards others. Unwittingly her generosity had the potential to implicate her in the drama surrounding Peter's escape. The narrator tells us that: "in the morning there was no small commotion

---

74. The "brothers" may refer either to believers as a whole or to the leadership of the Jerusalem church.

75. Italics are Witherington's. Witherington, *Acts of the Apostles,* 388.

among the soldiers as to what had become of Peter. After Herod had a thorough search made for him and did not find him, he examined the guards and ordered that they be executed." (Acts 12:18–19). Peter's disappearance was clearly a significant incident in Jerusalem. Knowledge of Peter's escape and his flight could have implicated Mary and her household in his escape.

Summary of Narratival Propositions

Ananias and Sapphira lie to the Spirit who is the guarantor of the existence, unity, and purity of the early church. Thus Luke does not idealize women, for female disciples may be involved in the worst kinds of sinful acts against God and his new people.

The seven take on a role which was usually carried out by women, which indicates that gender may not be the driving criteria for a ministry of service in the church. The whole community elected the seven, including men and women. This suggests that women may participate fully in the decision-making processes of the church.

Spirit-formed character was a primary characteristic of being set aside for a ministry of service in the early church. The Spirit empowers Stephen, a man outside the twelve, to prophesy and preach in addition to his diaconal role. This would indicate that a diaconal form of ministry does not preclude prophesying and preaching. As the Spirit is given to all believers, not the apostles alone, any believer may prophesy or preach.

Service is a positive mark for any disciple, not for those of female gender alone. This means that women and men who participate in the kingdom of God will not necessarily be channelled into stereotypical roles which correspond to expectations in wider society.

The work of the Spirit in a given context is the impetus for Christian ministries and ministry designations. We would therefore expect that the ministries of women would be Spirit led, and the tasks entailed by these ministries may vary according to different ministry contexts.

The word of God is personified in the book of Acts, and the personalization of the word of God and its advancement resist it being necessarily linked to apostolic ministry. Thus the apostles and the seven serve the word of the Lord, not vice versa. Therefore, a woman's gender does not disable her from authoritatively and effectively proclaiming the word of God.

Tabitha's story is paired with the story of Aeneas in such a way that she emerges as the more commendable character of the two. Tabitha's ministry takes the form of active service for the sake of the needy, and her life is strong within the social memory of the Christians of her region. The account of her life suggests that a woman may be the central figure in a Christian ministry of service. Further, Tabitha is a female disciple whose gender is not a barrier to discipleship, and neither is her discipleship a barrier to the expression of her gender. Therefore, female believers may be disciples in the fullest sense, and being a female disciple does not mean the suppression of her gender.

Mary hosted regular Christian gatherings in her home. Her servant Rhoda's announcement met similar incredulous resistance as did the women's proclamation of Jesus' resurrection. Yet her announcement was confirmed as true witness. By virtue of her inclusion in the Christian community, Rhoda operated beyond the sociological expectations of her gender and class. Consequently, the Christian faith not only allows women to operate within the sphere of the kingdom of God, but even to serve God and others beyond what their social circumstances would normally prescribe.

The Christian gathering in Mary's home played a pivotal role in the transition of leadership from Peter to James. In this context Mary embodies two qualities of discipleship, namely hospitality and generosity.

Theological Propositions

The narrative of Acts 3–12 gives rise to a number of theological propositions regarding female disciples of Jesus, particularly to do with their participation in the communal and missionary activity of the church.

1. God deals with women and men equally without favoritism with respect to sin and salvation.
2. The Spirit's work in the life of a person or community provides the power and direction around which forms of service are structured.
3. In the advancement of both God's kingdom and God's word, particular ministry designations or gender roles are fluid and a secondary concern.
4. God may include both single and married women in his work in the world.
5. Women may announce God's continuing works in the world.
6. Women may play a leading role in Christian gatherings.
7. God may establish a Christian community upon the foundational presence and work of a woman.
8. God may sustain a Christian community by means of the activities of a woman.

9. God may establish and sustain a Christian ministry based upon the foundational work of a woman.
10. God's character should be reflected in the lives of those who represent him to the world's cultures.
11. God carries out his mission to local cultures in such a way that Christian men and women may perform ministry roles which are supported by cultural norms.
12. God carries out his mission to local cultures in such a way that Christian men and women may perform ministry roles which are counter cultural.

CHAPTER 10

The Church in the Greco-Roman World (Acts 13–28)

The Conversion of Lydia (Acts 16:11–40)

IN RESPONSE TO A vision received at Troas, Paul and his companions[1] departed to preach the gospel in Macedonia. The first stop was the Roman colony of Philippi. The city was located on the Via Egnatia, the major east-west thoroughfare which connected Rome with provinces in the east. As a Roman colony its citizens enjoyed freedom from taxation, and lived under Roman law and government.[2] Tannehill contends that the overt mention of Philippi as a Roman colony was "not just to add local color but because the narrative is centrally concerned with the mission's encounter with the Roman world."[3]

Typically looking for a point of contact with the Jewish population, on the sabbath Paul journeyed outside the city gate looking for a place of prayer (προσευχήν). Commentators are divided as to whether προσευχή should be

---

1. This is the beginning of the "we" sections in Acts, as the author himself becomes part of the narrative. The most natural assumption, and the one that raises the least difficulties, is that Luke was a some-time companion of Paul. For a discussion, see Witherington, *Acts of the Apostles*, 480–86; Bock, *Acts*, 13–15; Schnabel, *Acts*, 38–41; Dunn, *Beginning from Jerusalem*, 64–66.

2. Ascough, *Lydia*, 19–27; Peterson, *Acts of the Apostles*, 459. Witherington, *Acts of the Apostles*, 488, notes that over 80 percent of the inscriptional evidence found at Philippi is in Latin rather than Greek.

3. Tannehill, *Narrative Unity*, 2:201.

understood here as a technical term for a synagogue—here located beyond the city walls,[4] or whether the description indicates a less formal meeting.[5] Favoring the latter is that it best explains why Paul immediately dialogues with the women. Paul's synagogue encounters typically deal with men, but here, perhaps surprisingly, they "spoke to the women who had gathered" (Acts 16:13).[6] This probably indicates that no men were present, which may explain the absence of a synagogue, for a Jewish synagogue required ten men to form a quorum.[7] Either way, the concerns of the synagogue, namely sabbath worship and prayer are still apparent.

Spencer comments that the location of the meeting outside the city and its composition of women rather than men, "betray its restricted, marginal status within the Roman colony."[8] This may be evident in the rather derogatory way in which the accusers of Paul and Silas later state the charge against them—"These men, being Jews, are troubling our city and are advocating customs which are not lawful for us, as Romans, to either accept or practice" (16:20–21).[9] In any event, here we see a break from the pattern of preaching the gospel in the synagogue within the town, with the focus on individual conversions and encounters, and the effect upon households.[10]

Lydia is the first Macedonian convert

The narrative then focuses on one woman who responded to the message. Lydia is characterized in a robust fashion and is clearly one of the leading female characters in Luke-Acts. The reader is told three things concerning Lydia. First, she was from Thyatira.[11] Second, she was a dealer in purple cloth (πορφυρόπωλις).[12] Thyatira was famous for its textile industry and the

---

4. Schnabel, *Acts*, 679–80; Bock, *Acts*, 533.

5. Peterson, *Acts of the Apostles*, 460; Bruce, *Acts of the Apostles*, 358; Thomas, "Place of Women," 117.

6. See Trebilco, *Jewish Communities in Asia Minor*, 104–26, for a discussion of the prominence of women in Jewish communities in this region.

7. *m. Sanh.* 1:6

8. Spencer, *Journeying Through Acts*, 174. Also Witherington, *Acts of the Apostles*, 490.

9. Thomas, "Place of Women," 117.

10. Peterson, *Acts of the Apostles*, 457.

11. Thyatira was in the region of Lydia in Asia Minor, and so this woman was named after the region from which she originated—Bruce, *Acts of the Apostles*, 358; Peterson, *Acts of the Apostles*, 460.

12. On this particular trade, see Ascough, *Lydia*, 58–81.

production of purple dye.[13] Purple was a color traditionally associated with wealth and royalty. Given the reference to "her household" it is likely that Lydia had established her business in Philippi rather than being a frequent traveller to the city.[14] Third, she was a "worshiper of God" (σεβομένη τὸν θεόν). Most understand this term to relate to Gentiles who attached themselves to the synagogue as worshipers of the God of Israel.[15]

It is likely that Lydia was a woman of some status as it was uncommon for women to be publicly mentioned by name in Greco-Roman society unless they were prominent.[16] She also appears to be head of her household, which tends to indicate that she was either widowed or divorced, or a single woman of considerable means.[17] Consequently she would have experienced a considerable degree of independence and mobility.

Lydia is central to God's purposes in Philippi and plays an integral role in the origins of that local church

It is significant, as Spencer notes, that although a Macedonian male appeared in the vision requesting Paul to come to Macedonia and preach the gospel, it is, in fact, a woman who first receives and responds to the message.[18] The fact that Lydia received direct instruction from a man also contrasts the position of women in Judaism, where "she could share only peripherally in the ritual and liturgy of Israel."[19] Her response is divinely prompted (Acts 16:14), which conveys to the reader that Christian origins in Philippi centering on the female Lydia were not the result of a circumstantial encounter between her and Paul but were divinely orchestrated.[20]

This again underlines the lack of gender discrimination that is typical of Luke-Acts and the significant role that women play at various places in the nascent Christian movement. "That the first candidate for baptism in

---

13. *ABD* 6:546.

14. Bruce, *Acts of the Apostles*, 359, mentions epigraphic evidence of a guild of purple merchants resident in Philippi.

15. See ibid., 252–53. Ascough, *Lydia*, 87–90, contends that the term simply indicates that Lydia was a devout worshiper of Greco-Roman deities.

16. Witherington, *Acts of the Apostles*, 492.

17 Ascough, *Lydia*, 35–45. There are texts indicating that women could act independently of their legal guardian in certain situations. For example, freeborn women with three children and freed women with four children had this and other legal privileges. See *New Docs.* 2.29, 32.

18. Spencer, *Journeying through Acts*, 174.

19. Thomas, "Place of Women," 117.

20. Peterson, *Acts of the Apostles*, 461.

Philippi was the woman Lydia points to a new status for women, a new estimate of the value and place of women in the purpose of God."[21] Luke clearly believes that *women are not marginal members of the kingdom of God nor of its expression in a given locale. Further, a woman may be a central figure in God's purposes with respect to the establishment of a church community in a given location.*

Lydia is a model disciple of Jesus who demonstrates hospitality and service

Following Lydia's acceptance of the message "she and her entire household were baptized" (Acts 16:15). This accords with common cultural practice, and is a familiar pattern in Acts (11:14; 16:33; 18:8).[22] She then enthusiastically offered hospitality to Paul and his entourage, thus echoing other female characters in Luke-Acts who support Jesus and/or his followers from their means (Luke 8:1–3; Acts 12:12). There is no indication in the narrative that Paul initially refused Lydia's offer because she, being a woman, was untrustworthy.[23] Rather, the Greek term παρεβιάσατο ("urge"/"persuade") reflects the Middle Eastern custom of initially refusing an offer only to have it repeated and accepted on the second or third occasion.[24] Her discipleship and piety is exemplified by her hospitality and generosity.[25]

Lydia is the ideal God-fearer. She is open to the message of God's kingdom, and in her baptism and that of her household she precisely echoes the response that Peter called for in his Pentecost address (Acts 2:38). Although wealthy, she has the same humble disposition towards God as do the lowly in Luke-Acts. In all the above, and in her offer of hospitality she parallels the earlier story of Cornelius (10:48).[26]

Lydia becomes the patroness of the fledgling church at Philippi

There is a turn in the narrative as Paul and Silas are thrown into prison at the instigation of the owners of a slave girl angry at their potential loss of business after a spirit of divination was driven from her (Acts 16:16–40). After

---

21. Thomas, "Place of Women," 118.

22. This not only parallels the Jewish practice of proselyte baptism of families (Peterson, *Acts of the Apostles*, 461). It also attests to the function of the head of the household in setting the religious agenda for those within the house.

23. Contra Schottroff, *Lydia's Impatient Sisters*, 110.

24. Ascough, *Lydia*, 47.

25. Peterson, *Acts of the Apostles*, 462.

26. Schnabel, *Acts*, 681.

the episode with the jailer and the release of the apostles they returned to the house of Lydia where "they met with the brothers and encouraged them" (16:40). It is unlikely that "the brothers" were only the traveling companions of Paul waiting for him at Lydia's house. Rather, they should be understood as new converts meeting in Lydia's home.[27] We know that the jailer and his household were also converted and it is highly likely that others were as well. The narrative is highly condensed and the "many days" (16:12) they remained in the city allows a much wider scope for evangelistic activity and conversions than are explicitly described.[28] These likely resulted not only from Paul's evangelistic activity, but also from Lydia's social and economic networks.[29] The new believers would have needed a place to meet and Lydia had both the means and the sense of hospitality to make it happen.[30]

In hosting the believers in her home, Lydia was not stepping outside the bounds of Roman culture. Beginning with Augustus, Roman women had been given increasing freedom, and as we saw in chapter 2, women regularly participated in religious rites and leadership of religious cults. Ascough comments, "she would not have been alone among women of the *kolōnia* in finding Eastern cults attractive and becoming involved in hosting and leading a group of cult devotees in her home."[31]

Moreover, in terms of Luke's narrative, here we find a further parallel between Lydia and Cornelius. Just as the conversion of Cornelius is the paradigmatic key that opens up the ministry to the Gentiles, so Lydia's conversion and ministry makes possible a new paradigm for female leadership over Christian households. Lydia's home had clearly become the meeting place for Christians in Philippi, "a strategic base of operation for Paul."[32] In this she may have had the responsibility of preparing and presiding over the shared meal in which believers remembered the death of Jesus.

Lydia thus functions as a paradigm for supportive Christian ministry in general, and more particularly as an example of generosity which would characterize the growing Philippian church (see Phil 4:10-20). Indeed, the

---

27. So Peterson, *Acts of the Apostles*, 474.

28. Schnabel, *Acts*, 682, 695. Witherington, *Acts of the Apostles*, 487, is probably correct in stating, "It is no accident that he focuses in 16:11-40 on the conversion of one woman and one man in Philippi in order to stress the equality of women and men in God's plan of salvation and their equal importance in the new community."

29. Ascough, *Lydia*, 55-57.

30. It is quite possible that Luke stayed behind in Philippi to attend to certain aspects of the work there, as the first person plural references cease at this point, and recommence in 20:5 from Philippi (Bruce, *Acts of the Apostles*, 367; Schnabel, *Acts*, 695).

31. Ascough, *Lydia*, 93.

32. Bock, *Acts*, 546.

references to Lydia frame the entire ministry in Philippi. This highlights her significance for the development of Christianity in this town and her role as patroness of the Christian community.[33] As Tannehill states, "In this way the narrator acknowledges the important role that local sponsors played in the establishment of the church and demonstrates the necessary partnership between traveling missionaries and local supporters."[34] Here Lydia anticipates other leading women whom Luke mentions by name: the leading women of Thessalonica (Acts 17:4), and the Greek women of high standing in Beroea (17:12). With respect to Philippi, Lydia also anticipates other leading women in this church, namely Euodia and Syntyche, whom Paul commends as his co-workers in his letter of friendship (Phil 4:2–3).

Priscilla (Acts 18:1–28)

Acts 18 shifts the reader from Athens to Corinth.[35] At Corinth Paul connects with one of the most prominent couples in early Christianity: Aquila and Priscilla.[36] This couple has been referred to as "the most prominent couple involved in the first-century expansion of Christianity."[37] They are referred to and held in high regard in a variety of passages in Acts (18:2–3, 18, 26) and the Paulines (Rom 16:3–5; 1 Cor 16:19; 2 Tim 4:19).[38] Paul "found a

---

33. Peterson, *Acts of the Apostles*, 458; Tannehill, *Narrative Unity*, 2:196–97. The relationship between Lydia and Paul is more complex. Lydia was indebted to Paul because he brokered access to the divine. Thus the hospitality she provided did not place her in a position of Paul's patron, but was an act of reciprocity for the benefits she had obtained through him (Ascough, *Lydia*, 53).

34. Tannehill, *Narrative Unity*, 2:197.

35. Paul likely arrived in Corinth in February or March of 50 AD. Schnabel, *Early Christian mission*: 2:1181.

36. Priscilla is the diminutive form of Prisca. For lengthy (though highly speculative) discussions on the nature of the diminutive. See Kurek-Chomycz, "Is there an 'Anti-Priscan' Tendency in the Manuscripts? Some Textual Problems with Prisca and Aquila." and Walker Jr., "The Portrayal of Aquila and Prisiclla in Acts: The Question for Sources."

37. Murphy-Connor, "Prisca and Aquila," 40.

38. The stories of Priscilla and Aquila in Acts are complemented and filled by the details about this couple in the Pauline epistles. The relationship also works in the other direction. The information we have about Priscilla and Aquila in the Paulines is enhanced by the accounts from Acts. The underlying reason for this is that both sources provide information on the missionary circles within which both Paul and Priscilla and Aquila worked. Outlining this mission and the characterization of women within its expansive reach could well be a topic of fruitful research. Richter Reimer, *Frauen in der Apostelgeschichte des Lukas*, 202. Marguerat's three-fold typology for interpreting Paul with special reference to non-Pauline works such as Acts provides

Jew named Aquila, a native of Pontus, recently come from Italy with his wife Priscilla, because Claudius had commanded all the Jews to leave Rome. And he went to see them" (18:2). The verb "went to them" (προσῆλθεν) indicates deliberate action on Paul's behalf; he sought them out. Given that the story of Acts concentrates on Peter and Paul and their closest associates, the fact that Priscilla and Aquila are recorded indicates their strategic influence and activity regarding key events in the Pauline Mediterranean mission.[39] They make powerful contributions to the mission in three key centers of Christian and imperial activity: Rome, Ephesus, and Corinth.

Priscilla and Aquila suffered for the cause of Christ

The reason for Aquila and Priscilla's presence in Corinth was an edict by the emperor Claudius (AD 41–54), one of two edicts which ordered the Jews to leave Rome. The Roman historian Dio Cassius (b. AD 155) records that Claudius issued a decree in his first year (AD 41) which ordered Jews to follow their ancient practices and not to deviate from them. This appears to have been legislated due to the civil complaints being made by Jews about the missionary activity of Jewish Christians.[40] The second decree, to which the author of Acts is most likely referring (Acts 18:2), was made in AD 49. The historian Suetonius (b. circa AD 70) recorded that Claudius expelled people of foreign birth from Rome on account of Jews who "constantly made disturbances at the instigation of Chrestus."[41] *Chrestus* is taken by most to be a misinterpretation of the name *Christos*, referring to Jesus the Christ. The likely conclusion is that "the disturbances were provoked by the missionary outreach of Jewish Christians who preached Jesus as Messiah ('Christos')

---

helpful methodological avenues for exploration in this direction. Marguerat, "Paul aprés Paul: une historie de réception." See also Marguerat, *Reception of Paulinism in Acts [= Réception du Paulinisme dans les Actes des apôtres]*. Further Marguerat, *Paul in Acts and Paul in his letters*.

39. Richter Reimer, *Frauen in der Apostelgeschichte des Lukas*, 202. McCarty writes "the witness to Priscilla, [in] the Acts 18 text, is rich in everyday details and conditions of missionary life in the emerging church; it offers an invaluable picture of the origins of Christianity among the Corinthians, and it helps to contextualize Paul's own more impressionistic account provided in 1 Corinthians 3–4. Both the Lucan and Pauline sources attest to Prisca and Aquila as among 'Paul's most strategic allies in his gentile mission.'" McCarty, "Prisca—Fellow Tent-maker and Fellow Missionary of Paul: Acts 18:2–3; Romans 16:3–4; 1 Corinthians 16:19; 2 Timothy 4:19," 45. In the final sentence above, McCarty cites Köstenberger, "Women in the Pauline Mission," 228.

40. Cassius Dio 60.6.6. Cited in Schnabel, *Acts*, 756.

41. Suetonius, Life of Claudius, XXV.4, cited in Stevenson, *A New Eusebius*, 1.

in the synagogues of Rome."[42] If this dating is correct, Aquila and Priscilla probably arrived in Corinth in the year 49.[43] Soon after they met Paul, also a recent arrival in Corinth. There is no indication from the narrative that Aquila and Priscilla were converted during their stay in Corinth or through Paul's ministry. Rather, the text implies that they are mature Christians and had been Christians when they resided in Rome. Given that they arrived in Corinth before Paul, it is possible that they may have laid the basis for what became the Pauline church.[44]

Paul was theologically comfortable with Aquila and Priscilla's faith and ministry

Aquila and Priscilla were tentmakers as was Paul (Acts 18:3a). For this reason Paul "stayed and worked with them" (18:3b). This detail is significant because it contributes to the characterization of Priscilla (and Aquila) as well as suggesting the kind of interactions which Paul had with them. In terms of characterization, the couple are presented as entrepreneurial artisans.[45] The characterization of Priscilla is strong and positive; despite being ejected from Rome and frequent travel and relocation, she manages a successful business with her husband. This fact is paired with her well-regarded Christian ministry. The narrative thus presents the reader with a character whose work ethic enables her to contribute significantly to church and world.[46]

The fact that Paul "stayed and worked with them" (18:3b) is also significant as this would have entailed close proximity and regular interaction. It is easy for contemporary readers of Acts to underestimate the degree of this intimacy. For this reason, we have included a well-regarded (reconstructed)

---

42. Schnabel, *Acts*, 756.

43. Witherington, *The Acts of the Apostles*, 545.

44. "Luke's account gives the impression that Aquila and Priscilla were believers when Paul met them in Corinth. If they had been involved in missionary outreach to other Jews in Rome, it is not impossible to assume that they were 'independent' missionaries who engaged in missionary work before Paul arrived. Nevertheless, Paul implies in 1 Cor. 2:1–5 that he founded the church in Corinth." Schnabel, *Acts*, 756. In 1 Corinthians 1:11 Paul refers to Chloe, a prominent woman in the Corinthian church. Schnabel believes that another prominent woman in the Pauline churches was Phoebe who was a merchant. Schnabel, *Acts*, 766.

45. Klauck, *Hausgemeinde und Hauskirche im frühen Christentum*, 3 ff.

46. This is a significant reason for Richter-Reimer's claim that Priscilla is portrayed as an "outstanding/brilliant missionary." ("ausgezeichnete Missionarin"). Richter Reimer, *Frauen in der Apostelgeschichte des Lukas*, 218.

description of their living and working arrangements in Corinth's North Market for the sake of today's reader:

> The shops gave on to a wide, covered gallery running round all four sides of the square. They had a uniform height and depth of 4 m (13 feet). The width varied from 2.8 m (8 feet) to 4 m (13 feet). There was no running water or toilet facilities. In one of the back corners, a series of steps in stone or brick was continued by a wooden ladder to a loft lit by an unglazed window centered above the shop entrance, which at night was closed by wooden shutters. Prisca and Aquila had their home in the loft, while Paul slept below amid the tool-strewn work and the rolls of leather and canvas.[47]

The narrative suggests a very positive and strong relationship between Paul and Priscilla and Aquila.[48] When read in conjunction with the Epistle to the Romans it is also apparent that they had a long-term ministry partnership. When Paul left Corinth for Ephesus after a year and a half of ministry, Aquila and Priscilla travelled with him (Acts 18:19). Years later, when greeting them as leaders of their home church in Rome, Paul recounts that they "risked their lives" for him (Rom 16:4). This long term association suggests that Paul would have been comfortable with them theologically and in terms of their ministry practice.[49]

---

47. Murphy-O'Connor, *Paul*, 263. Cited in Schnabel, *Acts*, 757. The market would have been a place where Paul would have had frequent contact with women as well as with men, meaning that both genders would have come into contact with Paul's message. "Tent-making would have brought patrons to their shop and the opportunity to persuade people on a one-to-one basis about the good news in Jesus Christ. The marketplace would have given Paul and Priscilla daily access to a great variety of people, including women. It is important to note that, especially in the poorer sectors of the first-century economy, it was not possible for women to be tucked away in private homes, secluded from the activities and lively conversations of the marketplace. As Paul was working at tent-making not only did Prisca likely share the labor alongside her husband at their craftwork, but Paul would have come in contract with women vendors and patrons alike on a daily basis." McCarty, "Prisca—Fellow Tent-maker and Fellow Missionary of Paul: Acts 18:2–3; Romans 16:3–4; 1 Corinthians 16:19; 2 Timothy 4:19," 51–52. McCarty also notes Cohick's work and her statement that "Inscriptions, epitaphs, and visual art all suggest the active presence of women in the economy of the ancient world." Cohick, *Women in the World of the Earliest Christians*, 242.

48. "Aquila and Priscila are introduced in 18:2. They are important, first of all, because they enable Paul to work at his trade. Later they will travel with Paul from Corinth to Ephesus (1:1) and will play a role in the mission as teachers during Paul's absence from Ephesus (1:26). Thus they are more than [his] employers." Tannehill, *Narrative Unity*, 2:221.

49. Indeed, this raises intriguing questions and suggestions: "it is fascinating to consider what influence Prisca's life partnership with Aquila may have had on Paul's

A church in the early Christian missionary movement was likely patroned and led by a married couple

The house shared by Priscilla, Aquila and Paul would have lent itself towards being the initial meeting place for local Christians and inquirers.[50] Aquila and Priscilla would naturally be the patrons of this church.[51] However, on the conversion of the "many" in Corinth (Acts 18:8), the church meetings would have moved to a larger space.

Priscilla was a travelling mission partner in the early Christian mission beyond Jerusalem

Paul's strategy was to establish a network of churches which were led by able men and women.[52] He would then revisit these churches where possible in order to provide strength and encouragement. Aquila and Priscilla were part of this expansive mission network and they too were travelling teachers. Tannehill describes the example they provided and their important role: "Priscilla and Aquila are examples of Christians who not only support a local community but also travel and link communities.... There is a suggestion here of the benefit to the mission from folk who are able to travel and who use that opportunity for mission and the new communities."[53]

---

evolving missionary strategy during his time sharing the tent-making trade with them and living in their home." McCarty, "Prisca," 53.

50. Schnabel, *Acts*. 575.

51. Given this, and the fact that a church met in Priscilla and Aquila's home in Rome, it is not surprising that Schüssler Fiorenza notes that Prisca is one of the "eminent missionaries and founders of house churches." Schüssler Fiorenza, *In Memory of Her*, 178.

52. Paul is part of a larger missionary endeavor which began in Jerusalem. His role was to expand this mission and strengthen it as a travelling evangelist, apologist, and community mentor. Paul clearly understood himself as part of this larger picture, hence his inclusion of other devoted Christians in this work. Tannehill writes: "Paul was not a loner, founding a separate Pauline church, but a major figure in one mission that began in Jerusalem and was effectively continued from Antioch.... Once churches have been established in an area, Paul will visit them again in order to strengthen them. Only then is Paul's work in an area relatively complete." Tannehill, *Narrative Unity*, 2:230.

53. Tannehill, *Narrative Unity*, 2:222–23. Furthermore, in Acts 18:18, there is a reference to another one of these churches in Cenchreae, also in the Corinthian region. Schnabel suggests that this church had "Phoebe as a patron of the congregation, a woman of means who, five years later, travelled to Rome taking Paul's letter from Corinth to the Roman Christians (Rom. 16:1–2)." Schnabel, *Acts*, 767. The explicit prominence of women in the Pauline church in this area is astounding. Priscilla and Chloe were prominent in the church at Corinth and Phoebe was naturally so as a patroness in nearby Cenchreae. In Col 4:15, another woman by the name of Nympha is a house

*Paul's confidence in Priscilla and Aquila is justified by
their ministry to Apollos and his subsequent success*

Priscilla and Aquila travelled with Paul in order to support the missionary expansion of the early church. The three depart Corinth together: "Paul... set sail for Syria, accompanied by Priscilla and Aquila" (Acts 18:18). After Paul spends some limited time in the synagogue at Ephesus debating with the Jews, he then departs and leaves behind Priscilla and Aquila. Given their ministry to Apollos which is described in vv. 26-27, any suggestion that they were not continuing in Christian ministry after Paul's departure runs counter to the narrative. It is clear then that Priscilla and Aquila were not merely pursuing a tent-making trade in Ephesus.

The city of Ephesus looms large in the book of Acts, with unique narratival attention and detail suggesting its significance. In Acts 18:23,

> Paul begins a journey to strengthen established churches. We hear of missionary preaching only in Ephesus, and even there some of the previous work had been done. We really have a settled mission in Ephesus incorporated into a journey of church visitation. . . . Ephesus is not just another stop in a series. It is Paul's last major place of new mission work; indeed, it is the sole center of mission noted in the last stage of Paul's work as a free man. The special importance of Ephesus appears already in 18:19-21, where Paul's brief visit to the Ephesian synagogue is indicated even though there is little to report except an initial responsiveness and Paul's promise to return. The fact that Paul's farewell speech will be addressed to the Ephesian elders is further indication of the special importance of Ephesus.[54]

Paul's refusal to stay on at Ephesus is initially jarring given the significance of this locale. Who will lead such a strategic mission, especially given the conflict which erupted around Paul's ministry? The narrative suggests that it will be Aquila and Priscilla. The fact that such a significant work as the Ephesian ministry would be left by Paul in the hands of his travelling companions, Priscilla and Aquila, confirms the high regard in which they were held by Paul

---

church leader directly greeted by Paul. In Acts 18, therefore, we have references to two locations in the Corinthian area in which Christian churches are present. One house church is led by a couple (Aquila and Priscilla), one is led by a woman (Phoebe). This suggests that leadership in early mission churches was not based on gifting within the range of male gender alone. It was based, rather, on God's providential work of conversion. In any given location, the converts and other Christians would gather around those Christians whom God had enabled (both materially and spiritually) to lead them.

54. Tannehill, *Narrative Unity*, 2:231.

THE CHURCH IN THE GRECO-ROMAN WORLD (ACTS 13–28)   195

and by the author of Acts. In this narrative account we are undoubtedly being introduced to two of the true gems of the early Gentile mission.

Priscilla may have been Apollos' primary theological instructor

Apollos enters the narrative in a straightforward manner. He was an Egyptian Jew, from Alexandria. Contrary to Aquila and Priscilla there is no description of his vocational trade nor his association with Paul. What sets him apart as a character is that he was "a learned man, well versed in the Scriptures" (Acts 18:24). He is portrayed as a believer in Jesus whose ministry was empowered by the Spirit, yet he may have been confused about the nature of Christian baptism.[55] Given such a lofty presentation of Apollos, it is significant that the narrative indicates Priscilla and Aquila as his hospitable teachers.[56] The record tells us that "when Priscilla and Aquila heard him, they invited him to their home and explained to him the way of God more adequately" (18:26 b, c).

The author of Acts conveys the qualities of their profound ministry to Apollos. These are: (1) they must have known the Scriptures more deeply than Apollos, (2) they were teachers, (3) they were hospitable. Furthermore, the word for "explained" (ἐκτίθημι) is reserved only for Peter and Paul aside from Priscilla and Aquila in the Acts narrative (11:4; 28:23).[57] By means of this ministry, the narrative presents them as the instructors of a gifted and godly teacher.[58] This presentation gives them high standing in the eyes of the audience of Acts.

Defying cultural convention, Priscilla's name is placed before her husband Aquila's in three out of the four uses of their names in Acts 18. Even more striking is that the only time Luke places Aquila's name before Priscila's is when he initially introduces the couple. By this the narrative suggests her prominence in three particular situations. Once the teaching ministry is in focus, her name is placed first. In our opinion, this communicates a

---

55. Schnabel proposes that "he may have baptized people with an emphasis on repentance and forgiveness of sins, without explaining the association of immersion in water with the life, death and resurrection of Jesus. This would certainly have been confusing for new converts and would have to be rectified." Schnabel, *Acts*, 785.

56. "With his competency in the scriptures, Apollos is invaluable for the transmission of the gospel, and Prisca and Apollos are described taking him aside, after hearing him preach boldly in the synagogue and explaining the Way of God to him more accurately. The couple was perhaps also useful in drawing him away from the synagogue to the growing congregation at the house church of Titus Justus, or perhaps to believers gathering for fellowship and prayer in Prisca's house." McCarty, "Prisca," 57.

57. Richter Reimer, *Frauen in der Apostelgeschichte des Lukas*, 221.

58. Ibid., 220.

deliberate task assignment by the author.[59] There have been other proposals for why Priscilla's name is placed before Aquila, but these are largely speculative. Some, for example, suggest that Priscilla was of a higher socio-economic status than Aquila.[60] There is not enough information to ground this claim, but the narrative does provide the context of a teaching activity as the basis for her prominent name.

On the likely assumption that the name priority for Priscilla is deliberate with respect to her teaching role, this reveals Luke's tacit support of female involvement in such ministries.[61] McCarty comments:

> [I]n this endeavour Priscilla is named first by Luke, a suggestion that there may have been a remembered tradition of her as the more persuasive tutor of Apollos and therefore at least in this respect, the more prominent member of the mission team. Since she was teaching Apollos, who was well-educated and well-versed in scripture, the reader might surmise that Prisca was herself well-educated and competent in scripture. This is reinforced as the story unfolds after this didactic episode in the positive outcome of Apollos' ministry with its subsequent success in Corinth; here he was able effectively to establish Jesus as the Messiah, using the proof of the scriptures (Acts 18:28).[62]

---

59. There is some disagreement on this in evangelical scholarship. For example, Schnabel is tentative with respect to Priscilla being in the lead role. He states Apollos was instructed "perhaps with Priscilla taking the lead." Schnabel, *Acts*, 786. This is a longstanding issue. It has even lead to manuscript alteration and apparently deliberate miscopying. As Peterson notes "The Western text mentions Aquila before Priscilla here and refers to Aquila without Priscilla in vv. 3, 18, and 21, apparently demonstrating an antifeminist tendency." Peterson, *Acts of the Apostles*: 526 n 84. Peterson himself seems to shy away from the issue of Pricilla's prominence in the couple's teaching ministry. However, he does acknowledge that Priscilla and Aquila's ministry was carried out "together."

60 A number of these speculative positions, as well as his own proposal, are outlined in Walker Jr., "Portrayal of Aquila and Prisiclla in Acts, 489 ff. . The "higher socio-economic status" argument does not work based on the information yielded by the narrative. McCarty writes: "Since she is described as working alongside her husband in their tent-making trade (Acts 18:3), it seems unlikely that Prisca either outranked Aquila socially or financially, in which case she would not have needed to work." McCarty thus concludes: "Therefore, some acknowledgement of Prisca's prominence in the life of the emerging Church may indeed be implied in the reversal of the traditional biblical form of naming the husband before the wife." McCarty, "Prisca," 49.

61. Witherington, *Women in the Earliest Churches*, 156, probably overstates the case with: "By including this story, Luke reveals the new roles women ought to be assuming in his view in the Christian community."

62. McCarty, "Prisca," 59.

Apollos' ministry highlights the fruit of Priscilla and Aquila's labors. When Apollos went to Achaia "he was of great assistance to those who through grace had become believers, for he vigorously refuted the Jews in public, demonstrating form the Scriptures that Jesus was the Messiah" (Acts 18:27–28). This serves to validate the teaching role of Priscilla in particular. It is hard to resist the fact that she is a key Christian character in the narrative and in the early Christian mission.

The Apollos account also serves another important theological and narratival role. It highlights the fact that the early Christian mission is expanding beyond the twelve apostles in Jerusalem, and even beyond Paul and his associates. It now lies in the hands of those mentored by disciples such as Priscilla and Aquila.

The influence of this couple continued for a number of years in various locations. By about AD 56 Aquila and Priscilla had returned to Rome, where they had a church meeting in their home (Rom 16:3, 5).[63] In Romans, where Priscilla is referred to as "Prisca," Paul writes: "Greet Prisca and Aquila, my fellow workers in Christ Jesus and who risked their lives for me, to whom not only do I give thanks, but also all the churches of the Gentiles" (Rom 16:3–4). In 1 Corinthians Paul also sent greetings from them to others: "The churches of Asia send greetings. Aquila and Prisca, together with the church in their house, greet you warmly in the Lord" (1 Cor 16:19), whilst they in turn receive greetings from Paul in 2 Timothy 4:19, "Greet Prisca and Aquila, and the household of Onesiphorus."

In sum, Priscilla is characterized as a female disciple who is willing to suffer for Jesus, to serve his worldwide mission, and to do so in partnership with others. She is presented as a character in whom the audience can have the utmost confidence. Priscilla was a co-missionary and house church leader with her husband in the nascent stages of Christianity. Her teaching role with respect to Apollos in particular makes her a standout character. By means of her teaching ministry, Priscilla embodies the principle and outcomes which were prized in Pauline communities. This is laid out in 2 Timothy 2:2, ". . . and the things you have heard me say in the presence of many witnesses entrust to reliable people who will also be qualified to teach others."

With respect to a number of areas, Priscilla is functionally able to live out the same forms of discipleship and gift expression as both her husband and Paul. These areas involve: (1) being willing to suffer for Jesus, (2) being a co-partner in mission, (3) leadership in the early Christian movement, and (4) teaching. Priscilla is a standout character in the narrative, but is not an atypical female disciple. Therefore, the narrative suggests that *women*

---

63. Schnabel, *Acts*, 757.

may carry out the same ministries as men, and to the same extent, including leadership and teaching within the larger Christian mission. Therefore, in the character and actions of Priscilla, a number of narratival threads in Luke-Acts concerning women converge.

The Daughters of Philip (Acts 21:1-16)

Here Luke narrates Paul's final journey to Jerusalem following the third missionary journey. At Miletus Paul had given instructions to the elders of Ephesus and said a final farewell, convinced that they would never see him again (Acts 20:17-38). The reader is not privy to the source of Paul's pessimism in this respect, but it is certainly vindicated in the narrative that follows. Luke then depicts the voyage to Caesarea via Cos, Rhodes, Tyre, and Ptolemais.

At Caesarea, Paul and his entourage lodge at the home of "Philip the evangelist, one of the Seven" (21:8). The reader is thereby drawn back to chapter 6 where seven men were chosen by the apostles to administer the daily distribution of food to the widows (6:1-7). Philip was also instrumental in the conversion of the Samaritans (8:1-25) and the Ethiopian eunuch (8:26-40). At the close of chapter 8 the narrative leaves Philip at Caesarea, the place where he appears to have taken up residence.

In fulfilment of the Joel oracle, women in the early church continue to prophesy

Luke tells his readers that Philip "had four unmarried daughters who prophesied" (Acts 21:9).[64] It is possible that the use of παρθένοι ("virgin," "unmarried") highlights their piety.[65] We should probably take the force of the participle προφητεύουσαι as signifying those who prophesied regularly (i.e., the "gift of prophecy"—NRSV), rather than denoting particular prophetic activity on the arrival of Paul. Although the language of "gift" is more Pauline than Lukan, it is probably appropriate in this context as Luke is clearly designating certain individuals who operate in the prophetic sphere.[66] This is made even more apparent with the mention in the following verse of "a prophet by the name of Agabus."

---

64. Eusebius (*HE* 3.39.9) relates that Papias of Hierapolis gleaned information about the early church from Philip's daughters. There is some evident confusion here, however, between Philip the apostle and Philip the evangelist.

65. Bock, *Acts*, 637.

66. See Acts 11:27-28; 13:1; 15:32.

The focus in the following verses falls upon Agabus and his prophecy to Paul regarding the imprisonment that awaits him in Jerusalem (21:10–16). It is not said that Phillip's four daughters participate in this prophecy. So the obvious question is, why mention them at all? Obviously, prophecy is important for Luke, as it constitutes one of the three modes of proclamation.[67] It is also hard to avoid the conclusion that women are important for Luke. So a combination of these two concerns likely informs the inclusion of this passing reference.

But more can probably be said. At a narrative level, Luke is also able to show how the Joel citation (2:17–21) has its outworking in the life of the early church. Here is a concrete example of "your daughters shall prophesy." So Joel is not employed merely to demonstrate what happened in the initial Pentecost event, the text is understood as paradigmatic with respect to the gender-inclusive gift of prophecy. It is also noteworthy that here, toward the end of the Acts narrative, Luke presents the reader with a choir of prophetic voices. True, the daughters of Philip do not speak, but linked in such close proximity with Agabus they serve to amplify the prophetic event. We find a similar choir of prophetic voices at the beginning of Luke's Gospel, where another five characters prophesy (Zechariah, Elizabeth, Mary, Simeon, Anna). In both cases, women outnumber the men. This helps underscore the importance of the prophetic for Luke and again demonstrates his gender inclusive approach to this aspect of life in the early church. Clearly, *women have a divinely-ordained prophetic role within the church.*

Summary of Narratival Propositions

Lydia is the first Macedonian convert. She is central to God's purposes in Philippi and plays an integral role in the origins of that local church. Lydia is a model disciple of Jesus who demonstrates hospitality and service, and becomes the patroness of the fledgling church at Philippi. Luke clearly believes that women are not marginal members of the kingdom of God nor of its expression in a particular locale. Further, a woman may be a central figure in God's purposes with respect to the establishment of a church community in a given location.

Churches in the early Christian missionary movement were likely patroned and led by married couples. This is exemplified by the ministry of Priscilla and Aquila, who suffered for the cause of Christ and were travelling mission partners in the early Christian mission beyond Jerusalem. Paul was

---

67. Together with straightforward witness and tongues. On this, see Keener, *Acts*, 1: 823–31.

theologically comfortable with Aquila and Priscilla's faith and ministry and this confidence was justified by their ministry to Apollos and his subsequent success. It is quite possible that Priscilla was Apollos' primary theological instructor. In the character and actions of Priscilla, a number of narratival threads in Luke-Acts concerning women converge. Given the unqualified and multifaceted nature of her discipleship and gift expression, the narrative suggests that women may carry out the same ministries as men, and to the same extent, including leadership and teaching within the larger Christian mission.

In fulfilment of the Joel oracle (Acts 2:18), women in the early church continue to prophesy. This is exemplified in the ministry of Philip's daughters. Hence, women have a divinely-ordained prophetic role within the church.

Theological Propositions

The narrative of Acts 13–28 gives rise to several theological propositions regarding female disciples of Jesus, particularly concerning their participation in the life of the missionary church.

1. There is no discrimination between men and women as recipients of salvation.
2. Women participate in God's new community as fulfilment of his end-time promises.
3. Women are empowered within God's new community by the Holy Spirit, in fulfilment of his end-time promises.
4. As far as they are empowered by the Spirit, women may have equal ministry roles to men.
5. Being a disciple of Jesus does not deny the gender of the disciple.
6. Female gender is not muted by a full expression of Christian discipleship and particular gifting.
7. There is no discrimination between men and women as agents of God's salvation and care.
8. The Spirit's work in the life of a person or community provides the power and direction around which forms of service are structured.
9. The advancement of both God's kingdom and God's word have a missionary priority over particular ministry designations or gender roles.
10. Ministry designations and gender roles are fluid to the extent that they serve God's mission.

11. God includes both single and married women in his work in the world.
12. Women may teach about God's continuing works in the world.
13. Women may be leaders, even the main leader, in Christian gatherings.
14. God may establish a Christian community based around the foundational presence of a woman.
15. God may sustain a Christian community by means of the activities of a woman.
16. God may establish and sustain a Christian ministry based upon the foundational work of a woman and her ministry partners.
17. God may establish a missionary network in which women are integral participants with respect to acts of service, hosting, leading and teaching.
18. Female disciples may be central to the local expansion of the kingdom of God as teachers, leaders, hosts and those who carry out acts of service.
19. God may gift believing women so that they are the primary instructor in a married couple, in a Christian ministry or in a Christian community.
20. God continues to speak to his church and to the world through women who serve as God's prophetic mouthpieces.
21. God's character should be reflected in the lives of those disciples who represent him to the world's cultures.
22. God carries out his mission to local cultures in such a way that Christian men and women may perform ministry roles which are supported by cultural norms.
23. God carries out his mission to local cultures in such a way that Christian men and women may perform ministry roles which are counter cultural.
24. God's mission may be functionally and culturally attuned whilst also being free to thoughtfully extend itself beyond these parameters.

CHAPTER 11

Summary and Conclusions

THE AIM OF THIS concluding chapter is to first of all summarize the narratival propositions that have emerged from our study of Luke-Acts. These will be grouped according to theme and will be briefly stated rather than argued at length, as the detailed argument can be found within the relevant chapter.[1] Biblical chapter and verse will be provided only when it may be unclear as to what passage is being referenced. We will then summarize the theological propositions that have resulted from the narratival propositions. This, in turn, will enable us to make some concluding comments regarding Luke's theology of women and suggest some directions for further study.

Summary of Narratival Propositions in Luke and Acts

First of all, and most obviously, God's creation of a new people includes women. There is no restriction on their inclusion aside from forgiveness by Jesus and a response of faith on their behalf. Consequently, women are equal participants in the covenant community of God's people; in Luke's Gospel even those women who are socially marginalized can experience the shalom of God. When women are mentioned as part of the circle of believers, they

---

1. Given our focus on women, we will not include here a summary of the narratival propositions regarding Jesus and his ministry that appear at the opening of chapter 4. They were discussed there in order to place his interactions with women within the broader context of his kingdom ministry.

are to be understood as full-orbed disciples without qualification. In fact, the role the women play in the resurrection narrative requires their long standing inclusion in the group of Jesus' disciples.

In Acts, the women remain part of the inner circle of Jesus' followers and are understood to be present when the entire group is mentioned. Undeniably, this inclusion of women alongside men was an essential mark of the early church. It is also apparent that women participated in the decision-making processes of the early church. This is seen in the selection of the replacement for Judas, and the entire community's participation in electing the seven. This would suggest that women may participate fully in the life of the church, including decision-making processes.

Time and time again throughout the narrative women model true discipleship. In this sense they function as a practical example of the "good soil" from the parable of the Sower. Women repeatedly embody true discipleship regarding the use of wealth and possessions (Luke 8:1-3; 21:1-4), and they are representative of those who forsake family ties for the sake of Jesus and the kingdom. In parable, the persistent widow (18:1-8) functions as a model for discipleship with respect to prayer and also for seeking justice in an unjust world. In Acts, Tabitha's ministry takes the form of active service for the sake of the needy, Mary (mother of John Mark) embodies the qualities of hospitality and generosity, whereas Lydia is a model disciple of Jesus who demonstrates hospitality and service.

Women are also introduced as examples of true piety. In the infancy narratives Elizabeth, Mary and Anna are all paradigms of Jewish piety. Women of pedigree or high standing also play a key role in the narrative. Elizabeth is a woman of pedigree, whereas Lydia is a well-to-do Greco-Roman woman of considerable means.

In Luke-Acts women are constantly portrayed as the recipients of God's compassion and blessing, often via the miraculous. For example, right at the opening of Luke's story Elizabeth is barren but experiences the intervening power of God. Mary is also the recipient of God's favor and grace, which involves an unexpected religio-cultural reversal sanctioned by God's presence and activity. She is presented as the one who is unexpectedly drawn into God's reversal of the fortunes of Israel and the whole world. As the ministry of Jesus commences, women are the equal beneficiaries of God's compassion expressed through Jesus' kingdom ministry and healing power. He shows concern for a crippled woman's plight (Luke 13:10-17), he has compassion on the daughter of a prominent Jew (7:40-56), and a chronically ill and therefore unclean woman (7:43-48). In Luke's Gospel, Jesus never wavers in his interest and concern for women and is mindful of their plight, even on the way to the cross.

In Acts, Tabitha is a recipient of the ultimate miracle of restored life. In fact, the story of Tabitha exemplifies Luke' interest in the presence of women throughout the story of Jesus and his people. It is clearly evident that God's compassion reaches to all, without differentiation in gender, age, or socio-religious status, and those who are participants in God's covenant community, including women, are entitled to the full blessings that derive from it.

One of the interesting features of the narrative is that women often function as positive examples, sometimes compared to men who do not. This is evident in the following: Elizabeth is unlike her husband Zechariah who doubted; the response of a sinful woman to Jesus surpasses that of a Pharisee (Luke 7:36–50); the Queen of Sheba was better able to comprehend the work of Yahweh than the generation of Jesus' day; and finally, unlike the male disciples, the women were faithful to Jesus, even to the devastating end of his life. In Acts this male-female contrast can be seen in the pairing of Tabitha's story with that of Aeneas in such a way that she emerges as the more commendable character of the two.

The narrative also depicts women who are faithful to God even under adversity. Mary, for example, is active and caring despite adversity. She is a protagonist who unknowingly plays her part in God's plan despite personal dislocation. In a sense, Mary is portrayed as a tragic figure. Her piety does not exempt her from conflict and misunderstanding with Jesus and her suffering parallels Jesus' own travails for the sake of God's mission.

This is not to say that Luke paints an idealized picture of women, yet it is interesting that Sapphira is the only female protagonist in Luke-Acts who is portrayed negatively. However, she does not act alone; she is caught up in the sin of her husband in lying to the Spirit who is the guarantor of the existence, unity, and purity of the early church. Nevertheless, this incident does demonstrate Luke's acknowledgment that women may be involved in the worst kinds of sinful acts against God and his new people.

Women also display a proper attitude and response to God. For example: Elizabeth shows gratitude to God with this gratitude finding expression in faithfulness and obedience; Mary is submissive to God's plan and considers herself the Lord's servant; the sinful woman (Luke 7:36–50) instantiates the characteristics that Jesus embodies and teaches about in future meal scenes; the crippled woman immediately praises God when healed by Jesus, and Lydia's response to God working in her life is to offer hospitality to Paul and his companions.

The Holy Spirit features prominently in both the Gospel and Acts, as it is the Spirit who directs and controls God's actions in history first of all through Jesus, and then through his followers. Right at the commencement of the narrative women are filled with the Holy Spirit or are receptive to the Spirit. Elizabeth is filled with the Holy Spirit and makes prophetic statements that are Christological and reinforce other narrative threads. In this respect Elizabeth anticipates the faithful disciple of Jesus: obedient, filled with the Holy Spirit, and a conveyor of the prophetic word. Furthermore she embodies the narrator's concerns and so forms an important link between the stated purpose in Luke's preface and the unfolding of later events. Unlike Elizabeth, Anna is actually described as a prophetess, a role that is implicitly Spirit directed. It is her status as a prophet, together with her exemplary piety, that confirms the reliability of her statements about the child Jesus.

In Acts, the presence of the Spirit is again evident in prophetic activity. With respect to women this activity begins at Pentecost where the women disciples receive the power of the Holy Spirit and declare the gospel in foreign languages. So, in fulfilment of the Joel oracle, women in the early church continue to prophesy. While this finds concrete expression in ministry and activity of Philip's daughters later in Acts, the narrative suggests that as the Spirit is given to all believers, not just the apostles alone, any believer may prophesy. In fact the cumulative and diverse prophetic activity linked with women in Luke-Acts indicates that women have a divinely ordained prophetic role within the church. They may engage in prophetic utterances and be reliable spokespeople for God under the inspiration of the Holy Spirit. Furthermore, with respect to Acts, it is the work of the Spirit in a given context that is the impetus for Christian ministries and ministry designations. We would therefore expect that the ministries of women would be Spirit led, and the tasks entailed by these ministries may vary according to different ministry contexts.

In Luke-Acts women rightly interpret Scripture, testify, or make insightful theological or Christological affirmations. Elizabeth makes such an insightful Christological affirmation in recognizing that Mary was "the mother of my Lord," whereas Mary is presented as a valid communicator and astute interpreter of salvation history. Mary is actually the first person in Luke-Acts to link Israel's salvation history with God's actions in her own time and is furthermore able to communicate this to others. As the narrative progresses, women testify faithfully to the events of which they are a part. The Queen of Sheba, for example, was attuned to God's work and made right theological judgments with respect to the Lord. It is clear that, for Luke, the gender of the Queen of Sheba was not a barrier or limitation to her comprehension of God. Women also make accurate conclusions with respect to unforeseen events. The women from Galilee, for instance, had the ability to rightly interpret Jesus' words concerning his resurrection and correctly applied Jesus' words to their situation. Indeed, throughout

Luke-Acts women are often keenly insightful with respect to people and their significance.

One of Luke's more dominant motifs is that of reversal. While women are not the only recipients of the reversal of fortunes, they do play a significant part. The narrator clearly expects the reader to change their perspective with regards to the lowly in society, particularly in relation to women, for it becomes clear that God uses ordinary women to achieve his purposes. This is supremely seen in Mary, who is an ordinary faithful Jewish woman, yet is the mother of the divine Son of God. As the narrative unfolds, God's inversion of expectations finds its fullest socio-religious expression with respect to Gentile women (Queen of Sheba, Lydia).

One the recurring features of Luke's narrative is the presentation of women as proclaimers or witnesses. In the Gospel, the ministry of the seventy resulted in joy and success. In this mission, female disciples of Jesus were given a proclamatory role together with the male disciples. Not only so, but the ministry of the seventy missionaries was deemed to be more effective by the narrative than the initial ministry of the twelve. In the resurrection account, the women from Galilee were sufficient witnesses of the empty tomb and were considered to be appropriate heralds with respect to the resurrection of Jesus. Women were also amongst those commissioned to proclaim forgiveness in the name of Jesus to the world. Further on in the Acts narrative we find that Rhoda's announcement meets the same incredulous resistance as did the women's proclamation of Jesus' resurrection, yet her announcement, as that of the women witnesses to the resurrection, is confirmed as true witness. All this demonstrates that women may be the first witnesses to God's works, and they are fit to interpret what they witness and to herald these things to others.

As the Acts narrative unfolds the word of God is personified. This personalization of the word and its advancement resist it being necessary linked to apostolic ministry. On the one hand, this is demonstrated in the Spirit's empowerment of Stephen and Philip, men outside the twelve, to prophesy and preach in addition to their diaconal role. This would indicate that a diaconal form of ministry does not preclude prophesying or preaching, for it is clear that the apostles and the seven serve the word of the Lord, not vice versa. On the other hand, the fact that there is not a one-to-one correspondence between the proclamation of the word and apostolic ministry is demonstrated in Acts 2, where women are part of the larger group empowered by the Spirit at Pentecost to share the gospel in foreign languages. This would indicate that a woman's gender does not, in an *a priori* sense, disable her from authoritatively and effectively proclaiming the word of God. This is confirmed in the character of Priscilla, a travelling mission partner in the early Christian mission beyond Jerusalem. It is clear that Luke and Paul were theologically comfortable with Aquila and Priscilla's faith and ministry; in fact Paul's confidence in the couple is vindicated by their ministry to Apollos and his subsequent success. Furthermore, it is quite possible that Priscilla was Apollos' primary instructor. It is evident that in the character and actions of Priscilla, a number of narratival threads in Luke-Acts concerning women converge. Given the unqualified and multifaceted nature of her discipleship and gift expression, the narrative suggests that women may carry out the same ministries as men, and to the same extent, including leadership and teaching within the larger Christian mission.

It is unavoidably apparent that Luke and Luke's Jesus do not follow stereotypical roles for women, and women in God's kingdom are no longer defined by socially regulated roles. Mary (sister of Martha), for example, is commended by Jesus for listing to his words as her first priority, even at the expense of the fulfilling a socially regulated role. Undeniably this story indicates that the first priority for a female disciple is to listen to the teaching of Jesus, for women who hear the word of God and do it are part of the blessed company of disciples and form part of the true family of Jesus. Membership in his true family provides the coordinates for a new realm of life for women who believe.

Members of the Christian community (in Acts) at times appear to operate beyond the sociological strictures of their gender and class status. Merely by virtue of her inclusion in the Christian community, Rhoda operated beyond the sociological expectations of her class. Consequently, the Christian faith not only allows women to operate within the sphere of the kingdom of God, but even to serve God and others beyond what their social circumstances would normally prescribe. In addition, the criteria for the various forms of female and male ministry in the early church appear to be functional and contextual. Women and men who participate in the kingdom of God will not necessarily be channeled into stereotypical roles which correspond to expectations in wider society.

In the ministry of the seven, men take on a serving role which was usually carried out by women. By this it is seen that Spirit formed character rather than gender was the primary characteristic of being set aside for a ministry of service in the early church. Furthermore, service is a positive mark for any disciple, not for those of female gender alone. A prime example of service is seen in Tabitha, a female disciple whose life is strong within the social memory of the Christians of her region. The account of her life suggests that a woman may be the central figure in a Christian ministry of service. Further, her gender is not a barrier to discipleship, and neither is her discipleship a barrier to the expression of her gender.

Luke's positive characterization of women is seen not only in living encounters between women and Jesus, but also in parables whose central character is a woman (Lost Coin, Judge and the Widow). We see here that Luke's Jesus is not averse to using women as examples of God's character, and pictures his own kingdom ministry in terms of a housewife. Luke's overall portrayal of women is thereby rich and diversified.

Finally, it is apparent that churches in the early Christian missionary movement could be patroned and led by women or mixed gender couples. Mary, mother of John Mark, hosted regular Christian gatherings in her home in Jerusalem. In fact, her home played a pivotal role in the transition of leadership from Peter to James. Lydia, the first Macedonian convert, is central to God's purposes in Philippi and performed an integral role in the origins of that local church. The narrative points to her role as patroness of the fledgling church in that strategic city. Luke clearly believes that women are not marginal members of the kingdom of God or of its expression in a given locale. Further, a woman may be a central figure in God's purposes with respect to the establishment of a church community in a given location. The ministry of Priscilla and Aquila also indicates that churches in the early Christian missionary movement were likely patroned and led by married couples.

In our analysis of the roles of women in Jewish and wider Greco-Roman society in chapter 2, we found that although there was an inherent ambiguity in the source material itself, it was possible to make some broad generalizations. The evidence suggests that Roman women would have had more freedom and movement in society than their Palestinian counterparts. Although class obviously played a crucial role here as well, geographical location was seen to be a significant factor.

When we examine the narratival propositions regarding women that emerge from Acts, it is interesting to note that they are largely commensurate with the above findings. It is observable that women play a more significant ministry role in the church in the Greco-Roman world than they do in Palestine. Once the church moves beyond Jerusalem (Acts 13–28) women's roles undeniably expand. There are exceptions, and we also need to recognize that the narrative is selective. This notwithstanding, the vital roles played by Lydia and Priscilla are certainly more at home in a Roman environment than they would have been in Palestine.

This, in turn, supports the essential historicity of Luke's portrayal of women. Luke does not engage in fictional characterization, where he has women regularly performing roles way outside of the cultural norm. Although the kingdom of God and the presence of the Spirit has broken down cultural stereotypes to some extent, women are engaged in ministry and practice in a way that is not subversive to the progress of the gospel in the wider culture. Consequently, even if Luke has an agenda regarding women, he has still presented a narrative that is culturally attuned.

Summary of Theological Propositions in Luke and Acts

We now move on to summarize the theological propositions that have emerged from each section of our study. Drawing these together serves a number of purposes. Presenting the theological propositions in a stand-alone section hopefully enables the reader to appreciate the breadth of Luke's theology of women. In addition, a full orbed presentation of Luke's work allows the reader to understand the theological relationships between propositions. Such an appreciation of these theological relationships, in turn, permits the coherence of Luke's view to emerge. The propositions are grouped topically in order to avoid repetition and to help to more clearly convey their distinctives.

We have included at the outset theological propositions concerning God's kingdom action and salvation through Jesus because that is the context in which the other theological propositions must be understood. In the same way that narratival propositions have a narratival context, theological propositions have a theological context. Luke's theological framework to do with God's salvation and a new people is decisive for understanding how he views women and their participation in God's Spirit-led eschatological community.

Theological propositions which relate to the kingdom of God and its relationship to humanity, particularly women

1. God's return to Israel in the person of Jesus reconfigured the nation of Israel, including women, according to the kingdom of God.
2. God's kingdom is a theo-social order in which men and women may equally receive his compassion.
3. God's compassion is extended to people through Jesus' ministry of proclaiming the kingdom of God and demonstrating it via a ministry of restoration.
4. As the Spirit-led Messiah, Jesus restored people to God and saved them from afflictions which resulted from distortions in nature, humanity (including some of its cultural norms) and the angelic realm.

5. The kingdom of God is the eschatological context for life and ministry which reconfigures a believer's native socio-cultural backgrounds.

Theological propositions which involve women and salvation via the presence of the Spirit and the kind of discipleship which this entails

1. Women are as important to God as men are.
2. Women are as constitutive of the new people of God as are men.
3. God includes women within his new people as full orbed disciples of Jesus.
4. God includes both men and women into his new community life by virtue of their trust in Jesus, receiving the Holy Spirit and the forgiveness of sins.
5. God's new community includes both men and women who will be obedient to Jesus.
6. God fulfils his promise that he will give his Spirit to men and women irrespective of age, gender and social status.
7. Women participate by the Spirit in the new people of God as fulfilment of his end-time promises.
8. God's kingdom requires that those who receive his compassion respond by listening to him and reflect his character to others through word and deed.
9. God's character may be clearly reflected by female believers through instances of generosity and faithfulness.
10. The disciple responds to God's work by acting with purpose and care despite various difficulties and a limited understanding of God's plan.
11. Being a disciple of Jesus does not deny the gender of the disciple.
12. The fullest basis and expression of male and female gender is achieved within the identity provided by being a disciple of Jesus.

Theological propositions to do with women and their participation by the Spirit in the communal and missionary activity of the new people of God

1. God may involve and empower any person, including a woman, to play a key role in the unfolding of salvation history.
2. God's mission may include women as primary figures through whose preaching he establishes his kingdom despite Satanic and socio-cultural adversity.
3. God's mission may include women as primary figures through whose works he establishes his kingdom despite Satanic and socio-cultural adversity.
4. God can employ female disciples to be the primary theological interpreters of scripture and salvation history in their context.
5. Women may hear from God and be called to prophetically apply their scriptural-historical insights to their own contexts.
6. God's presence in the lives of female believers by his Spirit empowers women for work towards end-time kingdom expansion.
7. God is a God of the humanly impossible, thus factors such as age, social status and gender are never insurmountable impediments to a person being the means through whom God ministers to others.
8. There are no gender restrictions upon the expression of discipleship in terms of the ministries of men and women.
9. God authorizes women to hear, teach and confirm Jesus' words.
10. God authorizes women to hear, teach and confirm Jesus' words through signs, prayer and living justly.
11. Women may speak the truth with authority and announce the resurrection of Jesus to male and female disciples.
12. God's words may be rightly interpreted and contextually applied by women.
13. God employs women as his prophetesses.
14. Women are included in God's mission to the extent that they may announce the good news of his salvation.
15. Women also participate in God's mission by reflecting his character to others through word and deed, obedient suffering for his sake, miraculous works, prayer, and living justly.

16. The Spirit's work in the life of a person or community provides the power and direction around which forms of service are structured.
17. In the advancement of both God's kingdom and God's word, particular ministry designations or gender roles are fluid and a secondary concern.
18. God may include both single and married women in his work in the world.
19. Women may announce God's continuing works in the world.
20. Women may be leaders in Christian gatherings.
21. God may establish a Christian community upon the foundational presence and work of a woman.
22. God may sustain a Christian community by means of the activities of a woman.
23. God may establish and sustain a Christian ministry based upon the foundational work of a woman.
24. God may establish a missionary network in which women are integral participants with respect to acts of service, as hosts, leaders and teachers.
25. Women may be central to the local expansion of the kingdom of God as teachers, leaders, hosts and those who carry out acts of service.
26. God may gift women so that they are the primary instructor in a married couple, in a Christian ministry or a in a Christian community.
27. God continues to speak to his church and to the world through women who serve as God's prophetic mouthpieces.
28. God's character will be reflected in the lives of those who represent him to the world's cultures.
29. God carries out his mission to local cultures in such a way that Christian men and women may perform ministry roles which are supported by cultural norms.
30. God carries out his mission to local cultures in such a way that Christian men and women may perform ministry roles which are counter cultural.
31. God's mission may be functionally and culturally attuned whilst also being free to thoughtfully extend itself beyond these parameters.

A Lukan Theology of Women

Biblical scholars and critics are keen to speak about Luke's theology (e.g., Christology) and its particular emphases. Our contention, based on the findings of this study, is that Luke operates with a particular theology of women. This theology is reflected in the kinds of stories he uses and the way he constructs the characters and the plot. This is significant because it speaks to the deliberateness of his stories to do with women, and the narratival argument that he mounts through these stories. Our study of the narratival construction and argument of Luke-Acts has established numerous narrative propositions regarding women in Luke's work. These suggest a number of theological propositions regarding female disciples of Jesus. Both the narratival and theological propositions have been summarized above.

Given Luke's theology of women in Luke-Acts, two major questions arise. The first is whether or not there is a generalized canonical theology of female disciples beyond Luke-Acts. Second is the related question of the normativity of Luke's theology for the church today. In what follows we offer a number of principles along which these avenues for further research could be pursued. Our hope is that by following the leads presented below, researchers will provide considered and well-resourced answers to these important questions.

The canonical "so what?" Towards a theology of female disciples of Jesus

Witherington suggests that in order to make generalized claims regarding women in the early Christian movement the data from Paul's theology and mission needs to be included. Our purpose here has been solely to provide Luke's perspective. However, a further profitable area of research would be an integration of the Pauline and the Lukan perspectives on the nature of female involvement in the earliest Christian churches and mission.

However, the issue is wider than Luke and Paul. Our work is written with the knowledge that Luke's voice provides us with one perspective on women disciples of Jesus amongst the variegated witness of the NT. Therefore, a final integrated theology of women disciples needs to address this variegated witness. In drawing together the views of the authors of Scripture, two hermeneutical points from within the historic Christian tradition are vital to ensuring that the voices within the canon are rightly co-ordinated and weighted with respect to each other. These principles are the "analogy of Faith" and the "analogy of Scripture."

1. "The Analogy of Faith." On this principle the clearer portions of Scripture serve as the passages which shed light on the obscure ones. In other words, the difficult passages of scripture are interpreted in the light of the clearer ones.[2] Narrative, such as Acts, is by nature clearer than occasional documents such as Paul's epistles because the narrative provides the context for statements, whereas occasional letters do not always supply such a context. Thus, the reader of an occasional letter is more likely to have to engage in "mirror reading."[3]

2. "The Analogy of the Canon." Under God's providence, the Bible has a settled canonical form with a particular order of its contents. In this order the first book in which we read about the earliest Christians and their expansion is the book of Acts. As such it functions as the narratival backdrop for the smaller and more particular works which follow. Thus, the content of the epistles is most appropriately read in light of the story of the earliest church expansion. Given the canonical order, the ideal reader of Scripture will approach the epistles with Acts in mind.

These two classic methodological principles will aid a canonical theology of women who are disciples of Jesus. They will ensure that God's providential ordering of the canon as well as the degrees of clarity which he has given to particular works will be taken into account. By means of employing these guidelines, the tasks of drawing together the various theologies of women in the NT, and assessing the relative significance of each author's theology and contribution, will hopefully be more rigorous and less contentious.[4]

---

2. A classic example of an obscure passage which needs to be interpreted in the light of clearer ones is Paul's writing on baptism on behalf of the dead (1 Cor 15:29).

3. Mirror reading is an attempt to reconstruct the circumstances that gave rise to a particular saying or situation. Such reconstruction is by nature speculative, although that does not invalidate the task itself.

4. The use of these principles will need to be aided by establishing criteria which will aid the selection of one theory over another in the case where competing theories arise. The establishment of these criteria will aid discernment between competing theories on a canonical theology of female disciples as well as its normative significance for the church today. These are beyond the bounds of this particular work, yet we hope others will take up the challenge. Millard Erickson recently undertook this line of investigation to do with various proposed models about the inner life of God the Trinity. See Erickson, *Tampering*.

The contemporary "so what"? Normativity and the question of the application of Luke's theology to today

Are the depictions of the roles played by Jesus' earliest female disciples in Luke-Acts normative for Christians today? Bauckham pointedly raises this issue. He contends that although we need to make the move from the Bible to contemporary practice with care, we must also acknowledge the remarkable role that women played in early Christianity. He writes:

> Any argument from the Gospels to the role women played in the Christian communities must proceed with extreme caution. But, in the case of the resurrection narratives . . . we can discern not the roles of Christian women in general, but the role of the specific women who witnessed the empty tomb and the risen Lord. These women . . . acted as apostolic eyewitness guarantors of the traditions about Jesus, especially his resurrection but no doubt also in other respects. . . . [T]hat their witness acquires textual form in the Gospels implies that it can never be regarded as superseded or unimportant.[5]

Further:

> For as long as these women were alive, their witness, "We have seen the Lord," carried the authority of those the Lord himself had commissioned to witness to his resurrection. . . . [The female witnesses] were well known figures and there were a large number of them. They surely continued to be active traditioners whose recognized eyewitness authority could act as a touchstone to guarantee the traditions as others relayed them and to protect the traditions from inauthentic developments.[6]

Bauckham is not a lone voice. Drawing upon his decades-long studies on women in early Christianity, Witherington notes the multifaceted nature of Luke's presentation of women believers. He also emphasizes that women played a number of significant roles in the earliest churches to do with Luke and Paul.

> Luke and Paul, like other early Christians, believed that their faith committed them to the reforming of some of the existing patriarchal structures so that women could play more vital and varied roles in the community of faith. The reform was to take place within the community. To this end, Luke presents five

---

5. Bauckham, *Gospel Women*, 295.
6. Ibid.

cameos of important Christian women and the variety of roles they assumed. In the mother of John Mark (Acts 12:12-17) and in Lydia (Acts 16:12-40) we see women assuming the role of 'mother' or patroness and benefactor to the then fledgling Christian communities in Jerusalem and Philippi respectively. Like them, in the story of Tabitha (Acts 9), a notable female disciple with an ongoing ministry, we find someone providing material aid to a particularly needy group of early Christians -widows (cf. Acts 6). Luke's mention of Philip's daughters is brief (Acts 21:9), but when compared to Acts 2:17 it is sufficient to show that women played important roles of inspired proclaimers in the early church. Perhaps most important is Luke's reference to Priscilla as a teacher of a notable early Christian evangelist, Apollos, in Acts 18. Luke's portrayal of Priscilla is unreservedly positive ....[7]

Are these portrayals merely descriptive or are they normative for Luke's readers and the communities which would be established by these readers?

Above we noted the need for criteria which will aid in drawing together the various scriptural voices on female disciples. In like manner, another area for further research may be to outline clear criteria by which Luke's view is assessed and applied in the church and world today.[8] In doing so one needs to beware of a number of pitfalls. By way of example, we can cite the mistake of assessing Luke's view according to contemporary notions of what constitutes a full human voice and existence.[9] For example, the concept of

---

7. Witherington, *Acts of the Apostles*, 338. Witherington also suggests that Luke's circumstances may have compelled him to write extensively and positively about women believers. In Witherington's mind: "the reason Luke took the pains to portray women in these varieties of roles is because when he wrote in the last quarter of the first century perhaps there was still much resistance—perhaps increasing resistance—to such ideas, and so the case had to be made in some detail." Ibid., 339. Witherington also writes on the attempts by later copyists to "disguise [Priscilla's] role." See Ibid., 562ff.

8. Witherington comments: "One . . . needs to ask whether the modern notion of being an independent, self-determining person is an appropriate concept by which to evaluate either men or women in antiquity." Ibid., 339 n 42.

9. Catalan feminist and writer Monserrat Roig is an example of independence as the primary criterion for female selfhood. Her powerful (and now classic) poem, "La mirada tuerta," urges women to break with, and fly away from, all that has gone before in order to drive themselves towards the discovery and expression of their own selfhood. This includes breaking with theological, social, literary models. It reads: "We invent a mythical past for ourselves, seduced by the ideas of an as yet unproven Great Mother Goddess, a past constructed in the context of the utopias of the final years of the twentieth century. However, the word of a woman strains to fly alone, urged on, seeking its own beat, conscious that imitation leads to the abyss, because real women, free from mythical feminine images are neither novel nor innocent." This is our own

an "independent Christian ministry" is for some a central contemporary criterion for purposeful and valued discipleship. However, this criterion may well be irrelevant to Luke's theology as it is very distant from Luke's *a priori* view of people and relationships as the context for the expression of the gifts of the Spirit.

A positive example of a criterion for the translatability of Luke's theology to contemporary practice may be termed 'missionary mindfulness.' This criterion refers to Luke's missionary considerations for Christian practice. Though Luke's theology of female disciples is driven by his powerful ideas about the kingdom of God, his theology of women is communicated subtly. This subtlety is driven by his apologetic concern, or, 'missionary mindfulness.' This term highlights the fact that Luke's understanding of Christian practice was open to it being lived out in various ways according to the particulars of the different Christian communities scattered throughout the Greco-Roman world.

In other words, Luke wrote in such a way that his readers would understand that Christian mission would not directly undermine the Roman empire. By avoiding the charge of being a direct threat to the empire, the Christian message and apologetic *itself* would not be undermined (in the eyes of the empire) by the practices of those who embraced it. Therefore, Luke's characterization of female disciples is done in such a way that does not undermine his apology to Rome. Hence at times he trades on the ambiguity in Greco-Roman society to do with women. However, as far as possible, he extends the roles and ministries of women in Luke and Acts as far as they have Greco-Roman precedent. Therefore, *the way he presents* his theology does not come across as subversive. Thus, a criterion such as 'missiological mindfulness' could mean that the reader must appropriate Luke's theology of women (and the portrayals of women which he provides)

---

translation of Roig, "La mirada tuerta," 61–62. Monserrat's work has been critiqued by fellow feminists, but this is not to say it has been left behind. For example, Rosalía Cornejo-Parriego argues that views such as Monserrat's need to be held in tension with being a woman of "flesh and bone" who live in the real world of "creation." This is the only way, she argues, that a *post-feminist* feminist proposal can bring to expression the full range of the female voice and the desires which underlie it. Cornejo-Parriego, "¿Feminismo posfeminista?" 610. In our view, Luke writes about women along the lines suggested by Cornejo-Parriego. He emphasizes the particularity of each woman as distinct character with her own sets of values, gifts and experiences. However, women are most often portrayed as essential within communities. In this way, women are at once unique as well as socially interdependent with others. Hence, for Luke there is no such thing as an independent woman per se; all Christians are vitally connected by the Spirit and by fellowship based upon teaching, prayer, common meals and common care. The flip-side of this reality is that there is no community of believers which is independent from the strong influence of women.

in a manner which is likewise sensitive to their own culture and context. These contextually attuned appropriations of Luke's theology and models of female disciples would be expressed in such a way that it enhances mission and does not undermine it.

A Final Word

The aim of our work has been to bring to light Luke's narratival presentation of women and the theology that undergirds it. We have found that this narrative presentation and theology is rich and quite remarkable given the socio-religious climate in which Luke wrote. Now that we have made our own "orderly account" of what Luke wrote, we turn these conclusions over to the broader Christian community for discussion. We did not set out to make final claims in any complementarian, egalitarian, or "other" theological direction to do with women. In this spirit we would like to offer these results to all sides of the debate on the roles of women in the church and the world. More pointedly, our hope is that all sides of the debate include the insights from Luke-Acts into their respective theologies.

In some senses, the debate over the role of women in the church today can be likened to a card game. The game consists of a number of players who represent the many sides of the debate over the status and role of women in the Christian community. The card deck is representative of the data used in the debate. Many of the players in the debate appear to be playing with a limited set of cards. Some play Galatians 3:28 as their sole card, others play it as their trump card. On the other side, 1 Timothy 2:11–15 is played as the trump card; for others it is played in tandem with 1 Corinthians 11:3. Others play with an 'all-star deck' which comprises a number of significant women of faith in the OT and the NT. Still others play a deck of gender cards. These (Eastern orthodox) players do not have verses on their cards but have instead the gender of God incarnate and the gender of the twelve apostles.

We firmly believe that the debate should proceed using a full deck of playing cards. Our work has contributed to the deck by adding crucial data regarding Luke's multi-faceted theology of women disciples of Jesus. It is our contention that any argument that ignores this data is deficient.

Leaving the illustration of the card game aside, we would like to offer suggestions for the various positions in the debate on women in ministry. To egalitarians we would particularly commend the use of narrative to communicate theological proposals as well as the tone and missionary sensitivity with which Luke applies his strong view of women as members and agents within the kingdom of God. To complementarians, we would also recommend the significance of theology communicated via narrative. This may enhance their view by amending a propensity to proof text from occasional documents. Furthermore, we would hope that the narratival data from Luke and Acts might have an influence on their normative data and final schema. We believe that this is possible without shifting their overarching complementarian structure. To those who are undecided, we simply commend the richness of Luke's view and would suggest pursuing the canonical and normative 'so what' questions.

Naturally, the debate over the status and roles of women is a very serious matter with massive implications for mission, Christian identity and purposefulness, discipleship, and witness to the wider world. Thus, we close this book with the humble reiteration that readers take into account Luke's remarkable work. Luke is a vital conversation partner in the discussion about the kingdom of God and its saving and socio-cultural consequences for women. However, we must do more than take up and read. We must also consider Luke's canonical and contemporary significance because his accounts of Jesus' life and that of the early church were written in order to secure the ultimate beliefs and practices of a Christian community.

We began this book with a quote from Barbara Reid. She states:

> If one chooses to teach and preach Luke's stories uncritically, they continue to reinforce patriarchal role divisions. On the other hand, if one engages in the difficult task of reinterpreting the text from a feminist perspective, reading against Luke's intent, then the stories can be recontextualized to proclaim the message of good news for women and men called equally to share in the same discipleship and mission of Jesus.[10]

Our conclusions have demonstrated that Luke's stories do not need to be "re-contextualized" to achieve this purpose, nor do we have to "read against Luke's intent." Ironically, the very result that Reid seeks arises from Luke's narrative itself.

---

10. Reid, *Better Part*, 205.

Bibliography

Agua Pérez, Agustín del. "El Testimonio Narrativo De La Resurrección De Cristo." *Estudios eclesiásticos* 77 (2002) 241–73.
Alexander, Loveday. *Acts in its Ancient Literary Context*. Library of New Testament Studies 298. London: T. & T. Clark, 2005.
―――. *The Preface to Luke's Gospel: Literary Convention and Social Context in Luke 1.1–4 and Acts 1.1*. SNTSMS 78. Cambridge: Cambridge University Press, 1993.
Alter, Robert. *The Art of Biblical Narrative*. New York: Basic, 1992.
―――. *The Five Books of Moses: A Translation with Commentary*. 1st ed. New York: Norton, 2004.
Anderson, Kevin L. *"But God Raised Him from the Dead": The Theology of Jesus' Resurrection in Luke-Acts*. Paternoster Biblical Monographs. Milton Keynes, UK: Paternoster, 2006.
Arjava, Antti. *Women and Law in Late Antiquity*. Oxford: Clarendon, 1996,
Arlandson, James Malcolm. *Women, Class, and Society in Early Christianity: Models from Luke-Acts*. Peabody, MA: Hendrickson, 1997.
Ascough, Richard, S. *Lydia: Paul's Cosmopolitan Hostess*. Collegeville, MN: Liturgical, 2009.
The Authorized Daily Prayer Book of the United Hebrew Congregations of the British Empire. London: Eyre & Spottiswoode, 1912.
Bar-Efrat, Shimeon, and Johannes Klein. *Das Erste Buch Samuel: Ein narratologisch-philologischer Kommentar*. Beiträge zur Wissenschaft vom Alten und Neuen Testament Neunte Folge. Stuttgart: Kohlhammer, 2007.
―――. *Das Zweite Buch Samuel: Ein narratologisch-philologischer Kommentar*. Beiträge zur Wissenschaft vom Alten und Neuen Testament. Stuttgart: Kohlhammer, 2009.
―――. *Narrative Art in the Bible*. Bible and Literature Series. Sheffield, UK: Almond, 1989.
Batten, Alicia. "Neither Gold nor Braided Hair (1 Timothy 2.9; 1 Peter 3.3): Adornment, Gender and Honour in Antiquity." *New Testament Studies* 55 (2009) 484–501.
Bauckham, Richard. *Gospel Women: Studies of the Named Women in the Gospels*. London: T. & T. Clark, 2002.

Beale, Gordon. K., and D. A. Carson. *Commentary on the New Testament Use of the Old Testament.* Grand Rapids: Baker Academic, 2007.

Bearsley, Patrick. "Mary the Perfect Disciple: A Paradigm for Mariology," *Theological Studies* 62 (2001) 464–68.

Bellis, Alice O. "The Queen of Sheba: A Gender-Sensitive Reading." *Journal of Religious Thought* 51.2 (1994) 17–28.

Benéitez, Manuel. *"Esta salvación de Dios" (Hech 28,28): análisis narrativo estructuralista de "Hechos."* Madrid: UPCM, 1986.

Bird, Michael F. "Jesus Is the 'Messiah of God': Messianic Proclamation in Luke-Acts." *Reformed Theological Review* 66.2 (2007) 69–82.

Bird, Phyllis A. "Women (OT)." *ABD* 6.951–52.

Boatwright, Mary Taliaferro. "Plancia Magna of Perge: Women's Roles and Status in Roman Asia Minor." In *Women's History and Ancient History,* edited by Sarah B. Pomeroy, 249–72. Chapel Hill, NC: University of North Carolina Press, 1991.

Bock, Darrell L. *Acts.* BECNT. Grand Rapids: Baker Academic, 2007.

———. *Luke.* BECNT. 2 vols. Grand Rapids: Baker Books, 1994.

———. *Proclamation from Prophecy and Pattern: Lukan Old Testament Christology.* Sheffield, UK: JSOT, 1987.

———. *A Theology of Luke and Acts.* Grand Rapids: Zondervan, 2012.

Börstinghaus, Jens. *Sturmfahrt und Schiffbruch: zur lukanischen Verwendung eines literarischen Topos in Apostelgeschichte 27,1–28,6.* Tübingen: Mohr Siebeck, 2010.

Bovon, François. *Luke the Theologian: Thirty-Three Years of Research (1950–1983).* Princeton Theological Monograph Series. Allison Park, PA: Pickwick, 1987.

———. *Luke.* 3 vols. Hermeneia. Minneapolis: Fortress, 2002–12.

Bow, Beverly, and George W. E. Nickelsburg. "Patriarchy with a Twist: Men and Women in Tobit," In *Women Like This,* edited by Amy-Jill Levine, 127–43. Atlanta: Scholars, 1991.

Brawley, Robert L. *Centering on God: Method and Message in Luke-Acts.* Literary Currents in Biblical Interpretation. Louisville, KY: Westminster/John Knox, 1990.

———. *Luke-Acts and the Jews: Conflict, Apology, Reconciliation* SBLMS. Atlanta: Scholars, 1987.

Brooten, Bernadette J. *Women Leaders in the Ancient Synagogue.* BJS 36. Atlanta: Scholars, 1982.

Brown, Jennine K. *The Disciples in Narrative Perspective: The Function and Portrayal of the Matthean Disciples.* Atlanta: Society of Biblical Literature, 2002.

Bruce, F. F. *The Acts of the Apostles: Greek Text with Introduction and Commentary.* 3rd ed. Grand Rapids: Eerdmans, 1990.

Burns, Rita J. *Has the Lord Indeed Spoken Only through Moses? A Study of the Biblical Portrait of Miriam.* SBLDS 84. Atlanta: Scholars, 1987.

Camp, Claudia V. "Understanding a Patriarchy." In *Women Like This,* edited by Amy-Jill Levine, 1–39. Atlanta: Scholars, 1991.

Cantarella, Eva. *Pandora's Daughters: The Role and Status of Women in Greek and Roman Antiquity.* Baltimore: John Hopkins University Press, 1987.

Casas Ramirez, Juan Alberto. "Los primeros días de Jesús según el cuarto Evangelio aproximacíon narrativa a Jn 1,19–2,12." *Theologica Xaveriana* 61 (2011) 369–96.

Chestnut, Randall D. "Revelatory Experiences Attributed to Biblical Women." In *Women Like This,* edited by Amy-Jill Levine, 107–25. Atlanta: Scholars, 1991.

Cohen, Shaye D. "Menstruants and the Sacred." In *Women's History and Ancient History*, edited by Sarah B. Pomeroy, 273-99. Chapel Hill, NC: University of North Carolina Press, 1991.
Cohick, Lynn H. *Women in the World of the Earliest Christians: Illuminating Ancient Ways of Life*. Grand Rapids: Baker Academic, 2009.
Coleridge, Mark. *The Birth of the Lukan Narrative: Narrative as Christology in Luke 1-2*. JSNTSup. 88. Sheffield, UK: JSOT, 1993.
Collins, Raymond F. "Mary." *ABD* IV:579-81.
Corley, Kathleen E. *Private Women Public Meals: Social Conflict in the Synoptic Tradition*. Peabody, MA: Hendrickson, 1993.
———. *Women and the Historical Jesus: Feminist Myths of Christian Origins*. Santa Rosa, CA: Polebridge, 2002.
Cornejo-Parriego, Rosalía. "¿Feminismo posfeminista? Reflexiones culturales a propósito de recuerda, cuerpo de Marina Mayoral." *Bulletin of Spanish Studies* 80.5 (2003) 593-609.
Craven, T. "Women As Teachers of Torah." In *Passion, Vitality, and Foment: The Dynamics of Second Temple Judaism*, edited by L. M. Luker, 275-89. Harrisburg, PA: Trinity, 2001.
Culpepper, R. Alan, and Fernando F. Segovia, eds. *Semeia 53: The Fourth Gospel from a Literary Perspective*. Atlanta: Society of Biblical Literature, 1991.
D'Ambra, Eve. *Roman Women*. Cambridge: Cambridge University Press, 2007.
Danove, Paul. "The Narrative Rhetoric of Mark's Ambiguous Characterization of the Disciples." *Journal for the Study of the New Testament* 70 (1988) 21-38.
Darr, John A. *Herod the Fox : Audience Criticism and Lukan Characterization*. JSNTSup. 163. Sheffield, UK: Sheffield Academic Press, 1998.
———. *On Character Building : The Reader and the Rhetoric of Characterization in Luke-Acts*. 1st ed. Literary Currents in Biblical Interpretation. Louisville, KY: Westminster/John Knox, 1992.
Dawsey, James M. *The Lukan Voice: Confusion and Irony in the Gospel of Luke*. Macon, GA: Mercer University Press, 1986.
deSilva, David A. *Honor Patronage Kinship and Purity: Unlocking New Testament Culture*. Downers Grove, IL: IVP, 2000.
Dettwiler, Andreas, and Poplutz, Uta. *Studien Zu Matthäus Und Johannes*. Zürich: Theologischer Verlag Zürich, 2009.
Dewey, Joanna. "Jesus' Healings of Women: Conformity and Non-conformity to Dominant Cultural Values as Clues for Historical Reconstruction." *Biblical Theology Bulletin* 24 (1994) 122-31.
Dornisch, Loretta C. "A Woman Reads the Gospel of Luke: Introduction and Luke 1: The Infancy Narratives." *Biblical Research* 42 (1997) 7-22.
———. *A Woman Reads the Gospel of Luke*. Collegeville, MN: Liturgical, 1996.
Downing, F. G. "'Theophilus' First Reading of Luke-Acts." In *Luke's Literary Achievement*, edited by C. M. Tuckett, 91-109. Sheffield, UK: Sheffield Academic Press, 1995.
Dube, Musa W. "Toward a Postcolonial Feminist Interpretation of the Bible." *Semeia* 78 (1997) 11-26.
Dunn, James D. G. "The Book of Acts as Salvation History." In *Heil und Geschichte: Die Geschichtbezogenheit des Helis und das Problem der Heilsgeschichte in der biblischen Tradition und in der theologischen Deutung*, edited by Jörg Frey, 385-99. Tübingen: Mohr Siebeck, 2009.

———. *The Acts of the Apostles*. Epworth Commentaries. Peterborough, UK: Epworth, 1996.

Durham, John I. *Exodus*. WBC. Waco, TX: Word, 1987.

Easton, B. S. "The Purpose of Acts." In *Early Christianity: The Purpose of Acts and Other Papers*, edited by F. C. Grant, 33–118. London: Seabury, 1955.

Eisen, Ute E. *Die Poetik der Apostelgeschichte: Eine narratologische Studie*. Göttingen: Vandenhoeck & Ruprecht, 2006.

Emmerson, Grace I. "Women in Ancient Israel." In *The World of Ancient Israel*, edited by R. E. Clements, 371–94. Cambridge: Cambridge University Press, 1989.

Erichsen-Wendt, Friederike. "Tabitha-Leben an der Grenze: Ein Beitrag zum Verständnis Von Apg 9,36–4." *Biblische Notizen* 127 (2005) 67–90.

Esler, P. F. *Community and Gospel in Luke-Acts*. SNTSMS 57. Cambridge: Cambridge University Press, 1987.

Evans, C. F. *St. Luke*. TPI New Testament Commentaries. London: SCM, 1990.

Fee, Gordon, D. "'One Thing Is Needful'? Luke 10:42." In *New Testament Textual Criticism: Its Significance for Exegesis; Essays in Honor of Bruce Metzger*, edited by Eldon Jay Epp and Gordon D, Fee, 61–75. Oxford: Clarendon, 1981.

Fiorenza, Elisabeth Schüssler, *In Memory of Her: A Feminist Theological Reconstruction of Christian Origins*. 2nd ed. London: SCM, 1994.

———. "A Feminist Critical Interpretation for Liberation: Martha and Mary: Lk 10:38–42." *Religion and Intellectual Life* 3.2 (1986) 21–36.

Fitzmyer, Joseph, A. *The Gospel according to Luke*. Anchor Bible. New York: Doubleday, 1981.

Forbes, Greg W. *The God of Old: The Role of the Lukan Parables in the Purpose of Luke's Gospel*. JSNTSup 198. Sheffield, UK: Sheffield Academic, 2000.

———. "Darkness over All the Land: Theological Imagery in the Crucifixion Scene." *Reformed Theological Review* 66 (2007) 83–96.

France, R. T. *The Gospel of Mark: A Commentary on the Greek Text*. NIGTC. Grand Rapids: Eerdmans, 2002.

Frey, J., C. K. Rothschild, and J. Schröter, eds. *Die Apostelgeschichte im Kontext antiker und frühchristlicher Historiographie*. Berlin: de Gruyter, 2009.

Frey, Jörg, and Uta Poplutz. *Narrativität und Theologie im Johannesevangelium*. Biblisch-Theologische Studien. Neukirchen–Vluyn: Neukirchener Verlagsgesellschaft, 2012.

Garland, David E. *Luke*. ZECNT. Grand Rapids: Zondervan, 2011.

Gathercole, Simon J. *The Preexistent Son: Recovering the Christologies of Matthew, Mark, and Luke*. Grand Rapids: Eerdmans, 2006.

Gaventa, Beverly R. *Acts*. Abingdon New Testament Commentaries. Nashville: Abingdon, 2003.

Gebauer, Roland. "Mission Und Zeugnis: Zum Verhältnis von missionarischer Wirksamkeit und Zeugenschaft in der Apostelgeschichte." *Novum Testamentum* 40.1 (1998) 54–72.

Gerber, Daniel. *"Il vous est né un Sauveur," La construction du sens sotériologique de la venue de Jésus en Luc–Actes*. Genève: Labor et Fides, 2008.

Grassi, Joseph A. *The Hidden Heroes of the Gospels: Female Counterparts of Jesus*. Collegeville, MN: Liturgical, 1989.

Green, C. M. C. *Roman Religion and the Cult of Diana at Aricia*. Cambridge: Cambridge University Press, 2007.

Green, Joel B. "Learning Theological Interpretation from Luke." In *Reading Luke: Interpretation, Reflection, Formation*, edited by Craig G. Bartholomew, Joel B. Green and Anthony C. Thistleton. 55–78. Grand Rapids: Zondervan, 2005.

———. *The Gospel of Luke*. NICNT. Grand Rapids: Eerdmans, 1997.

———. *The Theology of the Gospel of Luke*. New Testament Theology. Cambridge: Cambridge University Press, 1995.

Groppe, Elizabeth T. *Yves Congar's Theology of the Holy Spirit*. Oxford: Oxford University Press, 2004.

Grossman, Maxine L. *Reading for History in the Damascus Document: A Methodological Study*. Leiden: Brill, 2002.

Grundman, Walter. *Das Evangelium Nach Lukas*. Berlin: Evangelische Verlagsanstalt Berlin, 1968.

Habner, S. "Living and Dying for the Law: The Mother-Martyrs of 2 Maccabees." In *They Shall Purify Themselves: Essays on Purity in Early Judaism*, edited by A. Reinhartz, 75–92. Atlanta: Society of Biblical Literature, 2008.

Harrill, Albert. "Divine Judgment against Ananias and Sapphira (Acts 5:1–11): A Stock Scene of Perjury and Death." *Journal of Biblical Literature* 130.2 (2011) 351–69.

Hengel, Martin. *The Charismatic Leader and His Followers*. New York: Crossroad, 1981.

Howell, David B. *Matthew's Inclusive Story*. Sheffield, UK: JSOT, 1990.

Hutson, Christopher R. "Martha's Choice: A Pastorally Sensitive Reading of Luke 10:38–42." *RestQ* 45.3 (2003), 139–50.

Hylen, Susan E. "Modest, Industrious, and Loyal: Reinterpreting Conflicting Evidence for Women's Roles." *Biblical Theology Bulletin* 44.1 (2014) 3–12.

Inyamah, Deborah C. "Contrasting Perspectives on the Role of the Feminine in Ministry and Leadership Roles in John 4 and 1 Timothy 2:11–15." *Journal of Religious Thought* 60 (2008) 87–108.

Iverson, Kelly R., and Christopher W. Skinner, eds. *Mark as Story: Retrospect and Prospect*. Society of Biblical Literature: Resources for Biblical Study. Atlanta: Society of Biblical Literature, 2011.

Johnson, L. T. *The Gospel of Luke*. Sacra Pagina 3. Collegeville, MN: Liturgical, 1991.

Karris, Robert J. "Women and Discipleship in Luke." *CBQ* 56 (1994) 1–20.

Kearsley, R. A. "Women in Public Life in the Roman East: Iunia Theodora, Claudia Metrodora and Phoebe, Benefactress of Paul." *Tyndale Bulletin* 50.2 (1999) 191–98.

Keener, Craig S. *Acts: An Exegetical Commentary. Introduction and 1:1—2:47*. Grand Rapids: Baker Academic, 2012.

———. *Acts: An Exegetical Commentary. 3:1—14:28*. Grand Rapids: Baker Academic, 2013.

Kingsbury, Jack Dean. *Matthew as Story*. 2nd ed. Philadelphia: Fortress, 1988.

Kitchen, Kenneth A. "Arabia, Arabians." In *Dictionary of the Old Testament Historical Books*, edited by Bill T. Arnold and H. G. M. Willimason, 36–39. Downers Grove, IL: IVP Academic, 2005.

Klauck, Hans-Josef. *Hausgemeinde und Hauskirche im frühen Christentum*. Stuttgart: Stuttgarter Bibelstudien 103, 1981.

Kraemer, Ross S., ed. *Maenads, Martyrs, Matrons, Monastics: A Sourcebook on Women's Religions in the Greco-Roman World*. Philadelphia: Fortress, 1988.

Kraemer, Ross S. "Women in the Religions of the Greco-Roman World." *Religious Studies Review* 9.2 (1983) 127–33.

———. "Women's Authorship of Jewish and Christian Literature in the Greco-Roman Period." In *Women Like This*, edited by Amy-Jill Levine, 221–42. Atlanta: Scholars, 1991.

———. *Her Share of the Blessings: Women's Religions among Pagans, Jews and Christians in the Greco-Roman World.* Oxford: Oxford University Press, 1992.

Kremer, Jacob. "Dieser ist der Sohn Gottes (Apg 9, 20)." In *Der Treue Gottes Trauen: Beiträge zum Werk des Lukas*, edited by Claus Bussman and Walter Radl, 137–58. Freiburg: Herder, 1991.

———. "Weltweites Zeugnis für Christus in der Kraft des Geistes: Zur Lukanischen Sicht Der Mission." In *Mission Im Neuen Testament*, edited by Karl Kertelge, 145–63. Freiburg: Herder, 1982.

Krüger, René. "La inclusión de las personas excluidas. La propuesta contracultural de Lucas 14:12–14." *Cuadernos de Teología* 24 (2005) 67–88.

Kuhn, Karl Allen. *The Heart of Biblical Narrative: Rediscovering Biblical Appeal to the Emotions.* Minneaplis, MN: Fortress, 2009.

Kurek-Chomycz, Dominika A. "Is There an 'Anti-Priscan' Tendency in the Manuscripts? Some Textual Problems with Prisca and Aquila." *Journal of Biblical Literature* 125.1 (2006) 107–28.

Lefkowitz, Mary R. "Did Ancient Women Write Novels?" In *Women Like This*, edited by Amy-Jill Levine, 199–219. Atlanta: Scholars, 1991.

Levine, Amy-Jill. "Second Temple Judaism, Jesus and Women: Yeast of Eden." *Biblical Interpretation* 2.1 (1994) 8–33.

———, ed. *"Women like This." New Perspectives on Jewish Women in the Greco-Roman World.* Atlanta: Scholars, 1991.

Levine, Lee. "Synagogue Leadership: The Case of the Archisynagogue," In *Jews in the Graeco-Roman World*, edited by M. Goodman, 195–213. Oxford: Clarendon, 1998.

Maddox, Robert. *The Purpose of Luke-Acts.* Edinburgh: T. & T. Clark, 1982.

Marc, Adeline. "L'esprit Saint Dans Les Écritures: Ananie et Saphire (Ac 5,1–11): 'Mentir à L'Esprit Saint': L'Esprit Saint, un juge Mortel?" *Théophylon* 2.1 (1997) 149–75.

Marguerat, Daniel. "Paul aprés Paul: une historie de réception." *New Testament Studies* 54.3 (2008) 317–37.

———. *Les Actes des Apôtres (1–12).* Commentaire Du Nouveau Testament. Geneve: Labor et Fides, 2007.

———. *Paul in Acts and Paul in His Letters.* Wissenschaftliche Untersuchungen Zum Neuen Testament. Tübingen: Mohr Siebeck, 2013.

———. *Reception of Paulinism in Acts.* Leuven: Peeters, 2009.

Marshall, I. Howard. *Commentary on Luke.* NIGTC. Grand Rapids: Eerdmans, 1978.

Martin, Francis, ed. *Narrative Parallels to the New Testament.* SBL Resources for Biblical Studies. Atlanta, GA.: Scholars, 1988.

Mattill, A. J., Jr. "The Purpose of Acts: Schneckenburger Reconsidered." In *Apostolic History and the Gospel*, edited by W. W. Gasque and R. P. Martin, 108–22. Exeter, UK: Paternoster, 1970.

Mbilizi, Étienne L. *D'Israël aux nations: L 'horizon de la rencontre avec le Sauveur dans L'œuvre de Luc.* Frankfurt am Main: Lang, 2006.

McCarty, V. K. "Prisca—Fellow Tent-maker and Fellow Missionary of Paul: Acts 18:2–3; Romans 16:3–4; 1 Corinthians 16:19; 2 Timothy 4:19." *International Congregational Journal* 11.2 (2012) 45–60.

Meeks, Wayne A. *The First Urban Christians: The Social World of the Apostle Paul.* New Haven: Yale University Press, 1983.
Meyer, Marvin, with Esther A. de Boer. *The Gospels of Mary.* San Francisco: Harper, 2004.
Meyers, Carol L. *Discovering Eve: Ancient Israelite Women in Context.* New York: Oxford University Press, 1988.
Moessner, David. *Jesus and the Heritage of Israel: Luke's Narrative Claim upon Israel's Legacy.* Harrisburg, PA: Trinity, 1999.
Moltmann-Wendel, Elisabeth. *The Women around Jesus.* New York: Crossroad, 1997.
Moxnes, Halvor. "Patron-Client Relations and the New Community in Luke-Acts." In *The Social World of Luke-Acts: Models for Interpretation*, edited by Jerome H. Neyrey, 241–68. Peabody, MA: Hendrickson, 1991.
Nielsen, Karen M. "The Private Parts of Animals: Aristotle on the Teleology of Sexual Difference." *Phronesis* 53 (2008) 373–405.
Nolland, John. *Luke.* WBC. 3 vols. Dallas, TX: Word 1989.
North, J. Lionel. "ὀλίγων δέ ἐστιν χρεία ἢ ἑνός (Luke 10:42) Text, Subtext and Context." *Journal for the Study of the New Testament* 66 (1997) 3–13.
Osiek, Carolyn. "Accusers, Mourners, Disciples: The Women of Luke's Passion Narrative." *Bible Today* 48.2 (2010) 75–79.
Oswalt, John N. *The Book of Isaiah: Chapters 1–39.* NICOT. Grand Rapids: Eerdmans, 1988.
Paffenroth, Kim. *The Story of Jesus According to L.* JSNTSup 147; Sheffield, UK: Sheffield Academic Press, 1997.
Pao, David W. *Acts and the Isaianic New Exodus.* Wissenschaftliche Untersuchungen Zum Neuen Testament. 2 Reihe. Tübingen: Mohr Siebeck, 2000.
Parsons, Mikeal. *Luke: Storyteller, Interpreter, Evangelist.* Peabody, MA: Hendrickson, 2007.
Paschke, Boris. "Matthäus 5,13–16 Als Antizipation des nachösterlichen Missionsbefehls? Narrativ-Kritische Überlegungen." *European Journal of Theology* 21.2 (2012) 100–106.
Percy, Sandra. *Christian Women Writers through the Ages.* Melbourne: Mosaic, 2012.
Pervo, Richard I. "Women in Jewish Narrative and in the Greek Novels." In *Women Like This*, edited by Amy-Jill Levine, 145–60. Atlanta: Scholars, 1991.
Peterson, David G. *The Acts of the Apostles.* Pillar New Testament Commentary. Nottingham, UK: Apollos, 2009.
Plutarch, John Dryden, and Arthur Hugh Clough. *The Lives of the Noble Grecians and Romans.* Chicago: Encyclopædia Britannica, 1955.
Poplutz, Uta. *Erzählte Welt: Narratologische Studien zum Matthäusevangelium.* Biblisch-theologische Studien. Neukirchen-Vluyn: Neukirchener Verlag, 2008.
Powell, Mark Allan. *What Is Narrative Criticism?* Guides to Biblical Scholarship New Testament Series. Minneapolis: Fortress, 1990.
Ranjini, Rebera. "Polarity or Partnership? Retelling the Story of Martha and Mary from Asian Women's Perspective (Luke 10:38–42)." *Semeia* 78 (1997) 93–107.
Reid, Barbara. "Choosing the Better Part." *Biblical Research* 42 (1997) 23–31.
———. *Choosing the Better Part? Women in the Gospel of Luke.* Collegeville, MN: Liturgical, 1997.
Resseguie, James L. *Narrative Criticism of the New Testament.* Grand Rapids: Baker Academic, 2005.

Rhoads, David M., Joanna Dewey, and Donald Michie. *Mark as Story: An Introduction to the Narrative of a Gospel*. 2nd ed. Minneapolis, MN: Fortress, 1999.

Ricci, Carla. *Mary Magdalene and Many Others: Women Who Followed Jesus*. Translated by P. Burns. Minneapolis: Fortress, 1994.

Richter Reimer, Ivoni. *Frauen in der Apostelgeschichte des Lukas: Eine Feministisch-theologische Exegese*. Gütersloh: Gütersloher Verlagshaus Gerd Mohn, 1992.

Roig, Montserrat. "La Mirada Tuerta." In *Dime que me quieres aunque sea mentira*, 61–62. Barcelona: Ediciones Península, 1992.

Rowe, C. Kavin. "Biblical Pressure and Trinitarian Hermeneutics." *Pro Ecclesia* 11.3 (2002) 295–312.

———. *Early Narrative Christology: The Lord in the Gospel of Luke*. Beihefte zur Zeitschrift für die Neutestamentliche Wissenschaft und die Kunde der älteren Kirche. Berlin: de Gruyter, 2006.

———. "History Hermeneutics and the Unity of Luke-Acts." *Journal for the Study of the New Testament* 28.2 (2005) 131–57.

———. "Luke and the Trinity: An Essay in Ecclesial Biblical Theology." *Scottish Journal of Theology* 56.1 (2003) 1–26.

Rüpke, Jörg. *A Companion to Roman Religion*. Blackwell Companions to the Ancient World Literature and Culture. Malden, MA: Blackwell, 2007.

Sánchez Navarro, Luis A. *Testimonios del Reino: Evangelios sinópticos y Hechos de los apóstoles*. Madrid: Palabra, 2010.

Sarasa, Luis Guillermo. "Una indicación exegética sobre el discípulo amado como un prototipo." *Theologica Xaveriana* 58.165 (2008) 253–86.

Sawicki, Marianne. *Crossing Galilee: Architectures of Contact in the Occupied Land of Jesus*. Harrisburg, PA: Trinity, 2000.

Sawyer, Deborah F. *Women and Religion in the First Christian Centuries*. London: Routledge, 1996.

Schnabel, Eckhard J. *Acts* ZECNT. Grand Rapids: Zondervan, 2012.

———. *Early Christian Mission*. 2 vols. Downers Grove, IL: IVP Academic, 2004.

Schollmeier, Paul. "Aristotle and Women: Household and Political Roles." *Polis* 20.1–2 (2003) 22–42.

Schottroff, Luise. *Lydia's Impatient Sisters: A Feminist Social History of Early Christianity*. London: SCM, 1995.

Schuller, Eileen. "Women in the Dead Sea Scrolls." In *The Dead Sea Scrolls after 50 Years: A Comprehensive Assessment*, edited by P. W. Flint and J. C. VanderKam, 2.117–44. Leiden: Brill, 1999.

Schultz, Celia E. *Women's Religious Activity in the Roman Republic*. Chapel Hill, NC: University of North Carolina Press, 2006.

Seim, Turid Karlsen. *The Double Message: Patterns of Gender in Luke-Acts*. Edinburgh: T. & T. Clark, 1994.

Serrano, Andrés García. "Anna's Characterization in Luke 2:36–38: A Case of Conceptual Allusion?" *Catholic Biblical Quarterly* 76.3 (2014) 464–80.

Sim, David C. "The Women Followers of Jesus: The Implications of Luke 8:1–3." *Heythrop Journal* 30 (1989) 51–62.

Simons, Roberto. "La pregunta de María (Lucas 1:34)." *Kairós* 36 (2005) 51–64.

Spencer, F. Scott. *Salty Wives, Spirited Mothers, and Savvy Widows: Capable Women of Purpose and Persistence in Luke's Gospel*. Grand Rapids: Eerdmans, 2012.

———. *Journeying through Acts: A Literary-Cultural Reading*. Peabody, MA: Hendrickson, 2004.
Squires, J. T. *The Plan of God in Luke-Acts*. SNTSMS 76. Cambridge: Cambridge University Press, 1993.
Stein, Robert H. *Mark*. BECNT. Grand Rapids: Baker, 2008.
Stevenson, James. *A New Eusebius: Documents Illustrating the History of the Church to A.D. 337*. Rev. ed. London: SPCK, 1999.
Swartley, Willard M. *Israel's Scripture Traditions and the Synoptic Gospels: Story Shaping Story*. Peabody, MA: Hendrickson, 1994.
Takács, Sarolta A. *Vestal Virgins, Sibyls, and Matrons: Women in Roman Religion*. Austin, TX: University of Texas Press, 2008.
Talbert, Charles H. "Once Again: Gospel Genre." *Semeia* 43 (1988) 53–73.
———. *Literary Patterns, Theological Themes, and the Genre of Luke-Acts*. Missoula, MT: Society of Biblical Literature, 1975.
———. *Luke and the Gnostics: An Examination of the Lucan Purpose*. Nashville: Abingdon, 1966.
———. *Reading Acts: A Literary and Theological Commentary on the Acts of the Apostles*. Reading the New Testament. Rev. ed. Macon, GA.: Smyth & Helwys, 2005.
———. *Reading Luke: A Literary and Theological Commentary*. Reading the New Testament Series. Rev. ed. Macon, GA: Smyth & Helwys, 2002.
Tannehill, Robert C. "Acts of the Apostles and Ethics." *Interpretation* 66.3 (2012) 270–82.
———. "'Cornelius' and 'Tabitha' Encounter Luke's Jesus." *Interpretation* 48.4 (1994) 347–56.
———. *Luke*. Abingdon New Testament Commentaries. Nashville: Abingdon, 1996.
———. *The Narrative Unity of Luke-Acts: A Literary Interpretation*. 2 vols. Philadelphia: Fortress, 1991.
———. *The Shape of Luke's Story: Essays on Luke-Acts*. Eugene, OR: Cascade, 2005.
Terrien, Samuel. *Till the Heart Sings: A Biblical Theology of Manhood and Womanhood*. Philadelphia: Westminster, 1985.
Tetlow, Elisabeth Meier. *Women and Ministry in the New Testament: Called to Serve*. Lanham, MD: University of America Press, 1980.
Thomas, W. Derek. "The Place of Women in the Church at Philippi." *Expository Times* 83.4 (1971–72) 117–20.
Thompson, Lindsay J. *The Role of Vestal Virgins in Roman Civic Religion: A Structuralist Study of the Crimen Incesti*. Lewiston, NY: Mellen, 2010.
Trebilco, P. *Jewish Communities in Asia Minor*. SNTSMS 69. Cambridge: Cambridge University Press, 1991.
Tribble, Phyllis. "Women in the OT." *IDBSup*. 963–66.
Tyson, Joseph, ed. *Luke-Acts and the Jewish People: Eight Critical Perspectives*. Minneapolis: Augsburg, 1988.
Verseput, Donald J. "The Faith of the Reader and the Narrative of Matthew 13:53–16:20." *Journal for the Study of the New Testament* 46 (1992) 3–24.
Walker Jr., William O. "The Portrayal of Aquila and Priscilla in Acts: The Question of Sources." *New Testament Studies* 54 (2008) 479–95.
Wall, Robert, W. "Martha and Mary (Luke 10.38–42) in the Context of a Christian Deuteronomy." *Journal for the Study of the New Testament* 35 (1989) 19–35.

Walsh, Jerome T., and David W. Cotter. *1 Kings*. Berit Olam. Collegeville, MN: Liturgical, 1996.

Warrior, Valerie M. *Roman Religion*. Cambridge Introduction to Roman Civilization. Cambridge: Cambridge University Press, 2006.

Wassen, Cecilia. *Women in the Damascus Document*. Atlanta: Society of Biblical Literature, 2005.

Webb, Barry. *The Message of Isaiah*. Leicester, UK: IVP, 2000.

Wegner, Judith Romney. "Philo's Portrayal of Women—Hebraic or Hellenic?" In *Women Like This,* edited by Amy-Jill Levine, 41–66. Atlanta: Scholars, 1991.

Wiley, Tatha. *Paul and the Gentile Women: Reframing Galatians*. New York: Continuum, 2005.

Witherington, Ben III. "Women." *ABD* 6.957–61

———. "On the Road with Mary Magdalene, Joanna, Susanna, and Other Disciples—Luke 8:1–3." Zeitschrift für die neutestamentliche Wissenschaft 70 (1979) 243–48.

———. *Women in the Ministry of Jesus*. SNTSMS 51. Cambridge: Cambridge University Press, 1984.

———. *The Acts of the Apostles: A Socio-Rhetoical Commentary*. Grand Rapids: Eerdmans, 1998.

Wright, Christopher J. H. *God's People in God's Land: Family, Land, and Property in the Old Testament*. Grand Rapids: Eerdmans, 1990.

Wright, N. T. "Jesus' Self-Understanding." In *The Incarnation: An Interdisciplinary Symposium on the Incarnation of the Son of God*, edited by Stephen T. Davis, Daniel Kendall, and Gerald O'Collins, 47–61. Oxford: Oxford University Press, 2002.

———. *The Resurrection of the Son of God. Christian Origins and the Question of God.* Vol. 3. London: SPCK, 2003.

York, J. O. *The Last Shall be First: The Rhetoric of Reversal in Luke*. JSNTSup. 46. Sheffield, UK: JSOT, 1991.

Index of Names

A

Agua Pérez, Agustín del, 133nn.26–27
Alexander, Loveday, 34n.91, 140n.5, 141n.9, 141n.11, 144–146
Alter, Robert, 2, 10n.57, 11, 44n.19, 57n.37
Ananias, 91n.106
Anderson, Kevin L., 143n.17
Aristotle, 28
Arjava, Antti, 31n.72
Arlandson, James Malcolm, 28n.51, 34n.90, 90n.96
Ascough, Richard, 184n.2, 185n.12, 186n.15, 186n.17, 187n.24, 188n.29, 188n.31

B

Bailey, Kenneth, 117, 118n.80
Bar-Efrat, Shimon, 2
Batten, Alicia, 30, 30n.66
Bauckham, Richard, 6–7, 82–87, 87n.80–81, 87n.83, 88n.86, 89–90, 92n.110, 105nn.17–18, 130n.18, 133n.28, 134n.31, 152n.11, 215–16
Beale, Gordon, 113n.56
Bearlsley, Patrick, 63n.62
Bellis, Alice O, 111n.53, 113n.59
Benéitez, Manuel, 2
Bird, Michael, 71
Bird, Michael F., 22n.7, 23n.13
Boatwright, Mary Taliaferro, 32n.77
Bock, Darrell, 6, 20n.1, 37n.2;6, 38n.3, 39n.7, 42nn.15–16, 52n.28, 86n.74, 93n.113, 103n.9, 114n.60, 115n.66, 115nn.68–69, 116n.70, 116n.73, 142, 143n.20, 148n.43, 151n.8, 154nn.21–22, 164nn.16–18, 169n.33, 184n.1, 188n.32, 198n.65
Börstinghaus, Jens, 2
Boudicca, 31
Bovon, François, 82n.50, 83n.57, 167
Bow, Beverly, 24n.23
Brawley, Robert L., 3, 11, 38n.6
Brown, Jennine K., 42n.17, 77n.32
Bruce, E. F., 148n.43, 151n.8, 185n.5, 185n.11, 186n.14, 188n.30
Burns, Rita J., 22n.10

INDEX OF NAMES

C

Caesar Augustus, 52
Callimorphus, 9n.45
Calvin, John, 67n.6
Camp, Claudia V., 25n.26
Carson, D. A., 113n.56
Cassius Dio, 190
Chestnut, Randall D., 24n.21
Claudia Metrodora, 32
Codex Bezae (D), 149n.2, 151n.8
Cohick, Lynn, 25n.30, 26, 28n.52, 29n.54-55, 29n.60-61, 30n.63-65, 31n.69-71, 31n.73, 32nn.76-78, 33n.85, 34
Cohick, Lynn H., 192n..47
Coleridge, Mark, 40n.8
Collins, Raymond, 84n.59
Corley, Kathleen, 82n.50, 86n.74, 89n.90, 89n.95, 90n.99, 106n.19, 108n.36, 109, 150n.7
Cornelia, 30-31
Cornelius, 12
Cotter, David W., 111n.49, 111n.52
Craven, T., 24n.24
Culpepper, R. Alan, 2n.5, 11, 15

D

D'Ambra, Eve, 31n.68, 31n.74, 32n.75
Danove, Paul, 101n.1, 102nn.2-3, 102nn.5-6
Darr, John A., 3, 11, 86n.78
David, 49-50
Dawsey, James, 3, 11
de Boer, Esther A., 85n.63
Demonax, 53-54
deSilva, David A., 93n.114
Dettwiler, Andreas, 2n.5
Dewey, Joanna, 95n.125, 95n.128, 177n.66
Diogenes Laertius, 9
Dionysius of Halicarnassus, 9n.45
Dornisch, Loretta, 4-5
Downing, F. G., 9n.45

Dunn, James D. G., 67n.3, 146n.35, 149n.1, 152n.12, 184n.1
Durber, Susan, 117
Durham, John I., 23n.18

E

Eisen, Ute E., 2n.5
Eliezer, R., 27n.42
Emmerson, Grace, I., 22n.11, 23-24, 26, 27n.43
Erickson, Millard, 214n.4
Erischen-Wendt, Friederike, 173nn.47-48, 175n.55
Esler, P. F., 86n.75
Eusebius, 198n.64
Evans, C. F., 86n.77, 109n.42

F

Fee, Gordon D., 107n.35
Fitzmyer, Joseph A., 86n.74
Forbes, Greg W., 21n.2, 91n.105, 119n.85, 120n.91, 124n.8, 127n.12
France, R. T., 11, 11n.64, 12n.66-68
Francis (Pope), 133n.30
Frey, J., 2n.5, 3

G

Garland, David E., 38n.5, 42n.15; 17, 55n.34, 56, 60n.41, 74n.21; 23, 75n.24; 26, 76n.30, 78n.38, 89n.90, 93n.115, 94n.117, 94nn.120-121, 95n.123, 95n.126, 96n.131, 104n.13, 106n.20, 108n.39, 113n.54, 124n.6, 125n.9, 126n.11, 128n.16, 131n.23, 133n.29, 137n.41, 137n.43
Gasque, W. W., 70n.12
Gathercole, Simon J., 72n.20
Gebauer, Roland, 166n.21

Gerber, Daniel, 2
Gracchi, 30–31
Grassi, Joseph, 85n.64
Green, Joel, 3, 11, 45n.20–21, 45nn.20–21, 46n.22, 47n.23, 51n.27, 61n.46, 69nn.10–11, 70n.12; 14, 71n.16, 78, 79n.40, 80nn.42–43, 107, 111n.51, 113n.55, 126n.11, 127n.14, 131nn.20–21, 132n.24, 136n.36, 137n.42
Grundman, Walter, 133n.25

H

Habner, S., 25n.25
Harrill, Albert, 158nn.6–7
Hengel, Martin, 76n.31
Herodias, 33n.78
Howell, David B., 75–76
Hutson, Christopher R., 108n.36
Hylen, Susan E., 34n.87

I

Inyamah, Deborah C., 82n.48
Iverson, Kelly R., 2n.5

J

Jeremias, 118n.81
Johnson, L. T., 69n.9, 141n.12
Josephus, 9n.45, 129–30
Juvenal, 33

K

Karris, Robert J., 88n.84, 89n.90
Kearsley, R. A., 32n.80
Keener, Craig S., 34n.86; 88–89, 107n.28, 139, 140n.8, 140nn.2–6, 145n.28, 146n.34, 149n.3, 150n.4, 151–52, 154n.25, 155n.26, 161nn.11–12, 166n.22, 170n.34, 171n.39, 172–73, 175n.56, 177–78, 179n.71, 199n.67
Kingsbury, Jack Dean, 77n.32
Kitchen, Kenneth A., 111n.50
Klauck, Hans-Josef, 191n.45
Köstenberger, 190n.39
Kraemer, Ross S., 21n.3, 24n.22, 29n.56, 29n.59
Kremer, Jacob, 49n.25
Krüger, René, 81n.47
Kuhn, Karl Allen, 3
Kurek-Chomycz, Dominika A., 189n.36

L

Lefkowitz, Mary R., 24n.22
Levine, Amy-Jill, 21n.3, 25–26
Lucian, 53–54
Lydia, 31, 32n.77

M

Marc, Adeline, 157n.2, 158nn.4–5, 159n.9
Marguerat, Daniel, 114n.62, 141n.10, 147n.39, 152nn.13–15, 153n.19, 154nn.23–24, 157n.1, 166n.20, 167–68, 171nn.36–38, 189n.38
Marshall, I. Howard, 67nn.4–5, 86n.74
Mbilizi, Étienne, 2
McCarty, V. K., 190n.39, 192n..47, 192n.49, 195n.56, 196
Meeks, Wayne A., 29n.58
Metrodora, Claudia, 32–33
Metzger, Bruce, 103n.8, 107n.35
Meyer, Marvin, 85n.63
Meyers, Carol L., 23n.12
Michie, Donald, 2n.5, 11, 177n.66
Moltmann-Wendel, Elisabeth, 91n.106
Moxnes, Halvor, 90n.100
Musonius Rufus, 33

N

Navarro, Sánchez, 2
Nickelsburg, George W. E., 24n.23
Nielsen, Karen M., 28n.50
Nolland, John, 17n.70, 21n.2, 36n.1,
    40n.10, 55nn.32-33, 61n.50,
    68n.7, 83n.56, 85n.66, 86n.74,
    106n.20, 108, 109n.43, 115n.67,
    123n.1, 124n.7
North, J. Lionel, 173n.50

P

Paffenroth, Kim, 94n.118, 158n.3
Pao, David W., 136n.35, 167, 168n.30
Papias of Hierapolis, 198n.64
Parsons, Mikeal C., 3
Paschke, Boris, 78n.37
Percy, Sandra, 21n.4, 27nn.45-46,
    29n.57, 30n.67, 33n.83
Pervo, Richard, 24n.22, 28n.47
Peterson, David G., 32n.75, 114n.61,
    141n.10, 148n.43, 151nn.7-8,
    153n.17, 161n.13, 163n.15,
    176n.57, 176n.61, 184n.2,
    185n.5, 185nn.10-11, 186n.20,
    187n.25, 188n.27, 189n.33,
    196n.59
Plancia Magna, 32n.77
Plato, 28
Poplutz, Uta, 2n.5
Powell, Mark Allan, 2
Priscilla, 63

Q

Quirinius, 52

R

Rahaba, 22
Regensdorf, Karl, 79n.39

Reid, Barbara, 3-4, 82n.50, 88n.85; 88,
    90n.99, 92, 94n.119, 95n.127,
    95n.130, 96n.133, 96n.135,
    107n.28, 109, 116n.70, 119, 219
Reimer, Richter, 176n.59, 176n.64,
    178n.69, 189n.38, 190n.39,
    191n.46, 195nn.57-58
Resseguie, James L., 2n.5, 11, 12n.65
Rhoads, David, 11
Rhoads, David M., 2n.5, 177n.66
Ricci, Carla, 82n.50, 83n.57, 85n.63,
    86n.77, 95n.125
Roig, Monserrat, 216n.9
Rothschild, C. K., 2n.5, 3
Rowe, C. Kavin, 3, 11, 65n.1, 66n.2,
    121n.93, 143, 145-47
Rüpke, Jörg, 28n.53

S

Sarasa, Luis Guillermo, 75n.25, 76n.29
Sawicki, Marianne, 86n.77
Sawyer, Deborah F., 29n.61, 30n.62
Schaberg, Jane, 4
Schnabel, Eckhard, 72n.19, 163n.15,
    172n.42, 174-75, 176n.58,
    176n.62, 184n.1, 185n.4,
    187n.26, 188n.28, 188n.30,
    191nn.42-43, 192n.47, 193n.50,
    195n.55, 196n.59, 197n.63
Schollmeier, Paul, 28n.50
Schottroff, Luise, 108n.40, 119n.87,
    187n.23
Schröter, J., 3
Schüssler Fiorenza, Elisabeth, 89n.95,
    106n.19, 109, 150n.7
Segovia, Fernando F., 2n.5
Seim, Turid Karlsen, 83n.52, 86n.76,
    87n.82, 89n.90, 90nn.97-98,
    90nn.102-3, 91n.104,
    91nn.106-7, 95n.124, 96n.135,
    106n.23, 107n.26, 107n.30,
    107n.34, 109n.44, 114n.63,
    116n.71, 123n.2, 124n.5
Serrano, Andrés Garcia, 60n.39; 41-43,
    61n.48

INDEX OF NAMES

Sim, David C., 88n.86, 89n.90, 89n.92, 91n.106
Simons, Roberto, 113nn.57–58
Socrates, 28
Spencer, F. Scott, 7–8, 82n.50, 86n.74, 87n.79, 88n.85, 89n.95, 90n.100, 90n.102, 105n.16, 106n.19, 106n.21, 118n.81, 118n.83, 119–20, 150n.7, 185, 186n.18
Stein, Robert H., 93n.112
Suetonius, 190n.41
Swartley, Willard, 2, 11

T

Takács, 28n.53
Talbert, Charles, 3, 9, 11, 68n.8, 81n.46, 95n.129, 115n.66
Tannehill, Robert C., 3, 11, 38n.4, 40n.9;12, 41n.13, 49n.24, 54n.31, 60–62, 70n.15, 71n.18, 74n.22, 80n.41; 44, 81n.45, 88n.87, 96n.132, 103n.8, 103n.10, 104nn.11–1, 104nn.14–15, 107n.31, 109n.41, 115n.66, 127n.13, 128n.15, 131n.22, 134n.32, 134n.34, 136nn.37–38, 137nn.39–40, 147, 150n.5, 151n.6, 154n.22, 158n.8, 159n.10, 168–169, 173n.49, 184n.3, 189, 192n..48, 193nn.52–53, 196n.54
Terrien, Samuel, 26
Tetlow, Elisabeth Meier, 85n.65, 89n.95, 106n.19, 140n.7

Thomas, W. Derek, 185n.5, 185n.9, 186n.19, 187n.21
Thompson, Lindsay, 28n.53, 142
Trebilco, P., 185n.6
Tribble, Phyllis, 26
Tübingen School, 155n.27

V

Verseput, Donald J., 76

W

Wainwright, Elaine, 85n.65
Walker Jr., William O., 189n.36, 196n.60
Walsh, Jerome T., 111
Warrior, Valerie M., 28n.53
Wegner, Judith Romney, 25
Wiley, Tatha, 23n.14, 32n.79, 33n.84
Witherington, Ben III, 5–6, 25–27, 28n.53, 82n.50, 88n.87, 92n.108, 92n.111, 107n.27, 116n.72, 163n.15, 169n.32, 172n.41, 176n.60, 176n.63, 180n.75, 184nn.1–2, 186n.16, 191n.43, 196n.61, 213, 216nn.7–8
Wright, N. T., 23n.17, 179n.72

Y

York, J. O., 38n.6

www.ingramcontent.com/pod-product-compliance
Lightning Source LLC
Chambersburg PA
CBHW051053230426
43667CB00013B/2279